Blockchain - Pioneering the Web3 Infrastructure for an Intelligent Future

Edited by Luyao Zhang, Mark Esposito and Terence Tse

Published in London, United Kingdom

Blockchain - Pioneering the Web3 Infrastructure for an Intelligent Future
http://dx.doi.org/10.5772/intechopen.1001657
Edited by Luyao Zhang, Mark Esposito and Terence Tse

Contributors
Agoye Olorunfemi David, Anton Kudin, Bogdan Carbunar, Carlos Alberto Durigan Junior, Carlos Roberto Martinez Martinez, Claudio Juan Tessone, Francisca Nonyelum Ogwueleka, Luyao Zhang, Mehdi Shafiee, Nasser Arshadi, Oleksii Baranovskyi, Paul Meeusen, Refik Caglar Kizilirmak, Rune Hylsberg Jacobsen, Saqib Rasool, Sergey Khvan, Volodymyr Tkach, Yulin Liu

First published in London, United Kingdom, 2025 by IntechOpen
IntechOpen is the global imprint of INTECHOPEN LIMITED, registered in England and Wales, registration number: 11086078, 167-169 Great Portland Street, London, W1W 5PF, United Kingdom

For EU product safety concerns: IN TECH d.o.o., Prolaz Marije Krucifikse Kozulić 3, 51000 Rijeka, Croatia, info@intechopen.com or visit our website at intechopen.com.

British Library Cataloguing-in-Publication Data
A catalogue record for this book is available from the British Library

Blockchain - Pioneering the Web3 Infrastructure for an Intelligent Future
Edited by Luyao Zhang, Mark Esposito and Terence Tse
p. cm.
Print ISBN 978-0-85466-701-7
Online ISBN 978-0-85466-700-0
eBook (PDF) ISBN 978-0-85466-702-4

If disposing of this product, please recycle the paper responsibly.

Meet the editors

Dr. Luyao (Sunshine) Zhang is an Assistant Professor of Economics and Senior Research Scientist at the Data Science Research Center (DSRC) at Duke Kunshan University, a US-China joint venture university dedicated to fostering global leaders for advancing humanity. Passionate about driving innovation across disciplines, Dr. Zhang's research, empowered by blockchain technology, spans a wide range of topics, including Decentralized Finance (DeFi), Decentralized Autonomous Organizations (DAOs), tokenomics and cryptocurrency models, blockchain interoperability, blockchain-AI integration, blockchain for sustainability, and open-access data and benchmarks, while also extending beyond blockchain to broader economic and computational challenges. As a rising scholar, her contributions have earned recognition and funding from national science foundations in the US, China, and beyond, as well as publications in top-tier computational science, interdisciplinary, and general-interest venues. Dr. Zhang actively promotes entrepreneurship and innovation by organizing workshops, leading conference programs, and curating journal special issues, helping to shape the evolving landscape of blockchain and its intersection with art and humanity, social science, and the natural and applied sciences. Her research bridges computational science and economic theory to develop transformative technologies that benefit society. Acknowledged as one of the "60 Pioneers in Blockchain Innovation," Dr. Zhang remains dedicated to fostering interdisciplinary collaboration and pioneering impactful solutions for the global good.

Dr. Mark Esposito is a Professor of Economics and Strategy at Hult International Business School, USA, where he directs the Futures Impact Lab. He is also on the faculty at Harvard University, where he serves as a social scientist with affiliations at Harvard Kennedy School's Center for International Development, Harvard University's Institute for Quantitative Social Science (IQSS), and the Davis Center for Eurasian Studies. He is a Berkman Klein Centre faculty associate for Internet and Society. He teaches a popular course on Artificial Intelligence for the Division of Continuing Education and runs a seminar on AI and International Development at the Harvard Kennedy School's CID. He co-founded the Machine Learning research firm Nexus FrontierTech and TheChart ThinkTank. Dr. Esposito has written or co-written more than 150 peer-reviewed and non-peer-reviewed publications and 13 books, two of which are Amazon bestsellers: Understanding How the Future Unfolds and The AI Republic. His most recent books include The Emerging Economies under the Dome of the Fourth Industrial Revolution, The Great Remobilization: Strategies and Designs for a Global Smarter World, and Digitizing the Emerging Economies. His forthcoming books are Tectonic Shifts: How Technology is Remaking Global Power Dynamics and Becoming AI Native: A Playbook for Businesses. He has a doctorate from Ecole des Ponts Paris Tech and lives across Boston, Geneva, and Dubai.

Dr. Terence Tse is a thought leader at the intersection of finance, technology, and business transformation. As Professor of Finance at Hult International Business School and visiting professor at ESCP Business School and Cotrugli Business School, he is also the co-founder and Executive Director of Nexus FrontierTech, an AI company, and serves as Chair in Fintech & Business AI at The Chart ThinkTank. His latest work, The Great Remobilization: Strategies and Designs for a Smarter Global Future, was nominated for the 2023 Thinkers50 Strategy Award. His previous bestsellers include The AI Republic: Building the Nexus Between Humans and Intelligent Automation and Understanding How the Future Unfolds: Using DRIVE to Harness the Power of Today's Megatrends. The DRIVE framework introduced in the latter earned him a nomination for the prestigious CK Prahalad Breakthrough Idea Award. His technical work Corporate Finance: The Basics is now in its second edition. Looking ahead, Dr. Tse has two forthcoming titles slated for 2025: Charting the Next AI Frontier: Being AI Native and Tectonic Shifts: How Technology is Remaking Global Power Dynamics. Dr. Tse is a sought-after speaker and advisor who has addressed audiences ranging from the UN to major corporate boardrooms. His insights regularly appear in leading publications, including the Financial Times, The Guardian, Harvard Business Review, and WIRED. He has provided advisory services and workshops to numerous global organizations, including BNP Paribas, Johnson & Johnson, and the European Commission. Terence holds a doctorate from the Cambridge Judge Business School, University of Cambridge.

Contents

Preface

Blockchain technology has emerged as a transformative force, reshaping how we approach digital transactions, infrastructure, and security. In *Blockchain – Pioneering the Web3 Infrastructure for an Intelligent Future*, pioneering scholars and leading industrial practitioners explore blockchain's profound impact on a spectrum of applications. With insights that bridge disciplines, this collection highlights blockchain's role in building resilient digital foundations while demonstrating its power to drive technology that serves the greater good.

As with any powerful technology, blockchain can be used for both positive and negative purposes. Its potential to facilitate secure transactions, foster decentralized governance, and ensure data integrity is unparalleled, but it also requires mindful implementation to maximize its benefits and mitigate risks. Recognizing this dual potential, the authors in this collection emphasize collaboration across disciplinary and industry boundaries as essential to steering blockchain innovation toward positive societal impact.

In this book, readers will find discussions on key areas of blockchain, including early intrusion detection, cryptographic protocols, secure transactions, and decentralized frameworks. Authors delve into blockchain's applications across emerging areas such as the Internet of Things (IoT), self-sovereign identity, and renewable energy, revealing how it can advance technological innovation while supporting social and environmental objectives.

Through interdisciplinary collaboration and a shared commitment to ethical innovation, blockchain's capacity to shape a more secure, intelligent, and equitable digital future can be fully realized. This book is a resource for researchers, practitioners, and students, offering insights to inspire further advancements and applications that maximize blockchain's potential for societal good.

The Academic Editor Luyao Zhang is supported by the National Science Foundation China for the project entitled "Trust Mechanism Design on Blockchain: An Interdisciplinary Approach of Game Theory, Reinforcement Learning, and Human-AI Interactions" (Grant No. 12201266).

Luyao Zhang
Duke Kunshan University,
Suzhou, China

Mark Esposito
Hult International Business School,
London, United Kingdom

Harvard's Berkman Klein Center for Internet and Society,
Cambridge, Massachusetts, USA

Terence Tse
Hult International Business School,
London, United Kingdom

Section 1

Distributed Systems and Cybersecurity

Chapter 1

A Distributed System for Early Intrusion Detection and Assessment of Cybersecurity

Anton Kudin, Volodymyr Tkach, Oleksii Baranovskyi and Bogdan Carbunar

Abstract

Centralized intrusion detection and prevention systems (IDS/IPS) and Security Information Event Management (SIEM) systems often fail to analyze and respond to information and cybersecurity threats that occur in distributed and heavily loaded environments due to computational, storage, and license limitations. In this chapter, we propose a novel distributed hierarchical system concept for early intrusion detection and subsequent assessment of cyber and information security risks based on anomalous behavior analysis without using predefined patterns. The developed approach aims to increase the security of distributed systems against decentralized attacks including both DDoS and non-specific, non-DDoS attacks, such as advanced persistent threats (APT) conducted by high-skilled cybercrimes and state-sponsored adversaries. We expect the proposed concept to improve the performance of SIEM systems compared to centralized solutions. The increasing productivity effectiveness indicator depends on the possible number of hierarchy levels in the analyzed systems (the possibility of their decomposition into subsystems).

Keywords: Blockchain, intrusion detection, SIEM, anomaly detection, threat intelligence, IoC

1. Introduction

In the contemporary landscape of cybersecurity, ensuring the reliability of Indicators of Compromise (IoC) [1, 2] is paramount for security analysts striving to bolster threat intelligence. This chapter delves into the multifaceted realm of IoC data reliability, examining various factors that significantly influence its accuracy. Security analysts are required not only to comprehend the nuances affecting the credibility of intelligence sources but also to adeptly assess the relevance of collected data [3–6].

The assessment of intelligence source relevance is explored as a critical facet of achieving robust threat intelligence. This involves acquiring data from dependable sources that provide accurate and pertinent information. Moreover, the integrity of data must be preserved throughout the collection process, safeguarding against any inadvertent alterations.

In dissecting the factors that impact the credibility of intelligence sources, attention is given to challenges such as the potential lack of authenticity, inaccuracies within the provided data, and the presence of incomplete or insufficient information. Each of these factors poses potential threats to the reliability of the intelligence gathered.

Additionally, the chapter scrutinizes the influence of diverse data collection methods on the availability of data. It is recognized that varying collection methodologies may yield disparate amounts of data based on access levels, necessitating a nuanced understanding of their implications for the overall reliability of threat intelligence.

Furthermore, the study investigates the resource requirements associated with data storage and processing. Security experts often encounter challenges related to computational and storage limitations when dealing with the increasing number of events and incidents. This chapter sheds light on these challenges, offering insights into strategies for optimizing resource utilization in the face of growing data volumes.

Through this comprehensive analysis, security practitioners and researchers alike will gain a deeper understanding of the intricacies surrounding IoC data reliability, thereby contributing to the advancement of effective threat intelligence strategies.

2. Modern IDS: Trends, problems, and their relevance

While the rising popularity of cloud data centers is understandable and leaves no arguments against them except for maybe privacy issues, the outsourced SOC matter is questionable. The period of pandemic caused a rapid increase in demand for third-party security services, but as some surveys show, compared to 37% of companies that used outsourced services in 2021, current 22% look less appealing [7]. Whatever statistics may be, it is also undoubtful that both small and unspecialized companies will continue to use such SOC's help for managing their security due to cost and staff saves. It is often easier to use the already set-up mechanism than to build one from scratch, and though the third-party specialists may need more time to get familiar with a new infrastructure and will deal with all the sensitive data in the company, the outsourced SOC benefits can make up for it. The process of configuring security systems to effectively detect anomalies and threats may be trickier with the outsourced SOC than with its in-house version, but it will either way obviously create a huge number of false positives. Although, skilled in-house experts are more likely to overcome this problem by thorough tuning, this is not always an option.

To explore the problem, some fresh tendencies are worth mentioning:

1. Rising importance of communication channels in cloud. When relying mainly on cloud services for security or other issues, one must understand that if due to any reason a cloud is unreachable, the whole work stops inevitably. Among such reasons are of course the dreadful DDoS attacks that harm the availability of company's resources, bringing up not only financial but also reputational damage. According to Ref. [8], DDoS attacks remain in the top 10 cloud security risks; hence, the protection of communication channels between cloud and its clients is of great importance. To mitigate them, IDS usage and Firewall Traffic Inspection can be offered, as well as anomaly search and IP blocking, all of which will bring more false-positive alerts. Unfortunately, even respectable companies like Cloudflare cannot propose more than manually adding exceptions or

changing the sensitive level of the detection rule for cases when legitimate traffic is classified as malicious [9].

2. Increasing IoC's source authenticity requirements. By trusting immense lists of IoCs of arguable origin, a company decreases its detection efficiency and leaves both experts and system resources overwhelmed. IOC databases should be not only updated frequently but also validated for their confidence score and authoritative origin. Different methodologies can be used to evaluate IOC's confidence score, for example, as described in Ref. [10] or other ML-based decisions. Another option is to analyze the cyber kill chain [11], which in fact can also be automated *via* ML. Although a lot of companies are jealous when it comes to sharing a rather valuable experience of fighting against cyber threats, some open-source platforms for accounting IOC exist. Several examples include OpenIOC Framework, MISP, IBM X-FORCE, SANS Internet Storm Center, numerous open Github solutions, etc.

3. Trusted attacker. As cloud services gained their popularity, they became of great use not only to regular users but also to hackers, which led to an issue of a malicious user enjoying the same privileges inside the cloud service as a legitimate user. Moreover, a system is unlikely to check in-depth for example the internal traffic, than the one coming from outside. As Ref. [12] states, "over 35% of cloud security incidents occurred from attackers' use of valid, compromised credentials." These statistics reveal a significant problem of mitigating such insider-like attacks, especially taking into consideration the fact that such actions may not be as obviously evil as other incidents. The question arises: How to distinguish such a user's activity from normal? Best practices include giving the least needed privileges to users, implementing some behavioral detection algorithms and using the Data Security Posture Management (DSPM) approach that can prevent sensitive data breaches [13]. Just as finding anomalies can be the key, it will also create more detection noise.

4. Comprehensive analysis of user behavior. Owing to the advanced nature of modern cyber-attacks, a traditional signature-based attitude toward the detection of deviations from normal user behavior needs more comprehensive treatment. Hackers no longer threaten only high privileged accounts, and they prefer to play safe and gradually gain more and more access to the system by starting with lower profile users that often do not get the security attention they need. Hopefully, protection measures are aware of the described risks and some solutions are already presented. Oracle's CASB (Cloud Access Security Broker) Cloud Service, for example, has User Behavior Analytics (UBA) module that is able to perform "dynamic, user-risk scoring based on continual assessment of user behaviour," and create access patterns and control users' usage of applications [14]. Other changes, including any privileges or security configuration, are also crucial to monitor and validate. IBM QRadar too offers similar UBA service [15] that utilizes ML abilities to extract a behavior model from historical data of user activities. Another great instance of UBA implementation is Exabeam, which also by means of ML can detect deviations from the established baselines.

5. Increasing volumes of telemetry data. In response to new attacks, specialists are forced to add more detection rules, log sources, checks, all of which multiples

telemetry data annually. At some point, the company's resources are exhausted, and it no longer has full control over the situation. "38% of companies operate with limited awareness of what's happening in their software," states [16]. Excessive log gathering otherwise means not all of them are actually used or useful in investigations. Among already mentioned problems, Callaway [16] also remarks that "telemetry data is unstructured; varying formats make it hard to use; data preparation is time-consuming and sensitive data in logs may lead to compliance violations."

6. Not only IoC, but also other telemetry data should be considered comprehensively. It follows from the previous paragraph that all data can be gathered in vain when used without thought. For achieving early anomaly detection, it is never enough to conduct just IoC monitoring or other signature-based detection, as the whole landscape should be taken into account. Security specialists must observe not merely one alert, but rather the sequence of seemingly legitimate actions that result in some attacks. This can be done by means of complex detection rules, based on the knowledge of previous attack schemes, for example, MITRE propose. Alternatively, ML algorithms or neural networks can be fed with normal system activities and therefore learn to detect such suspicious patterns.

Considering current tendencies in cloud services, we can only conclude that all of them demand a more comprehensive approach for detecting anomalies and broadening information we gather from systems, which in turn creates more false-positive alerts unless we have the wisdom to tune the detection systems even more carefully or use advanced automated detection algorithms.

2.1 Indicators of Compromise

Several platforms offer Indicator of Compromise (IoC) feeds, delivering real-time, automated notifications regarding potential threats or vulnerabilities sourced from diverse outlets such as honeypots, sandboxes, and other threat intelligence repositories. These feeds serve to empower organizations in proactively addressing security risks by furnishing instantaneous updates. The conventional application of IoC feeds involves updating security systems to preemptively identify, intercept, and neutralize threats, thus mitigating potential damage. Over time, the confidence or value associated with Indicators of Compromise inevitably diminishes. However, gauging the temporal degradation of IoC confidence necessitates a more sophisticated parameter estimation process. The MISP project [6] presents an extensive taxonomy of parameters, some of which can be employed to assess the decay of IoCs over time. Notably, within the AlienVault framework, several parameters prove instrumental, including related alerts, pulses (indicating the IoC's validity and detection by other sources), source information, and others.

2.2 Model of decaying of indicators of compromise

Tkach et al. [10] introduced a scoring model for the assessment of indicators, which is potentially applicable to various types of indicators or data sources. This scoring model consists of a foundational score and a decay rate that diminishes the score of an Indicator of Compromise (IoC) over time. The initial value of the indicator's life cycle or score undergoes a reset upon the introduction of a new indicator. This initial value, combined with considerations of the confidence in its source and associated taxonomies, constitutes the base score. The decay rate, on the other hand, represents the speed at which the score diminishes, signifying a variable decay speed over time. The value of an IoC is assessed using this scoring mechanism. Typically, during IoC evaluation, the decay factor is calculated, although other influencing factors are also considered, as detailed in subsection A. The evaluation of an indicator can be conducted based on these parameters, as elucidated in the subsequent section. It is imperative to systematically evaluate indicators across all available data platforms, and notably, this evaluation should be performed regularly.

Trust values are employed to determine confidence levels. Understanding the behavior of these confidence levels allows for the assessment of an indicator's decay. By studying the correlation among alerts, IDs, related pulses, and file scores, along with the confidence level, the quality of an indicator can be determined throughout its lifecycle. The model was designed to calculate the confidence score of an IoC throughout its lifecycle. To explain the proposed scoring model, the pulse value for a certain i_{th} IoC should be introduced, as proposed in (1):

$$\text{pulse}_i = logistic\left(\sum_{j=1}^{N} trust_{ij}\right), \tag{1}$$

where $trust_{ij}$ is a level of trust to j_{th} source of pulse ranging $(0..1)$; N is the number of these sources; $score_i$ is the current confidence score for i_{th} IoC; finally, $logistic(\cdot)$ is the normalization function (3), bringing the sum of multiple sources trust to a range $(0..1)$. And as the confidence score also belongs to the same range, the pulse value is also normalized to $(0..1)$.

The general form of the logistic curve is depicted in (19) and **Figure 1**.

For each IoC, as the feed brings new pulses (IoC occurrences) from multiple sources, they all should be considered. However, we should never exceed the top limit of 1 for trust (which means trust is absolute, we take all the pulses from the source at 100%).

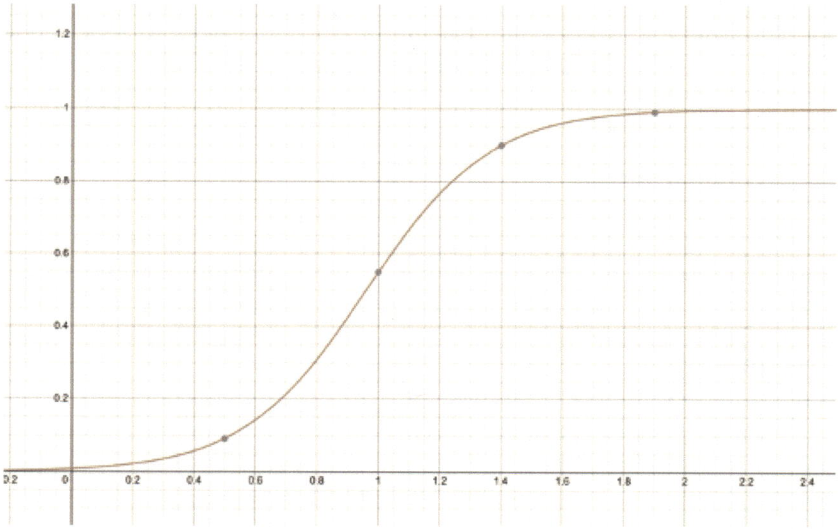

Figure 1.
Logistic curve to represent the function of $p_t = logistic$.

For simplicity and without losing the generality of the model, trust for an unknown source is put to be 0.5.

Many previous models estimated confidence levels over periods measured in days; however, the proposed model was tested against different time intervals to observe variations in the behavior of the confidence levels. Additionally, the model incorporated trust values into its calculations. This enhanced version allows for mapping the behavior of the estimated confidence level over various time frames, such as days and hours.

Based on the findings from the statistical analysis in the preceding sections, it was concluded that time is a critical parameter in the decay of an indicator or the confidence levels. For the time intervals during which pulses exist, the confidence level is calculated as proposed below:

$$c_t = logistic\left(c_t^{decayed} + pulse_i\right), \tag{2}$$

where $c_t^{decayed}$ is defined to be:

$$c_t^{decayed} = \frac{c_{t-1} - k \cdot c_{t-1}(m - c_{t-1})}{m^2}, \tag{3}$$

where c_t is a confidence level at the moment t; k is a constant to adjust the confidence decay speed according to maximum lifetime for IoC; i stands for the range of cases/periods, and finally, $logistic(\cdot)$ is a logistic function, having the main purpose of bringing the confidence level to the range of (0,1).

For the time intervals when there are no pulses, the c_t is calculated by (3) alone. The general view of an IoC confidence scoring method application is shown in Section 5.2 of this chapter.

It is worth mentioning here that Eq. (3) is a finite-difference form of reverse logistic function (Eq. (18) with $b < 0$). It is also important to mention that for any chosen time interval, if at a certain point there are no pulses, the value of $pulse_i$ equals 0. Eq. (3) is the core of the proposed model. The expression is a logistical function calculating the indicators' confidence level in the feed at a particular time and keeping it in a range of (0..1). For this method, we consider the value of trust, regardless of the value of i, as a constant.

2.3 Early intrusion detection

As the complexity of critical infrastructures increases, the impact of cyber threats correspondingly intensifies. This escalation is driven by continuous information flows and the rise of streaming data. Such data evolves over time, making the detection of patterns and the maintenance of high detection accuracy in a complex environment a priority [17, 18].

Research by Waite [19] indicates that higher functionality leads to greater complexity, which in turn reduces the security level of any system. Given the consistently increasing number of cyber attacks, as highlighted by Refs. [20, 21], the paramount task of a state's cyber defense is to protect its state institutions and entire critical infrastructure. One of the most significant challenges in the field of cyber defense is the absence of effective mechanisms for preventing attacks unless specific signatures of such attacks are identified. Consequently, it becomes imperative to develop mechanisms for the early detection and prevention of cyber threats before their complete implementation, known as early intrusion detection. This is crucial even in the absence of clearly defined information about potential threats and/or their signatures.

Early intrusion detection is crucial in safeguarding systems against cyber threats. Traditional signature-based approaches may overlook novel attack vectors, highlighting the need for non-pattern anomaly detection techniques. By analyzing deviations from normal behavior rather than relying solely on predefined patterns, non-pattern anomaly detection can identify emerging threats at their nascent stages, allowing for proactive response and mitigation. Integrating early intrusion detection with non-pattern anomaly detection enhances overall security posture by providing a more comprehensive view of system activity, enabling organizations to detect and respond to threats before they escalate into full-blown breaches. This proactive approach not only minimizes potential damage but also reduces the likelihood of false positives associated with signature-based methods, thus improving the efficiency and efficacy of intrusion detection systems.

An effective mechanism for anomaly detection involves analyzing deviations in agent behavior when interacting with observable objects. In this study, an agent refers to a user or any type of device. An anomaly is defined by the authors as behavior that significantly deviates from expected norms rather than "normal" behavior, which can vary subjectively across different systems. These deviations from expected behavior primarily rely on predictive models [21–23].

To develop a non-pattern anomaly detection approach, continuous and real-time data reflecting agent behavior is essential. A widely utilized tool for this purpose is Security Information and Event Management (SIEM) systems, capable of continuously gathering and analyzing data logs from various network devices, IDS, and applications. SIEM systems play a crucial role in achieving secure log correlation and event detection across the infrastructure, both within and outside the security perimeter [24, 25].

The ongoing discovery of zero-day vulnerabilities underscores the critical need for detecting anomalies that lack discernible patterns. However, detecting pattern-based anomalies in time series across critical infrastructures is challenging due to issues such as label scarcity, generalization, and efficiency concerns [26]. Current methodologies predominantly focus on pattern-based detection. Hence, the authors advocate exploring Non-Pattern based Anomaly Detection (NP-AD) in time series. In this context, "detection" refers to recognizing or distinguishing unusual or usual actions relative to the data [27].

This approach to anomaly detection not only addresses the complexity of varying definitions of "normal" behavior but also emphasizes the importance of real-time data analysis and the integration of diverse sources within the security framework.

2.3.1 Anomalies and security data gathering

Anomalous data, often perceived as an outlier, can be interpreted from various perspectives. Hawkins [28] defines it as "an observation that significantly deviates from others, arousing suspicion." In contrast, Barnett and Lewis [29] describe it as an observation inconsistent with the rest of the dataset. Data itself, merely a collection of bytes, lacks intrinsic value to a security specialist unless contextualized into actionable information that can inform detection, prevention, and defense against adversaries. Drawing from the definitions by Hawkins and Barnett [28, 29], we explore the nuances of data acquisition using security systems and its temporal sequencing. Research by Ahmed et al. [30] underscores the complexity of anomaly detection, emphasizing the identification of abnormal or anomalous data within datasets.

No	Task	Description
1	Gathering	Collection, processing, and analyzing security events that come into the system from diverse sources many sources
2	Detection	Real-time detection of attacks and violations of security criteria and policies
3	Assessment	Prompt assessment of the security of information, telecommunications, and other critical resources
4	Risk	Security risk analysis and management
5	Investigation	Conducting investigations into incidents
6	Security	Making effective decisions to protect information
6	Reporting	Reporting documents

Table 1.
Tasks mainly accomplished by a SIEM system.

Moreover, it highlights the detection of rare and significant events that necessitate immediate action due to their unusual behaviors [31].

While data and anomalies have been extensively studied from a broad perspective [21, 32, 33], many investigations focus on traditional anomaly detection methods, leveraging techniques such as nearest neighbor distances and clustering. An emerging trend involves the application of deep neural networks, as advocated by Markou [34], which shows promise in identifying anomalous data.

Security Information and Event Management (SIEM) systems serve as real-time platforms for analyzing security incidents [35]. These systems enable immediate analysis of security incidents originating from sensors within information and communication systems. SIEM systems manifest as applications, devices, or services and are instrumental in performing various tasks, as detailed in **Table 1**.

One of the widely used types of SIEMs capable of gathering data intelligently is SPLUNK [36–38]. SPLUNK collects a variety of relevant data, including log files, configuration files, system notifications, application alerts, metrics, scripts, and network data. The foundation of the information collected in the SPLUNK system is an index—a data repository that consists of a file or set of files that store data. SPLUNK can process any type of data, as it is designed to handle a vast majority of unstructured and poorly structured data automatically [36–38].

2.3.2 Time-series in anomaly detection

Since security events unfold over time, representing them as a time series is a common approach. Time series are essentially a sequence of observations ordered chronologically and derived from various phenomena [39]. Conceptually, they can be understood as an ordered sequence of values of a variable at equally spaced time intervals. Let us formalize this definition:

Definition 1: *A Time Series is a collection of points where measurements T are made, and the observations are indexed by time t. The set of these observations is represented as* $X(t), t \in T$ [39].

Here, T is assumed to be a finite set of points, typically denoted as $T = \{1, 2, \ldots, N\}$. Alternatively, T can be represented as a continuous parameter within a finite interval, expressed as $T = \{t : 0 \le t \le L\}$. Consequently, a stochastic process with random variables can be expressed by Eq. (4):

$$\{Y_t : t = 0, \pm1, \pm3, \dots\} \tag{4}$$

This equation encapsulates the essence of time series. It is notable that such a process is influenced by a set of distributions $s = \{0,1,2, \dots, n\}$ representing finite collections of Y [40].

In the realm of anomaly detection within time series, data can be represented as either univariate or multivariate. Univariate time series, as described by Ref. [41], consist of real-valued observations ordered by time, while multivariate time series involve ordered sets of dimensional vectors recorded over time [41]. Detecting anomalies within time series poses challenges, particularly in determining whether it is feasible to predict the novelty or normalcy of observed time series within a set of training data [42].

2.3.3 Non-pattern anomaly detection in time series

In this section, we briefly introduce the Non-Pattern based Anomaly Detection (NP-AD) approach implemented in the Distributed Data Intrusion Detection System (DDIDS), detailed in the paper [43].

The NP-AD method in time series is structured as a five-step process, depicted in **Figure 2**. The initial step (Step 1) involves receiving anomaly samples as input data, which are then categorized as either univariate or multivariate time series in Step 2. Subsequently, Step 3 entails algorithmic training/processing to acquire user time series, typically obtained from log files such as those generated by a Security Information and Event Management (SIEM) system, especially in a pattern-based approach. The NP-AD process, executed in steps 3 and 4, facilitates the identification of pattern-based and patternless observations, respectively. Pattern-based anomalies typically adhere to recognizable patterns, while patternless anomalies deviate significantly from the norm.

A Finite State Machine (FSM) serves as the underlying model for this approach. Formally defined as a sequential system with a graph of nodes, an FSM is represented by a set of five tuples, as shown in Eq. (5):

$$FSM = \{Q, \Sigma, \delta, q_0, F\} \tag{5}$$

Here, Q denotes a finite nonempty set of states $(q_1, q_2, \dots, n)$, Σ represents a set of input symbols $(\sigma_1, \sigma_2, \dots, \sigma_m)$, δ is the state transition function, q_0 is the initial state, and F is a set of end states.

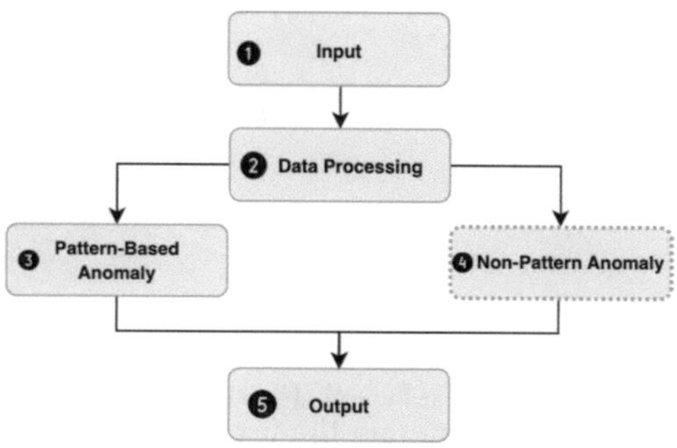

Figure 2.
Non-Pattern Based Anomaly Detection general schema.

The input information is represented as a vector of values, as shown in Eq. (6):

$$x = \langle a_1, a_2, a_3, \ldots, a_k \rangle \tag{6}$$

Each coordinate a_j of the vector corresponds to the value of log entry parameters, which can be either categorical or numeric. This allows for the association of input data with system states, considering elements like configuration files, system messages, and applications.

To facilitate FSM processing, numerical input vectors are converted into categorical ones by dividing them into intervals and assigning them to specific categories. For instance, a rational attribute's minimum and maximum values and the intervals between them can correspond to categories like "low," "medium," and "high." This results in an input alphabet representing all possible states of the vector x, with the total number of states determined by Eqs. (7) and (8), respectively.

$$X = \{x_1, x_2, x_3, \ldots, x_n\} \tag{7}$$

$$n = \prod_{i=1}^{k} |a_i| \tag{8}$$

where |•| is the operator of determining the power of the set of values, which takes a certain coordinate of the vector of input information. The output alphabet can be defined as the signals coming from the system, as shown in Eq. (9).

$$Y = \{y_1, y_2, y_3, \ldots, y_m\} \tag{9}$$

These output signals allow deviations from the normal conditions based on the transition matrix. Specific definitions for multiple outputs can be represented based on the following conditions: do nothing; increase the likelihood of anomaly; reduce the likelihood of anomaly; and signals. The set of states of the system is defined as shown in Eq. (10).

$$S = \{s_1, s_2, s_3, \ldots, s_d\} \tag{10}$$

where d is the number of all possible states.

Definition 2: Probability/Likelihood. *The likelihood estimator for n independent activity is denoted by Y_i, where Y_i is the i-th activity, and $i = 1, 2, \ldots, n$,* with a probability p observing the positive outcome [44]. This is shown in Eq. (11)

$$P_r = [Y_i = y] = P^y(1-p)^{(1,y)}, for\{y = 0, 1\} \tag{11}$$

where the likelihood for obtaining a sample from an activity $\{A_1, A_2, \ldots, A_n\}$ is given in Eq. (12)

$$P_r = [A_1, A_2 \ldots \ldots, A_n P] = \prod_{i=1}^{n} P^{A_i}(1-p)^{(1,A)} \tag{12}$$

In this paper, the terms "normal," "warning," or "anomaly" are utilized to denote different states of the system. However, the specific type of anomaly is not determined; rather, the focus is on determining the probability of its occurrence. The term "likelihood" is employed because it aligns with the mathematical definition of probability and better reflects the expectation of potential anomalies.

It is assumed that each value of the input vector is influenced by a likelihood function, implying that the values of each component of the vector are random within the range of possible values, forming a random vector. Therefore, it becomes crucial to evaluate anomalies probabilistically. To achieve this, a parameter is introduced to determine the likelihood of an anomalous state at a given time, based on state-to-state transition functions and output detection, as described in Eq. (13).

$$s_{t+1} = f\left(s_t, p_{t+1}\right) \tag{13}$$

where s_{t+1} and s_t are state values at appropriate times, and p_{t+1} is the current value of the anomaly likelihood. Because the FSM is a discrete-time model, it is necessary to define a transition function as a threshold function, which may be, for example, a transition to the opposite state in the presence of a likelihood value above/below a certain threshold. Depending on the current state and the likelihood value, it may change to the opposite state or again to the current state based on the behavior. In addition to this, based on a certain sequential ordering of the input vectors, the predictive value of the next input vector can be constructed. Note that in the context of this paper, it does not matter how the predictive value is determined. We assume this value has already been obtained using one of the multiple prediction functions. Hereafter, we assume that the predicted value is obtained as a function of μ (•) from the input dataset (for the time interval x_{t-m} to x_t) as is shown in Eq. (14).

$$\tilde{x}_{t+1} = \mu(x_{t-m}, \ldots, x_t) \tag{14}$$

Additionally, in order to assess the correspondence between the predicted and actual input vector values, it becomes essential to establish a measure quantifying the difference between the vectors within the feature space. This disparity is captured as the prediction error, depicted in Eq. (15).

In this equation, μ represents the predicted value derived from the sequence of input data over the specified time interval. The function f can encompass various modeling approaches, including statistical methods, machine learning algorithms, or time series forecasting techniques designed to capture trends and patterns in the data.

$$\delta x = \Delta(\tilde{x}_t, x_t) \tag{15}$$

where $\tilde{x}_t$ represents the predicted value of the vector at time t, and x_t denotes its actual value. After observing a measure of distance, we can now determine the function that describes the dependence of the anomaly likelihood of the state on that distance. The likelihood determination functions ρ can be defined as a function of the current likelihood and a measure of the distance, as described in Eq. (15), which measures the discrepancy between the predicted vector and the actual vector, as shown in Eq. (16).

$$\rho_{t+1} = \rho\left(p_t, \delta x\right) \tag{16}$$

The final step involves determining the thresholds highlighted in Eq. (13).

2.3.4 NP-AD requirements and functions

This section discusses NP-AD requirements and functions, building upon the NP-AD formalisms outlined in previous section. Two key aspects are addressed: the general prediction function and the Logistic Function. These functions are crucial for understanding anomaly identification and profiling based on FSM representations of states and transitions.

2.3.4.1 General prediction function

The prediction value prioritizes recent values over older ones. However, incorporating older values remains important due to their likelihood of occurrence. Several prediction functions meet this criterion, with Single Exponential Smoothing (SES) being a notable example [45]. SES is a key component in various time series analyses, making it essential for NP-AD in time series. Based on FSM dimensions and transitions, this study presents the prediction function as:

$$\tilde{x}t = \alpha x_t + (1-\alpha)\tilde{x}t - 1 \tag{17}$$

Here, α reflects the prediction function's memory depth, where a higher value implies less memory depth, leading to predictions based primarily on the most recent previous values.

where α is a parameter reflecting the "depth" of the prediction function memory. A higher value of α implies less memory depth, leading to predictions based primarily on the most recent previous values. Next, we introduce the logistic function, which is an integral part of this paper's scope.

2.3.4.2 Logistic function

The logistic function is utilized to calculate the likelihood of detecting an NP-AD, as shown in Eq. (18):

$$\text{logistic}(x) = \frac{1}{1+e^{b}(x-x_0)} \tag{18}$$

The logic behind this function lies in its ability to normalize the deviation and scale it to measurable and predictive values within the range of (0-1). This normalization enables the likelihood function, represented in Eq. (19), to maintain consistency:

$$p_t = \text{logistic}\left(p_{t-1} + \text{logistic}(\delta x)\right) \tag{19}$$

Here, p_t represents the current likelihood value, while δx denotes the normalized deviation of the time series actual value from the predicted (expected) value.

Using this function fulfills two key criteria: Firstly, it confines the likelihood value within the range of (0-1). Secondly, it normalizes the deviation to ensure consistent logistic function parameters, keeping the outer logistic function input within the range of (0-2). Eq. (19) highlights that logistic functions may have varying parameters, such as $\{b, x_0\}$, as specified in Eq. (18). For instance, assuming parameters $b = 5$ and $x_0 = 0.9$, a logistic curve is generated as depicted in **Figure 1**. Here, an anomaly likelihood value of 0.5 suggests a potential occurrence of unexpected behavior in the previous step. Subsequent unexpected behavior may lead to a deviation of ρx, resulting in $logistic(\delta x) = 0.7$. Consequently, the outer logistic function yields a value of 1.2, increasing the likelihood to $p_t \approx 0.77$.

Conversely, if a new value of logistic $(\delta x) \approx 0.4$ is obtained, the resulting likelihood value would be $p_t \approx 0.43$, lower than the previous anomaly likelihood value. This aligns with the intuitive understanding of deviation from expected behavior.

In defining the criteria for the inner logistic function and its parameters, it is acknowledged that these parameters b, x_0 could exhibit variability across different time series values and deviations. For example, a deviation of 20 might not raise concerns if the average value of the time series is 2000 within a specific time range. However, the same deviation of 0.2 could be considered significant for another time series with a different average value.

To tackle this challenge, a dynamic approach is adopted, employing a sliding window technique to continuously monitor and adapt to changes in the time series characteristics. By utilizing this method, the model can effectively calibrate its parameters based on the evolving nature of the data. This adaptive mechanism ensures that the anomaly detection system remains responsive and accurate across diverse scenarios and datasets.

Hence, to account for these variations, a family of logistic curves is considered instead of using static values in Eq. (18), meeting the following criteria:

- Its middle point (the point where $logistic\ (\delta x) = 0.5$) depends on the average of the last N values of δx
- Its parameter b is reciprocally proportional to the average of the last N values of δx.

The aforementioned average of the last values is calculated as follows:

$$\text{Average} = \frac{1}{N}\sum_{j=i-N}^{i} |x_j|, \text{ where } i \in [N, \text{len(timeseries)}] \tag{20}$$

This family of logistic curves is shown in **Figure 3**, illustrating the average of the last N values of δx equal to {0.25, 0.5, 1, 1.5, 2}, arranged from left to right. Having looked at essential aspects that have been used as basic building blocks for NP-AD, it has been observed and understood that the deviation of anomaly is dependent on the average prediction errors. Furthermore, it was observed that every deviation is normalized by average value.

Algorithm 1: NP-AD in Time-Series

Input: x_t,
Output: $A(x_t)$
Function AnomalyDetection (*timeseries*):
    initialize predicted, slidingwindow, deltas, likelihood, variance, anomalyset
    foreach *point in timeseries* **do**
        delta←*predicted* − *timeseries*[*point*]
        lastNaverage←*AverageofthemostrecentNdeltas*
        variance←*logistic*(*delta/lastNaverage*)
        likelihood←*logistic*(*likelihood* + *variance*)
        predicted←*Predict*(*timeseries*[*point* − *slidingwindow* : *point*])
        anomalyset.append(*likelihood*)
    end
    return *anomalyset*
End Function

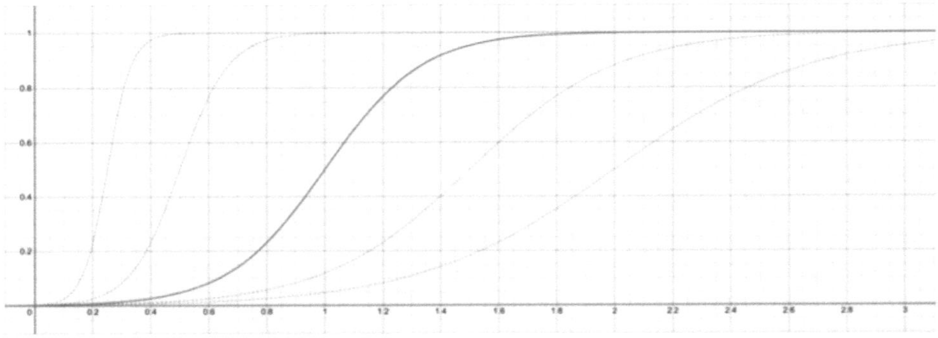

Figure 3.
Logistic function normalized for δx by its average value for the last N points in a sliding window, left to right: {0.25,0.5,1,1.5 *and* 2}.

3. Distributed and decentralized IDS

3.1 Blockchain on duty

The evolution of blockchain writing techniques has played a pivotal role in leveraging the immutable nature of blockchain for data storage. Kaminsky [46] introduced the pioneering blockchain writing solutions, utilizing the output address bytes in the scriptPubKey. The Pay-to-Pubkey-Hash (p2pkh) and Pay-to-Script-Hash (p2sh) techniques were proposed, with Apertus [47] specifically adopting the p2pkh writing method. This technique involves overwriting the 20 bytes of a destination address to store arbitrary data. However, it should be noted that, due to the nature of arbitrary data, the writer becomes unable to redeem this output. Early blockchain-writing systems, such as Catena [48] and Blockstack [49], focused on lightweight transaction usage, introducing cost-effective solutions for handling small payloads. They employed OP RETURN-based writing to mark a transaction as invalid and output unspendable transactions that could be promptly pruned from the unspent transaction set. Catena [48] went a step further, implementing transaction chains, where each transaction had two outputs—one storing data into an unspendable OP RETURN output and the other spent in the subsequent transaction in the chain.

3.1.1 Blockchain for storing data

Beyond the realm of writing techniques, blockchains have emerged as versatile solutions for storing diverse types of data. These encompass arbitrary user data [50–54], sensitive information such as medical records [55], decentralized Public Key Infrastructure (PKI) systems [49], data provenance in cloud environments [56], and privacy-preserving domain name systems [57]. Notably, some services utilize centralized blockchains [58–60], despite concerns over their security. Others employ custom-made blockchains, although their limited adoption makes them vulnerable to majority attacks [61]. For example, Miller et al. [53] proposed a Bitcoin modification integrating proof of retrievability for decentralized file storage. Solutions such as Sia [52], MaidSafe [51], and FileCoin [50] are currently supported by small gossip networks and mining infrastructure, exposing them to risks such as opportunistic attacks through platforms like NiceHash [62]. For instance, Sia clients store files for a fee, leveraging proof-of-store protocols, yet they rely on reputation systems and centralized service distribution, making them susceptible to attacks.

In their study [63], Recabarren and Carbunar developed techniques to embed data into transactions, disguising it from scrutiny by powerful adversaries within regular cryptocurrency operations. This research culminated in the development of an optimal data storage framework (**Figure 4**).

The objective of the Max-Size Data Storing Script is to devise methodologies for writing transaction scripts that optimize script usage, aiming to maximize input throughput while also preventing integrity attacks and adhering to blockchain constraints. These constraints dictate that optimal script utilization allows for a maximum of 3 large push operations per transaction, with an additional allowance for bytes per input script.

An intelligent contract is designed to achieve optimal utilization of available storage space within these constraints, while also safeguarding against integrity attacks. Notably, the inclusion of public key and signature verification in the redeeming script is maintained, ensuring each input script can handle up to 1568 bytes. Considering overhead, the typical size of a funding/spending transaction pair totals 1703 bytes.

Figure 4(a) illustrates max-rate transaction constructs developed to enable funding outputs that generate spending inputs across a network of transactions, aimed at minimizing storage overhead. This optimization is achieved by consolidating the maximum number of inputs into a single transaction, thereby reducing the overhead associated with multiple transactions serving this purpose.

The initial max-rate funding transaction, shown on the left side of **Figure 4(a)**, consolidates n funding outputs (with n maxing out at 2937) and includes an additional change output. Each output carefully references the redeeming script of the corresponding payload-storing input within a max-rate spending transaction,

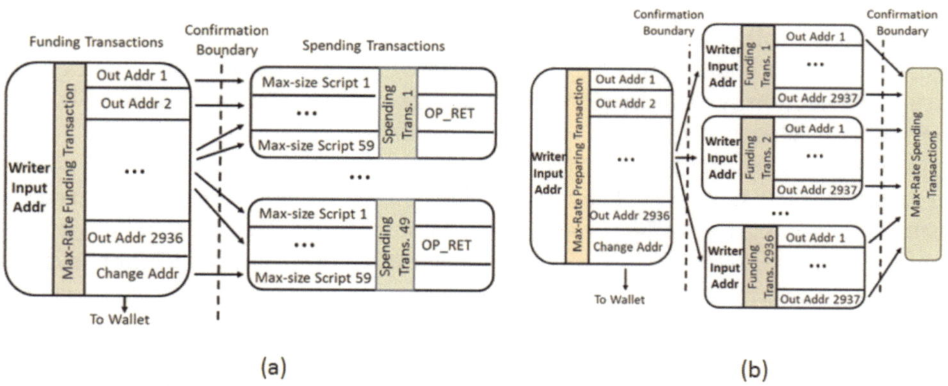

Figure 4.
(a) An optimal data storage construction is designed to establish a network of funding and spending transactions aimed at minimizing storage overhead. This foundational framework facilitates the storage of files up to a maximum size of 4.5 MB within a single confirmation epoch (a). Additionally, it incorporates an indexing technique that enables the linkage of associated funding transactions. This indexing strategy allows metadata to be stored as regular transaction inputs/outputs across different levels of indirection. At the final level, spending transactions are employed to store the actual data (as depicted on the right side of (a)). Transactions occurring between consecutive confirmation boundaries can be simultaneously transmitted up to the maximum block size, given that all their inputs have been confirmed in the preceding epoch.

depicted on the right side of **Figure 4(a)**. Since each spending transaction can accommodate up to 59 payload-storing inputs, a max-rate funding transaction should fund 49 complete spending transactions, with an additional spending transaction comprising 46 inputs. As a result, using this approach, up to 4.6 MB of data can be written (2936 × 1568), covering one funding and 50 spending transactions.

Moreover, it is crucial that the max-rate funding transaction and subsequent spending transactions are separated by a confirmation boundary, as depicted in **Figure 4(b)**, representing a new block mining event and its associated waiting period. This ensures that the funding transaction is mined and confirmed before any spending transactions are issued, adhering to the rule that chains of unconfirmed transactions must not exceed 101 KB in size. Consequently, every funding output is confirmed before any spending input enters the network, minimizing waiting times for payload-storing transactions by navigating the constraints of maximum unconfirmed transaction chains.

3.1.2 Blockchain for intrusion detection

Researchers have explored various approaches to integrate blockchain into IDS architectures to address the challenges of data integrity, trustworthiness, and decentralized threat intelligence sharing. For instance, in their study, Wang et al. [64] proposed a blockchain-based IDS framework that leverages smart contracts to automate threat intelligence sharing among network nodes, improving detection accuracy and response time. Similarly, the review by Malviya et al. [65] provides insights into the potential of blockchain for IDS, highlighting its role in ensuring data integrity and transparency in intrusion detection within Internet of Things (IoT) environments.

Moreover, recent advancements in blockchain technology have led to the development of innovative IDS architectures with enhanced security and resilience against cyber threats. Guo et al. [66] introduced a blockchain-enabled IDS that integrates machine learning techniques for anomaly detection, leveraging the transparent and immutable nature of blockchain to enhance the trustworthiness of detected threats. Additionally, the study by Farooq et al. [67] presents a blockchain-based IDS framework for cloud computing systems, which records security-related events and transactions in a decentralized ledger, ensuring the integrity and non-repudiation of digital evidence. These advancements highlight the potential of blockchain in revolutionizing intrusion detection systems by providing a secure and decentralized platform for real-time threat intelligence sharing and forensic analysis.

Furthermore, Shafagh [68] explores the role of blockchain technology in enhancing security in IoT networks. They discuss the potential applications of blockchain in ensuring data integrity, authentication, and secure communication in IoT environments, thereby augmenting intrusion detection capabilities. Similarly, Mahmood et al. [69] conduct a comprehensive review of intrusion detection systems using blockchain technology, addressing the issues and challenges associated with their implementation. They analyze various blockchain-based IDS frameworks, highlighting their advantages and limitations, and discuss potential research directions for overcoming existing challenges and optimizing the performance of blockchain-enabled intrusion detection systems.

3.1.3 Blockchain for information sharing

Blockchain technology can be a powerful tool for sharing information about cybersecurity threats, such as IoCs, along with their confidence levels. Blockchain's decentralized nature ensures that IoCs are stored across multiple nodes, reducing the risk of data tampering or loss. Once information is recorded on a blockchain, it cannot be altered. This immutability ensures the integrity of the IoCs shared among participants. Blockchain can store confidence levels associated with each IoC, providing users with information about the reliability and accuracy of the data. Blockchain networks can implement robust access control mechanisms to ensure that only authorized entities can add or view IoCs, enhancing security. As new threats are identified, they can be instantly added to the blockchain, allowing for real-time sharing and updates of IoCs. The transparent nature of blockchain helps in building trust among different entities sharing cybersecurity information.

3.2 Distributed and decentralized IDS concepts

Ideas of construction distributed intrusion detection system was famous from 90th of 20 century [70–72] but our approach differs with such way:

- decentralization storing of reputation's event source data
- used feedback for adaptive management by data gathering based on information radius [73]
- used a new complex index of anomaly behavior

Decentralized blockchain-based applications change information systems, and threats/attacks as well as security systems must change accordingly. Problems include both theoretical and practical ones:

Indistinguishably of anomalies caused by different types of events (which anomalies are attributed to attacks); existing models do not clearly answer and give no recommendations on the choice of parameters, the limits of the scales for measuring parameters, etc.; existing models do not fully consider the problem of working with primary/processed data (including the choice of the optimal solution for speed/accuracy); inconsistency of these observations from sensors with different metrics thus the focus should not be on creating a single unified metric, but rather on finding optimal solutions that can function effectively in this metric-less space. (general theory of optimal algorithms); trust and credibility of the data sensors.

The practical absence of modern models in commercial systems, alongside the predominant reliance on signature-based systems and the complexity of introducing anomaly detection systems, necessitates an architecture for the Decentralized Distributed Intrusion Detection System (DDIDS) that includes a set of agents deployed on appropriate network nodes.

Each agent serves three roles: a sensor for network events, a sensor for agent (endpoint) events, and a node of the blockchain. Furthermore, each agent may belong to a dynamic set of nodes determined by its hierarchical level (high, medium, and low).

3.3 DDIDS design

The concept leverages the decentralization inherent to blockchain technology to enhance cybersecurity through a collaborative approach to IDS. This system combines contributions from various stakeholders, including companies and governmental entities, to generate and evaluate IoCs. The breakdown of how this system operates:

- Stakeholders as sensors
  - Participating entities: Companies and governmental bodies act as sensors within this ecosystem. Each stakeholder contributes by monitoring their networks for potential security threats.
  - Anomaly detection systems: These entities employ both pattern-based and non-pattern-based anomaly detection methodologies to identify unusual activities that could indicate a security breach. Pattern-based approaches might rely on known signatures of malware or attack vectors, while non-pattern-based (or heuristic) methods focus on detecting deviations from normal behavior that might signal an intrusion.
- IoC generation and blockchain integration
  - Indicator of compromise generation: Upon detecting anomalies, the systems generate IoCs, which are digital artifacts or patterns (such as malicious IP addresses, URLs, file hashes) that indicate a potential security incident.
  - Blockchain "main": These IoCs, along with their metadata (including the time of generation), are recorded in a blockchain network named "main." This blockchain serves as an immutable ledger, ensuring the integrity and traceability of the IoC data shared across the network and tracking the origin (block producer).
- Quality evaluation and secondary blockchain
  - IoC quality evaluation: Stakeholders can assess the quality and applicability of the IoCs. This evaluation might include factors such as the relevance of the IoC to their specific context, the confidence level in the IoC's accuracy, and the potential impact of the threat it signifies.
  - Blockchain "quality storage": The results of these evaluations are stored in a second blockchain network, named "Quality storage." This separate blockchain maintains records of each IoC's assessed quality level, offering a transparent and immutable history of evaluations.
- Dynamic IoC feeds and enhanced security
  - Customizable IoC feeds: Stakeholders can filter and select IoCs from the "main" blockchain based on various attributes, such as the quality level, confidence level, and type of IoC. This enables entities to tailor the IoC feeds to their specific needs and threat landscape.
  - Integration with IDS/SIEM: The selected IoCs can then be integrated into the stakeholders' existing intrusion detection systems (IDS) or security information and event management (SIEM) systems. This ensures that the defense mechanisms are informed by the most relevant and reliable threat indicators.

By pooling resources and intelligence, the system enhances the ability of each participant to detect and respond to emerging threats more effectively. The use of blockchain technology ensures the integrity of the IoC data and the transparency of the quality evaluation process, fostering trust among stakeholders. The ability to select IoCs based on detailed criteria ensures that stakeholders are working with the most applicable and high-confidence threat intelligence, improving the overall effectiveness of cybersecurity measures. This decentralized IDS system represents a novel approach to cybersecurity, leveraging the collective intelligence and resources of a wide range of stakeholders, underpinned by the security and transparency of blockchain technology.

4. Blockchain protocol for decentralized IDS

Blockchain is used in distributed intrusion detection systems like databases but in a different way: It serves also as a trusted third party to regulate the role of each node.

The right to generate the next block in the consensus protocol is obtained by the participant with the highest S rating. The rating of each participant indirectly depends on the amount of valuable resources, which is the participant's IP address in the protocol. A lottery is used to calculate the S rating. Prizes for participation in the lottery do not increase the amount of valuable resources. The lottery is implemented using the function F computable at time t (until the t time the function F is incompatible due to incomplete input information). To do this, when the F function is calculated, a random variable R is used in the joint generation in which at least k protocol participants take part.

4.1 Step-by-step description of the protocol

Step 1. Initialization ("throw stones").

Negotiation of the current number and subset of protocol participants. Co-generation of secret and secret sharing ("first lottery") between all protocol participants (between all elements of set B).

All active participants with their IP addresses take part in the lottery, n participant's - $IP_1, \ldots, IP_n$.

To generate the i – block in the blockchain, select the thresholds of complexity $0 < l_i < 1$ and $k_i < n$. The choice of the k_i value is determined by the ratio of the required transaction speed and protocol resistance to a DSA attack. The choice of the l_i value determines the probability of calculating the predicate, which is determined by the number of attempts to generate a new block for each protocol participant.

Select the k_i protocol participants (by the smallest values of IP addresses, for example), which generate a random number R_i using the Diffie-Hellman group protocol. The selection of participants may be implemented by any other random procedure. The Diffie-Hellman protocol for groups is an extension of the Diffie-Hellman protocol to n members [74]. The length of R_i must be more than 1024 bits for security reasons.

Step 2. Accumulation ("collect stones").

Collect of secret parts (contained in set B) protocol participants from set A ("second lottery"). Computation for secret recovery for participants of the protocol from set A.

Function $F_{l_i} : \{0,1\}^* \rightarrow \{0,1\}$—the predicate, defined as $P(F_{l_i}(^*, R_i) = 1)) = l_i$, here $P(X)$—probability of random variable X. A predicate can be constructed as:

for each of participants $j = 1, k_i$ concatenating values: $X = H_{i-1} \parallel IP_j \parallel count_{1j} \parallel R_i$, where H_{i-1}—hash code of previous block in blockchain,

$count_{j1}, \ \ldots, \ count_{ju}, \ldots, \ count_{jm}$—count value, where m—maximum value of counter.

Calculating a hash code $H(X)$, used by the hash function $H : \{0,1\}^* \rightarrow \{0,1\}^t$ (the length of t must be more than 256 bits for security reasons).

Determining parity of $H(X)$ if value $l_i = 1/2$ (because value close to random, uniform distribution). The $F_{l_i}(H(X)) = 1$, if parity of $H(X)$ is 1.

For any $0 < l_i \approx \frac{C}{D} < \frac{1}{2}$—determining $H(X) mod \ D$ (the hash code from the concatenation of the values of the hash code of the previous block, IP address, random variable, and counter value, taken modulo D). If $H(X) mod \ D < C$ then the $F_{l_i}(H(X)) = 1$. If $H(X) mod \ D \geq C$ then the $F_{l_i}(H(X)) = 0$. Here, C and D are some integer numbers.

For i block generation each of n participants calculate m value $F_{l_i}(H_{i-1}, IP_j, count_{1j}, \ R_i)$, ... $F_{l_i}(H_{i-1}, IP_j, count_{mj}, \ R_i)$, H_{i-1} – hash code of previous block in blockchain, $count_{j1}, \ \ldots, \ count_{ju}, \ldots, \ count_{jm}$ – count value.

The winner is the one who for some value $F_{l_i}(H_{i-1}, IP_j, count_{uj}, \ R_i) = 1$. If for some $j_1 \neq j_2$ $F_{l_i}(H_{i-1}, IP_{j_1}, count_{*j_1}, \ R_i) = F_{l_i}(H_{i-1}, IP_{j_2}, count_{*j_2}, \ R_i)$, then the winner is the one who have minimum , $count_{*j_*}$. If the values of the counters are equal, then we have the situation of the "fork" of traditional blockchains, which is resolved by choosing the largest chain.

The winner generates a digital signature of the block transaction.

Step 3. Verification.

Minimizing the probabilities of "forks" and wrong block attacks. Check process of block generation participants of the protocol from set B.

For any participant checking F_{l_i} and verification of digital signature of block transaction are possible.

4.2 Step-by-step example of the protocol

Step 1. Initialization ("throw stones").

All active participants with their IP addresses take part in the lottery, $n = 5$ participant's - $IP_1, \ldots, IP_5$, let $IP_1 = 78.27.168.220$, $IP_2 = 104.31.255.255$, $IP_3 = 27.121.104.0$, $IP_4 = 5.39.126.236$, $IP_5 = 5.135.53.40$.

To generate the i-block in the blockchain, select the thresholds of complexity $0 < l_i < 1$ and $k_i < n$. Let $k_i = 3$, let $l_i = 0,5$.

For another example, we can also choose thresholds of complexity $0 < \mathrm{l_i} < 1$ and $\mathrm{k_i} < \mathrm{n}$. Let $\mathrm{k_i} = 3$, let $\mathrm{l_i} = 0,67 \cong \frac{2}{3}$, consequently $C = 2$, $D = 3$.

Select the $k_i = 3$ protocol participants (by the smallest values of IP smallest 3 decimal digits of addresses, for example (in the real world for the arrangement of participants we can calculate $H(IP_i)$ of each participant and approve they lexicographic order). We choose participants with IP_3, IP_5, IP_1 in our case. We generate a random number R_i using the Diffie-Hellman group protocol as follows:

We choose $p = 23$, $q|(p-1) = 11$, $\alpha = 5$ (generator group with order $p-1$). Participant with IP_3 address choose random number $r_1 = 7$, calculate "part or random number (down the text PR)" $PR_1 = 5^7 mod \ 23 = 17$ and put it (PR_1) to participant with IP_5 address. Participant with IP_5 address choose random number $r_2 = 4$, calculate $PR_2 = 5^4 mod \ 23 = 4$, $PR_{12} = 17^4 mod \ 23 = 8$, and put $PR_1 = 17, PR_2 = 4, PR_{12} = 8$ to participant with IP_1 address. Participant with IP_1 choose random number $r_3 = 15$, calculate $PR_{23} = PR_2^{r_3} = 4^{15} mod 23 = 3$, $PR_{13} = PR_1^{r_3} = 17^{15} mod \ 23 = 15$, $R_i = PR_{12}^{r_3} =$

$8^{15} mod\ 23 = 2$ and put P_{23} =3 to participant with IP_3, put $P_{13} = 15$ to participant with IP_5. Participant with IP_3 address calculates $R_i = PR_{23}^{r_1} = 3^7 mod\ 23 = 2$. Participant with IP_5 address calculates $R_i = PR_{13}^{r_2} = 15^4 mod\ 23 = 2$.

Another example. We choose $p = 557$, $q|(p-1) = 139$, $\alpha = 2$. Participant with IP_3 address chooses random number $r_1 = 73$, calculate $PR_1 = 2^{73} mod\ 557 = 162$, and put $PR_1 = 162$ to participant with IP_5 address. Participant with IP_5 address chooses random number $r_2 = 21$, calculate $PR_2 = 2^{21} mod\ 557 = 47$, $PR_{12} = PR_1^{r_2} mod\ p = 162^{21} mod\ 557 = 340$ and put $PR_1 = 162, PR_2 = 47, PR_{12} = 340$ to participant with IP_1 address. Participant with IP_1 chooses random number $r_3 = 12$, calculate $PR_{23} = PR_2^{r_3} = 47^{12} mod\ 557 = 547$, $PR_{13} = PR_1^{r_3} = 162^{12} mod\ 557 = 19$, $R_i = PR_{12}^{r_3} = 340^{12} mod\ 557 = 455$ and put P_{23} =547 to participant with IP_3, put $P_{13} = 19$ to participant with IP_5. Participant with IP_3 address calculates $R_i = PR_{23}^{r_1} = 547^{73} mod\ 557 = 455$. Participants with IP_5 address calculates $R_i = PR_{13}^{r_2} = 19^{21} mod\ 557 = 455 = 0x1c7$.

Step 2. Accumulation ("collect stones").

Collect of secret parts (contained in set B) protocol participants from set A ("second lottery"). Computation for secret recovery for participants of the protocol from set $A = \{IP_3, IP_5, IP_1\}$.

Function $F_{1/2} : \{0,1\}^* \rightarrow \{0,1\}$ – the predicate, defined as $P(F_{1/2}(^*, R_i) = 1)) = 1/2$, here $P(X)$ – probability of random variable X. A predicate can be constructed as:

Let H_{i-1} = 0x7be45e06e6993cd9bbe506594f3a09185953e60ee2f0a1ce80f7e2f 8eb56c350 be an example of the hash-code of text message = "Begin of blockchain chain." made by SHA-256 algorithms.

For participant with IP_3 let $count_{11} = 0x0000001$; $X = 0x7be45e06e6993cd9bbe 506594f3a09185953e60ee2f0a1ce80f7e2f8eb56c3502712110400000001 1c7$, where $R_i = 455 = 0x1c7$. Calculating a hash code: $H(X) = 0xa2d2746d63ebf7568 4effbec969996aa2813e5e683a9c72b5f9bffc45beed7bb$ used by hash function SHA-256. Determining parity of $H(X)$ ($l_i = 1/2$). The $F_{1/2}(H(X)) = 1$, because parity of $H(X)$ is 1. Participant with IP_3 becomes the winner! He generates digital signature of block transaction and send X all participants IP_1, IP_2, IP_4, IP_5.

4.3 Another example with $l_i = 0,67 \cong \frac{2}{3}$, consequently $C = 2$, $D = 3$

Function $F_{1/2} : \{0,1\}^* \rightarrow \{0,1\}$—the predicate, defined as $P(F_{2/3}(^*, R_i) = 1)) = 2/3$, here $P(X)$—probability of random variable X. A predicate can be constructed as:

Let H_{i-1} = 0x7be45e06e6993cd9bbe506594f3a09185953e60ee2f0a1ce80f7e2f8eb56c350 be an example of the hash-code of text message = "Begin of blockchain chain." made by SHA-256 algorithms.

For participant with IP_3 let $count_{11} = 0x0000001$; $X = 0x7be45e06e6993cd9bbe506594f3$.

$a09185953e60ee2f0a1ce80f7e2f8eb56c35027121104000000011c7$ where $R_i = 455 = 0x1c7$. Calculating a hash code $H(X) = 0xa2d2746d63ebf75684effbec969996aa2813e5e683a\ 9c72b5f9bffc45beed7bb$ used by hash function SHA-256. Determining $H(X) mod\ 3 = 2$ ($l_i = 2/3$). The $F_{2/3}(H(X)) = 0$, because $H(X) mod3 \geq 2$.

For participant with IP_5 let $count_{11} = 0x0000001$; $X = 0x7be45e06e6993cd9bbe 506594f3a09185953e60ee2f0a1ce80f7e2f8eb56c350513553400000000011c7$ where $R_i = 455 = 0x1c7$. Calculating a hash code.

$H(X) = 0x0b3480025d29973c711ec925e109a39496369ab200de9f3732b8 bba97c5dcc88$ used by hash function SHA-256. Determining $H(X) mod\ 3 = 1$ $(l_i = 2/3)$. The $F_{2/3}(H(X)) = 1$, because $H(X) mod 3 < 2$. Participant with IP_5 becomes the winner because $F_{2/3}(H(X)) = 1$ for IP_5 for minimum value of counter! He generates digital signature of block transaction and send X all participants IP_1, IP_2, IP_3, IP_4.

Step 3. Verification. Minimizing the probabilities of "forks" and wrong block attacks. Check process of block generation participants of the protocol from set B. All participants with IP_1, IP_2, IP_4, IP_5 address checking $F_{1/2}$ for participant with IP_3 address and verification of digital signature of block transaction.

5. Practical aspects of DDIDS implementation

5.1 Endpoint protection

Endpoint protection is a critical aspect of cybersecurity, particularly as organizations increasingly rely on interconnected devices and remote work environments. Anomaly detection techniques play a pivotal role in bolstering the security posture of endpoints by identifying and mitigating potential threats that evade traditional security measures. These techniques involve monitoring and analyzing the behavior of endpoints in real time to identify deviations from normal patterns or expected behavior. By leveraging machine learning algorithms and advanced analytics, anomaly detection empowers organizations to proactively detect and respond to emerging security threats before they escalate into full-scale breaches.

One of the key advantages of anomaly detection techniques for endpoint protection is their ability to detect novel and previously unseen threats. Traditional signature-based antivirus solutions are effective at identifying known malware based on predefined patterns or signatures. However, they often struggle to detect zero-day exploits or sophisticated attacks that deviate from known patterns. Anomaly detection, on the other hand, operates on the principle of detecting deviations from baseline behavior, enabling it to identify previously unknown threats that may exhibit anomalous patterns or behaviors. This proactive approach to threat detection helps organizations stay ahead of emerging threats and minimize the risk of compromise to their endpoints and sensitive data.

The utilization of the Non-Pattern-Based Anomaly Detection approach facilitates the detection of behavioral novelties in the absence of specific signatures or patterns for anomaly detection. As illustrated in **Figure 5**, this approach identifies two behavioral anomalies in the time series, both of which are outliers. However, there exists another anomaly that remains undetected due to two key factors: Firstly, the threshold level set for anomalies is excessively high; and secondly, the amplitude of fluctuations in the time series values gradually increases in the interval preceding this point, leading the model to adapt to such values.

Figure 6 further demonstrates the efficacy of the approach by detecting anomalies in a more intricate time series, representing the temperature of a hard-disk drive collected from a laptop, with the x-axis denoting time measured in seconds.

Figure 6 illustrates a non-seasonal time series containing outliers, specifically depicting the CPU battery voltage collected from a laptop, with time measured in

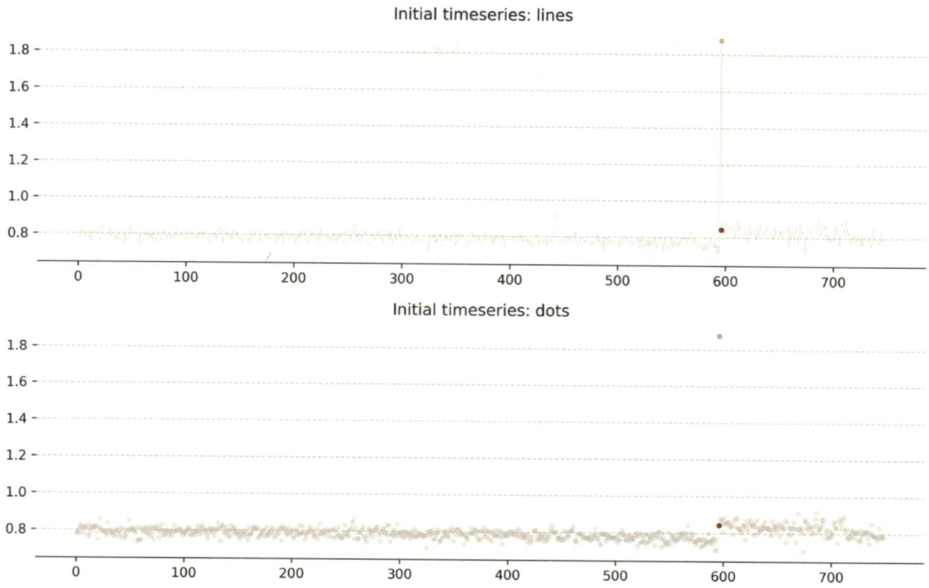

Figure 5.
Artificially made time series with outliers to demonstrate the approach. Non-seasonal time series with outliers.

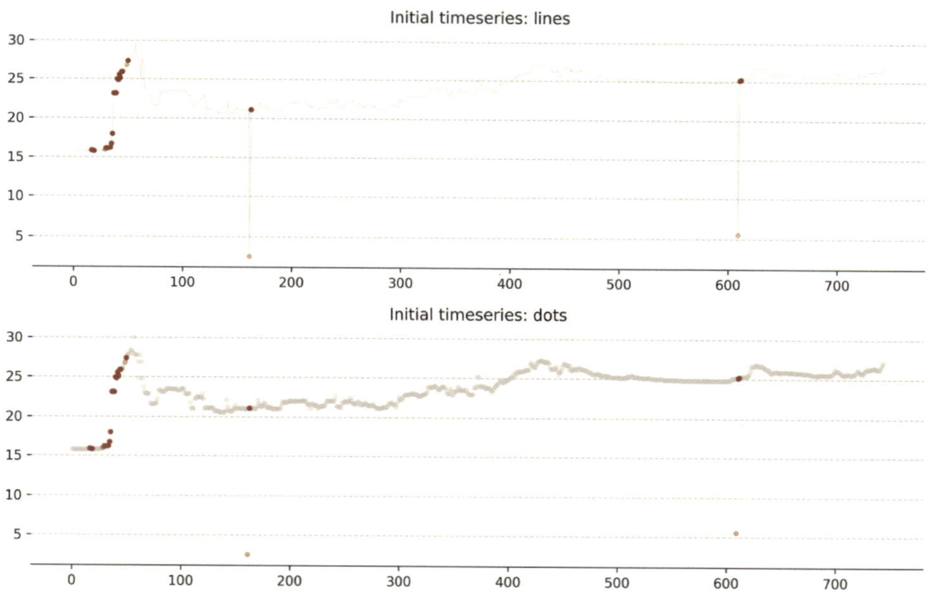

Figure 6.
Non-seasonal time series with outliers. Anomalies were found with an anomaly likelihood threshold of 0.95.

seconds. On the other hand, **Figure 7** portrays a time series exhibiting repeated values with the spike density anomaly, showcasing various anomaly likelihood thresholds sourced from the Numenta Anomaly Benchmark (NAB) dataset.

In selecting an appropriate anomaly likelihood threshold, adjustments are tailored to the number of alerts across different types of raw data, or the identification of new anomalies within repeated time series becomes necessary. For instance, **Figure 8** exemplifies a time series characterized by high variance and a seasonal component.

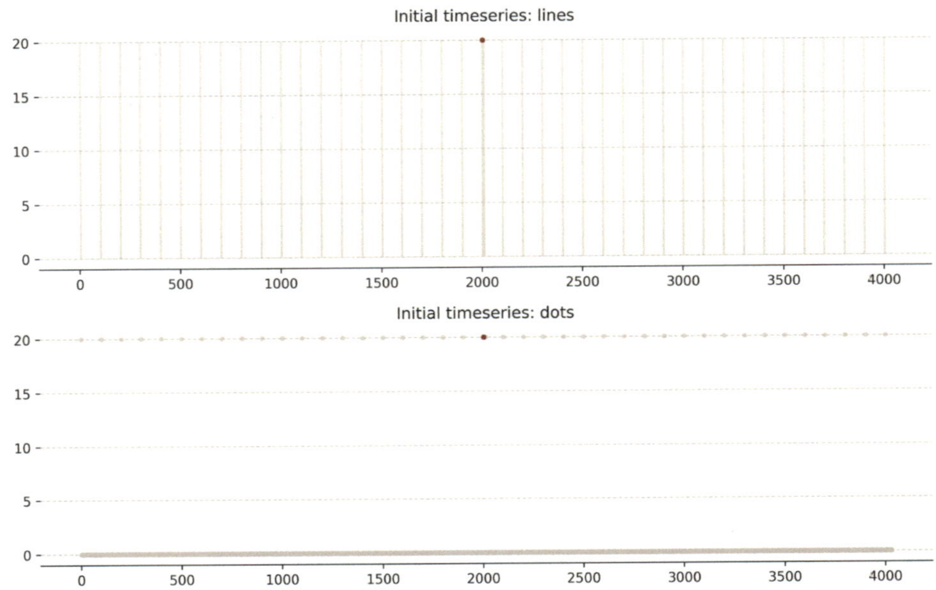

Figure 7.
Numenta Anomaly Benchmark spike density anomaly found with anomaly likelihood threshold 0.98.

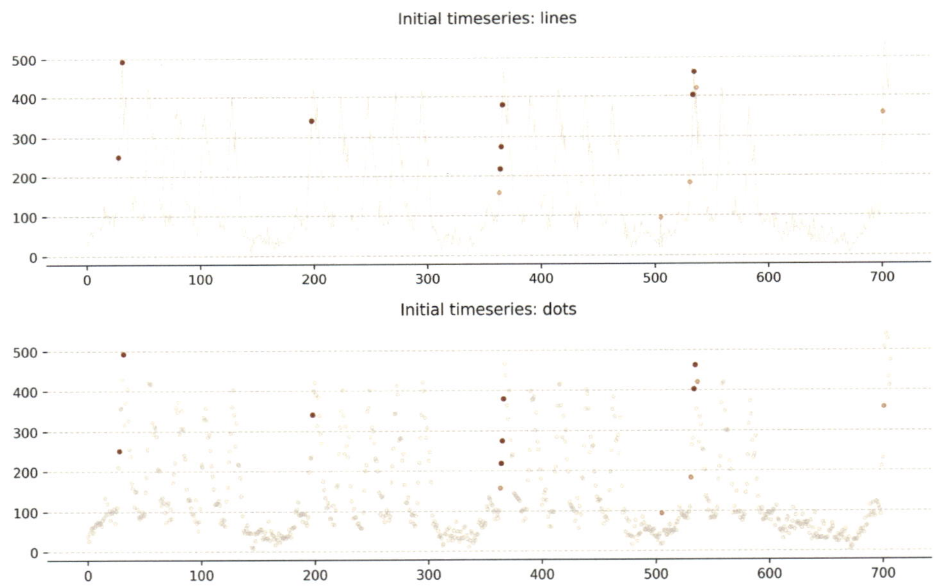

Figure 8.
Numenta Anomaly Benchmark time series with a seasonal component.

The anomaly depicted therein highlights a limitation of the proposed model employing Single Exponential Smoothing (SES) as the prediction function. To address such anomalies, the SARMA (SARIMA, SARIMAX) function is proposed as an alternative [75–78]. This avenue warrants further investigation in future research endeavors. The most interesting result is observed in a time series that is both non-seasonal and free of statistical outliers. As shown in **Figure 9**, the model is capable of

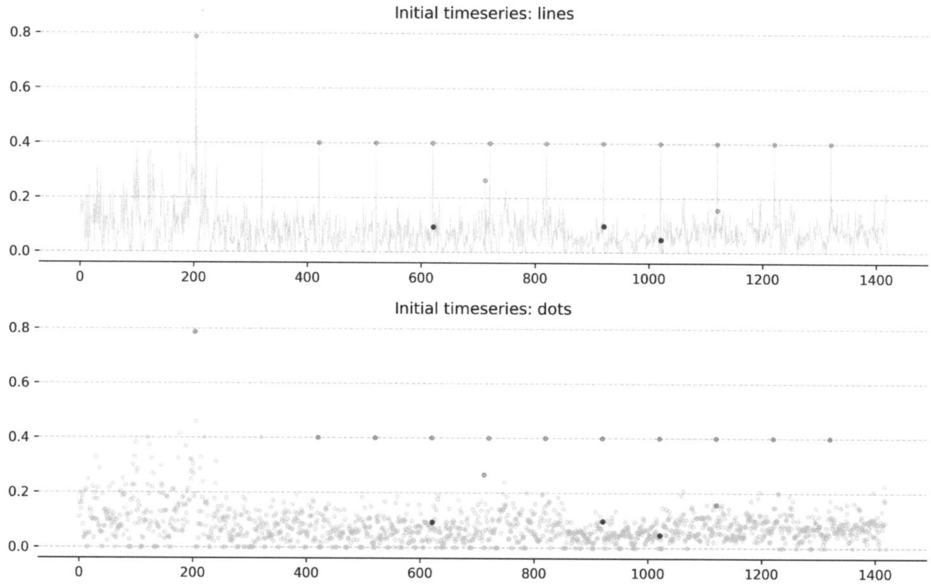

Figure 9.
Numenta Anomaly Benchmark time series with hidden context anomalies within repeating point anomalies set. Anomalies were found with an anomaly likelihood threshold of 0.9.

detecting contextual anomalies even when their values fall within the expected range of the statistical distribution.

Generally, the proposed method for anomaly detection is an essential part of an endpoint. Not only this method generates alerts for suspicious behavior but also assists in gathering additional information at these points. The digital artifacts collected by the system in points where anomaly likelihood reaches the threshold after consideration and investigation may be defined as Indicators of Compromise (IoC). At the initial stages, these digital artifacts may be considered Indicators of Risk (IoR) or Indicators of Attack (IoA).

5.2 NP-AD and IoC generation

The previous models were designed with certain specifications, such as being developed for a particular type of IoC (such as IP addresses) or for a specific data source. However, these studies did not consider confidence levels throughout the complete life cycle or analyze how confidence changes over time formats. Additionally, many factors and data were considered when creating these models.

The confidence level is crucial in determining the quality and quantity of an IoC's life cycle. Trust values are used to calculate confidence levels. The model introduced in 2.2 was designed to calculate scores with confidence levels over the entire IoC lifecycle.

5.2.1 Behavior pattern of confidence level over a period of days

The following figures illustrate graphs depicting confidence levels against days. On the y-axis, the confidence level is represented within the range of 0 to 1, while the x-axis denotes time intervals measured in days. It is important to note that the intervals employed here are in days, aiming to capture the behavior pattern of confidence

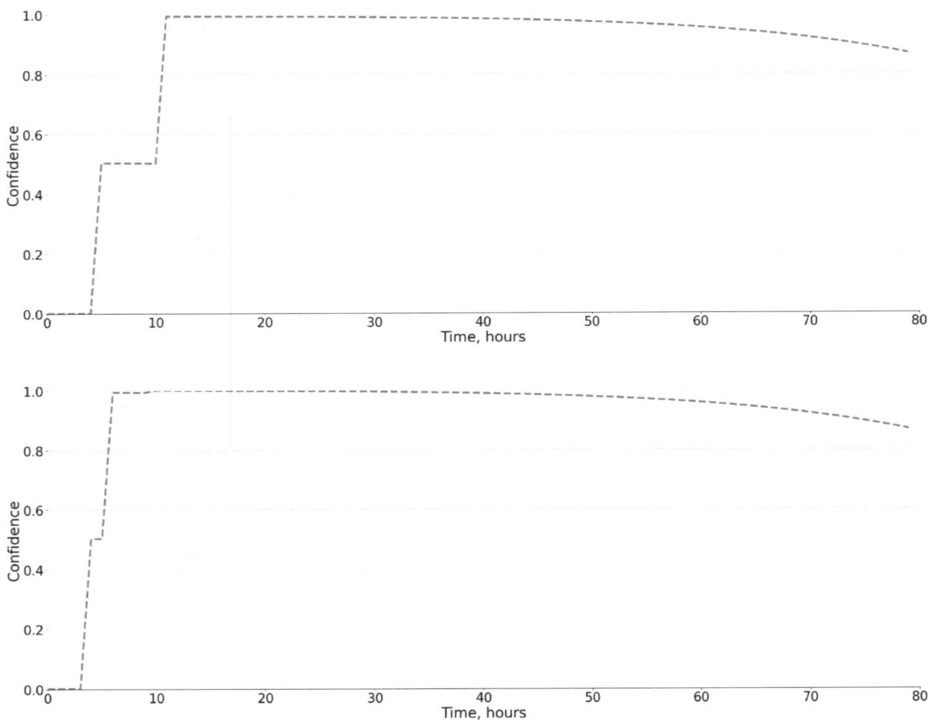

Figure 10.
Behavior pattern of confidence for the first feed (for 1-hour and 2-hour intervals).

levels. Consequently, a longer interval signifies an extended lifetime for an Indicator of Compromise (IoC).

For the provided feed, **Figure 10** illustrates a behavioral trend spanning 116 days, albeit with observable patterns only within the initial 20 days. Initially, the trend starts from zero and gradually ascends, remaining relatively constant for a significant duration, indicating consecutive testing of the indicator and yielding a 50% confidence level. Subsequently, confidence rapidly rises to approximately 1 and remains at that level for the remainder of the lifecycle.

In the case of the first feed, confidence builds gradually, taking a short duration to reach 50% and around 20 – 30 days to stabilize at 1. Conversely, for the second feed, peak confidence is attained within the initial 20 days, indicating a faster buildup of confidence due to more frequent testing. However, it is important to note that these observed patterns may not be indicative of a consistent confidence pattern, as they can be further analyzed at an hourly level to discern the true volatility of confidence.

5.2.2 Behavior pattern of confidence level on hourly basis

The model was deployed hourly to examine the volatile nature of confidence levels. Confidence levels exhibit considerable fluctuations, with sporadic pulses observed during testing intervals and minimal activity otherwise. Unlike the daily implementation, the hourly approach allows for a more detailed observation of confidence dynamics, capturing minute fluctuations in confidence levels. A constant peak

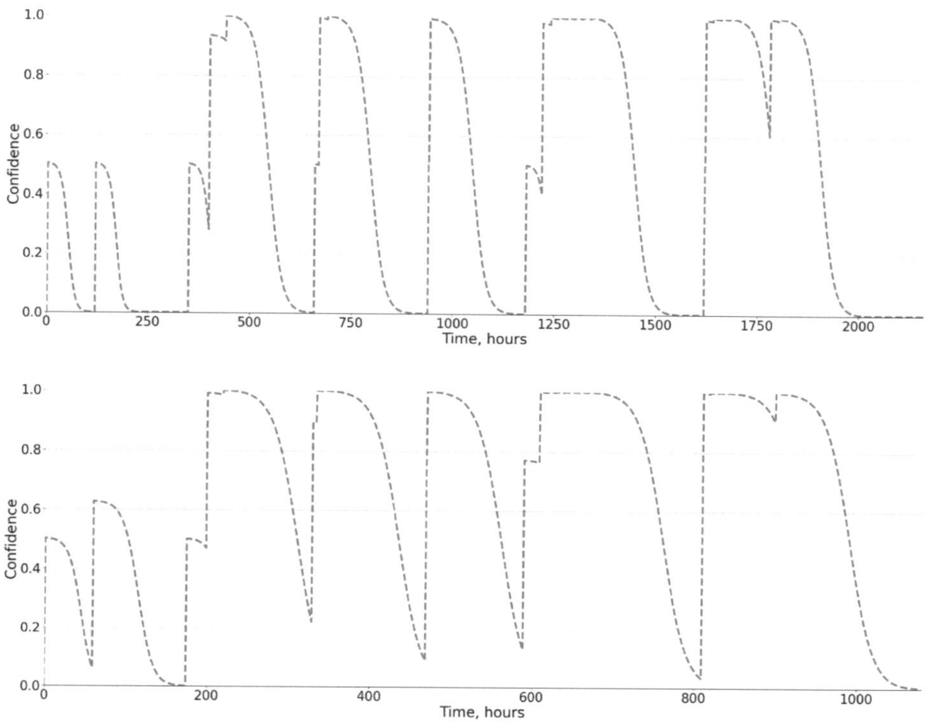

Figure 11.
Behavior pattern of confidence for the second feed (for 1-hour and 2-hour intervals).

in the graph suggests either minimal differences between testing times or multiple tests occurring within the same day, providing insights into the testing frequency and confidence stability.

5.2.3 Behavior pattern of confidence level over 2-hour interval

Confidence is also relative and dependent on various factors. Implementing the model against two-hour time intervals helped to observe the significant change compared to the hourly graph. Here the frequency was more on an hourly basis, there is more fluctuation, but in the interval of 2 hours, it is relative (**Figure 11**).

Comparing the confidence levels of IoCs using graphs across different time formats is a valuable method for analyzing their behavior. By comparing graphs of minutes and seconds with those of days and hours, researchers can observe how the confidence level changes over time, leading to more precise and accurate results as the dataset size increases. Time is a critical factor for IoCs, significantly influencing their behavior, and the nature of the confidence level for the same IoC feed can vary significantly depending on the time format being used.

Differences in the behavior of IoCs over different time formats can be attributed to various factors, such as changes in the threat landscape, variations in IoC creation methods, and shifts in attacker tactics and techniques. Analyzing the behavior of IoCs over different time formats can provide insights into how these factors affect IoC efficacy and how they can be improved. This approach can help organizations develop better threat detection and response capabilities, thereby enhancing their overall cybersecurity posture.

6. Conclusions and perspectives

In this chapter, we explored the concepts of distributed and decentralized intrusion detection systems (IDS) with a focus on leveraging blockchain technology. The evolution of blockchain writing techniques, such as Pay-to-Pubkey-Hash (p2pkh) and Pay-to-Script-Hash (p2sh), has paved the way for innovative approaches to data storage within blockchains. Early blockchain-writing systems such as Catena and Blockstack introduced lightweight transaction usage for handling small payloads, while recent advancements have extended blockchain's utility to store various types of data including arbitrary user data, sensitive medical records, decentralized Public Key Infrastructure (PKI) systems, and more.

Blockchain technology offers a versatile solution for storing different types of data securely and immutably. While some services resort to centralized blockchains, others opt for custom-made blockchains, each presenting its own set of security challenges. Solutions such as Sia, MaidSafe, and FileCoin require widespread adoption to minimize vulnerability to attacks. The development of optimal data storage construction, as proposed by Recabarren and Carbunar, aims to embed data into transactions indistinguishably from regular cryptocurrency use, ensuring data integrity and security.

Blockchain technology has garnered significant attention for enhancing intrusion detection systems (IDS) due to its decentralized and immutable nature. Researchers have proposed blockchain-based IDS frameworks leveraging smart contracts to automate threat intelligence sharing among network nodes, improving detection accuracy and response time. Integrating machine learning techniques for anomaly detection further enhances the trustworthiness of detected threats. These advancements highlight the potential of blockchain in revolutionizing intrusion detection systems by providing a secure and decentralized platform for real-time threat intelligence sharing and forensic analysis.

Blockchain technology facilitates secure and transparent information sharing about cybersecurity threats, such as Indicators of Compromise (IoCs), across multiple nodes. The decentralized nature of blockchain ensures data integrity and reliability, while robust access control mechanisms ensure that only authorized entities can add or view IoCs. Real-time sharing and updates of IoCs enable swift response to emerging threats, fostering trust among different entities sharing cybersecurity information.

Our approach to constructing distributed intrusion detection systems differs from traditional centralized systems by focusing on the decentralization of reputation event source data and using feedback for adaptive management based on information radius. The introduction of modern models and architectures for distributed and decentralized IDS presents both theoretical and practical challenges, including anomaly detection, parameter selection, data processing, and trustworthiness of sensor data.

The implementation of Distributed and Decentralized IDS (DDIDS) involves the deployment of agents on appropriate nodes of the network, each fulfilling multiple roles including sensor for network events, sensor for end-point events, and node of the blockchain. The blockchain serves as a trusted third party to regulate the role of each node, ensuring the decentralized and secure operation of the system.

The protocol for block generation employs cryptographic techniques such as Diffie-Hellman group protocol and hash functions to ensure security and integrity.

In conclusion, the integration of blockchain technology into intrusion detection systems offers promising avenues for enhancing cybersecurity by providing secure, decentralized, and immutable platforms for data storage, threat intelligence sharing, and anomaly detection. However, the practical implementation of distributed and decentralized IDS presents several challenges that require further research and development to address effectively.

Acknowledgements

This paper was published under the CRDF Global Ukraine-USA Grant Agreement with the National Technical University of Ukraine "Igor Sikorsky Kyiv Polytechnic Institute" (Kyiv, Ukraine), and Florida International University (Miami, FL, USA). Authors are grateful to the Blekinge Institute of Technology for supporting this publication.

Conflict of interest

The authors declare no conflict of interest.

Author details

Anton Kudin[1†], Volodymyr Tkach[1,3*†], Oleksii Baranovskyi[1,2†]
and Bogdan Carbunar[4†]

1 Igor Sikorsky Kyiv Polytechnic Institute, Kyiv, Ukraine

2 Blekinge Institute of Technology, Karlskrona, Sweden

3 George Mason University, Fairfax, VA, USA

4 Florida International University, Miami, FL, USA

*Address all correspondence to: vtkach@gmu.edu; vntkach@gmail.com

† These authors contributed equally.

References

[1] Asiri M, Saxena N, Gjomemo R, Burnap P. Understanding indicators of compromise against cyber-attacks in industrial control systems: A security perspective. ACM Transactions on Cyber-Physical Systems. 2023;7(2):1-33

[2] Dodiya B, Singh UK. Tithonus: A bitcoin based censorship resilient system. International Journal of Computer Applications. 2022;**183**(53): 68-86

[3] Iklody A, Wagener G, Dulaunoy A, Mokaddem S, Wagner C. Decaying indicators of compromise. arXiv preprint arXiv:1803.11052. 2018. DOI: 10.48550/arXiv.1803.11052

[4] Villalón-Huerta A, Ripoll-Ripoll I, Marco-Gisbert H. Key requirements for the detection and sharing of behavioral indicators of compromise. Electronics. 2022;**11**(3):321-338

[5] Preuveneers D, Joosen W. Sharing machine learning models as indicators of compromise for cyber threat intelligence. Journal of Cybersecurity and Privacy. 2021;**1**(1):140-163

[6] MISP Project. Open source threat intelligence and sharing platform. Available from: https://www.misp-project.org/ [Accessed: 2024-03-25]

[7] Fuchs M, Lemon J. Threat hunting: Focusing on the hunters and how best to support them. 2023. Available from: https://www.devo.com/wp-content/uploads/2023/08/Survey_Threat-Hunting-2023_DEVO.pdf [Accessed: March 25, 2024]

[8] Srivastava S. Top 10 cloud security risks solution in 2024 how to tackle them. 2024. Available from: https://appinventiv.com/blog/cloud-security-risks-and-solutions/ [Accessed: March 25, 2024]

[9] Cloudflare documentation. https://developers.cloudflare.com/ddos-protection/managed-rulesets/adjust-rules/false-positive/ [Accessed: March 25, 2024]

[10] Tkach V, Baranovskyi O, Kudin A, Godavarti N, Kliok O, Modali S. Indicators of compromise confidence scoring method. In: Proceedings of the 12th IEEE International Conference on Intelligent Data Acquisition and Advanced Computing Systems: Technology and Applications (IDAACS). Dortmund University of Applied Sciences and Arts; 2023. pp. 537-545

[11] Van Impe K. How to defend with the courses of action matrix and indicator lifecycle management. 2018. Available from: https://securityintelligence.com/how-to-defend-with-the-courses-of-action-matrix-and-indicator-lifecycle-management/ [Accessed: March 25, 2024]

[12] Caridi C. "Authorized" to break in: Adversaries use valid credentials to compromise cloud environments. 2023. Available from: https://securityintelligence.com/x-force/adversaries-use-valid-credentials-compromise-cloud-environments/ [Accessed: March 25, 2024]

[13] Boehm C. Avoiding the storm | how to protect cloud infrastructure from insider threats. 2023. Available from: https://www.sentinelone.com/blog/avoiding-the-storm-how-to-protect-cloud-infrastructure-from-insider-threats/ [Accessed: March 25, 2024]

[14] The importance of user behavior analytics for cloud service security.

Available from: https://www.oracle.com/assets/user-behavior-analytics-3497541.pdf [Accessed: March 25, 2024]

[15] IBM Documentation. Qradar user behavior analytics. Available from: https://www.ibm.com/docs/en/qradar-common?topic=app-qradar-user-behavior-analytics [Accessed: March 25, 2024]

[16] Callaway T. How to maximize telemetry data value with observability pipelines. Available from: https://devops.com/how-to-maximize-telemetry-data-value-with-observability-pipelines/ [Accessed: March 25, 2024]

[17] Ahmad S, Lavin A, Purdy S, Agha Z. Unsupervised real-time anomaly detection for streaming data. Neurocomputing. 2017;**262**:134-147

[18] Tan SC, Ting KM, Liu TF. Fast anomaly detection for streaming data. In: Proceedings of the Twenty-Second International Joint Conference on Artificial Intelligence (IJCAI 2011). Barcelona, Spain; IJCAI/AAAI Press; 16-22 July 2011. pp. 2329-2334. DOI: 10.5591/978-1-57735-516-8/IJCAI11-392 [Accessed: 30 November 2024]

[19] Waite A. InfoSec Triads: Security/Functionality/Ease-of-use. Infosanity's Blog; 2010. Available from: https://blog.infosanity.co.uk/2010/06/12/infosec-triadssecurityfunctionalityease-of-use/ [Accessed: November 30, 2024]

[20] Rainie L, Anderson J, Connolly J. Cyber-attacks likely to increase. Pew Research Center; 2014. Available from: https://www.pewresearch.org/internet/2014/10/29/cyber-attacks-likely-to-increase/ [Accessed: November 30, 2024]

[21] Chandola V, Banerjee A, Kumar V. Anomaly detection: A survey. ACM Computing Surveys (CSUR). 2009;**41**(3):1-58

[22] Munir M, Siddiqui SA, Dengel A, Ahmed S. Deepant: A deep learning approach for unsupervised anomaly detection in time series. IEEE Access. 2018;7:1991-2005

[23] Wei L, Kumar N, Lolla VN, Keogh EJ, Lonardi S, Ratanamahatana CA. Assumption-free anomaly detection in time series. In: Proceedings of the 17th International Conference on Scientific and Statistical Database Management (SSDBM 2005). Vol. 5. London, UK: Springer; 2005. pp. 237-242

[24] Hindy H, Brosset D, Bayne E, Seeam A, Bellekens X. Improving SIEM for critical SCADA water infrastructures using machine learning. In: Computer Security. Germany: Springer; 2018. pp. 3-19

[25] Di Mauro M, Di Sarno C. Improving siem capabilities through an enhanced probe for encrypted skype traffic detection. Journal of Information Security and Applications. 2018;**38**:85-95

[26] Ren H, Xu B, Wang Y, Yi C, Huang C, Kou X, et al. Time-series anomaly detection service at Microsoft. In: Proceedings of the 25th ACM SIGKDD International Conference on Knowledge Discovery & Data Mining (KDD 2019), 4-8 August 2019. Anchorage, Alaska, USA: ACM; 2019. pp. 3009-3017

[27] Alkharabsheh K, Alawadi S, Kebande VR, Crespo Y, Fernández-Delgado M, Taboada JA. A comparison of machine learning algorithms on design smell detection using balanced and imbalanced dataset: A study of god class. Information and Software Technology. 2022;**143**:106736

[28] Hawkins DM. Identification of Outliers. Vol. 11. Germany: Springer; 1980

[29] Barnett V, Lewis T. Outliers in Statistical Data. Wiley Series in Probability and Mathematical Statistics: Applied Probability and Statistics. 2nd ed. Chichester: John Wiley & Sons; 1984

[30] Ahmed M, Mahmood AN, Jiankun H. A survey of network anomaly detection techniques. Journal of Network and Computer Applications. 2016;**60**: 19-31

[31] Ahmed M, Mahmood AN. Novel approach for network traffic pattern analysis using clustering-based collective anomaly detection. Annals of Data Science. 2015;**2**(1):111-130

[32] Zimek A, Schubert E, Kriegel H-P. A survey on unsupervised outlier detection in high-dimensional numerical data. Statistical Analysis and Data Mining: The ASA Data Science Journal. 2012;**5**(5): 363-387

[33] Pimentel MAF, Clifton DA, Clifton L, Tarassenko L. A review of novelty detection. Signal Processing. 2014;**99**:215-249

[34] Markou M, Singh S. Novelty detection: A review—part 2: neural network based approaches. Signal Processing. 2003;**83**(12):2499-2521

[35] González-Granadillo G, González-Zarzosa S, Diaz R. Security information and event management (siem): Analysis, trends, and usage in critical infrastructures. Sensors. 2021;**21**(14): 4759

[36] Carasso D. Exploring SPLUNK. CITO Research, New York; 2012. pp. 154

[37] Fedorov M, Adams P, Brunton G, Fishler B, Flegel M, Wilhelmsen K, et al. Leveraging Splunk for Control System Monitoring and Management. Technical Report. Livermore, CA (United States): Lawrence Livermore National Lab. (LLNL); 2017

[38] Sigman BP, Delgado E. Splunk Essentials. Birmingham, UK: Packt Publishing Ltd; 2016. ISBN 978-1785889462

[39] Parzen E. An approach to time series analysis. The Annals of Mathematical Statistics. 1961;**32**(4):951-989

[40] Cryer JD. Time Series Analysis. Vol. 286. Berlin, Germany: Springer; 1986. ISBN 978-0871509635

[41] Blázquez-Garca A, Conde A, Mori U, Lozano JA. A review on outlier/anomaly detection in time series data. ACM Computing Surveys (CSUR). 2021; **54**(3):1-33

[42] Teng M. Anomaly detection on time series. Proceedings of the 2010 IEEE International Conference on Progress in Informatics and Computing, PIC 2010. Vol. 1. 2011. pp. 603-608. DOI: 10.1109/PIC.2010.5687485

[43] Tkach V, Kudin A, Kebande VR, Baranovskyi O, Kudin I. Non-pattern-based anomaly detection in time-series. Electronics. 2023;**12**(3):687-703

[44] Pan J-X, Fang K-T. Maximum likelihood estimation. In: Growth curve Models and Statistical Diagnostics. Germany: Springer; 2002. pp. 77-158

[45] Aue A, Norinho DD, Hörmann S. On the prediction of functional time series. arXiv preprint arXiv:1208.2892. 2012;**41**:43

[46] Kaminsky D. Blackops of tcp/ip2011. Available from: http://www.slideshare.net/dakami/black-ops-of-tcpip-2011-black-hat-usa-2011 [Accessed: December 26, 2023]

[47] Apertus 0.3.17-beta. archive data on your favorite blockchains. Available from: http://apertus.io/ [Accessed: December 26, 2023]

[48] Tomescu A, Devadas S. Catena: Efficient non-equivocation via Bitcoin. In: Proceedings of the IEEE Symposium on Security and Privacy (SP 2017), 22-24 May 2017. San Jose, California, USA: IEEE; 2017. pp. 393-409

[49] Ali M, Nelson J, Shea R, Freedman MJ. Blockstack: A global naming and storage system secured by blockchains. In: Proceedings of the Usenix Annual Technical Conference (ATC 2016), 20-22 June 2016. Denver, Colorado, USA: Usenix Association; 2016. pp. 181-194

[50] Filecoin. Available from: https://filecoin.io/ [Accessed: December 26, 2023]

[51] Maidsafe. Available from: https://maidsafe.net/ [Accessed: December 26, 2023]

[52] Sia: Fully Decentralized Cloud. Available from: https://sia.tech/ [Accessed: December 26, 2023]

[53] Miller A, Juels A, Shi E, Parno B, Katz J. Permacoin: Repurposing Bitcoin work for data preservation. In: Proceedings of the IEEE Symposium on Security and Privacy (SP 2014), 18–20 May 2014, San Jose, California, USA: IEEE; 2014. pp. 475-490

[54] Sengupta B, Bag S, Ruj S, Sakurai K. Retricoin: Bitcoin based on compact proofs of retrievability. In: Proceedings of the 17th International Conference on Distributed Computing and Networking (ICDCN 2016), 4-7 January 2016; Bangalore, India: ACM; 2016. pp. 1-10

[55] Dubovitskaya A, Zhigang X, Ryu S, Schumacher M, Wang F. Secure and trustable electronic medical records sharing using blockchain. CoRR. 2017. abs/1709.06528

[56] Liang X, Shetty S, Tosh D, Kamhoua C, Kwiat K, Njilla L. Provchain: A blockchain data provenance architecture in cloud environment with enhanced privacy and availability. In: Proceedings of the 17th IEEE/ACM International Symposium on Cluster, Cloud and Grid Computing (CCGrid 2017), 14-17 May 2017; Madrid, Spain: IEEE; 2017. pp. 468-477

[57] Wachs M, Schanzenbach M, Grothoff C. A censorship-resistant, privacy-enhancing and fully decentralized name system. In: Proceedings of the International Conference on Cryptology and Network Security (CANS 2014), 1-3 December 2014; Kyoto, Japan: Springer; 2014. pp. 127-142

[58] Ws blockchain partners: Accelerating your distributed ledger journey. Available from: https://aws.amazon.com/partners/blockchain/

[59] Ibm blockchain. Now delivering value around the world. . Available from: https://www.ibm.com/blockchain [Accessed: December 26, 2023]

[60] Microsoft azure blockchain. Develop, test, and deploy secure blockchain apps. Available from: https://azure.microsoft.com/en-us/solutions/blockchain/ [Accessed: December 26, 2023]

[61] Majority attack. Available from: https://en.bitcoin.it/wiki/Majorityattack [Accessed: December 26, 2023]

[62] Largest crypto-mining marketplace. Available from: https://www.nicehash.com/ [Accessed: December 26, 2023]

[63] Recabarren R, Carbunar B. Tithonus: A bitcoin based censorship resilient system. Proceedings on Privacy Enhancing Technologies. 2019;**68–86**(01):2019

[64] Xu H, Long J, Li H, Liu Y, Wang Y. Blockchain-based intrusion detection system for internet of things. Journal of Sensor and Actuator Networks. 2021; **11**(4):71

[65] Gupta A, Sharma A, Rani S, Malviya N. A review on blockchain-based intrusion detection systems for internet of things environments. Sensors. 2021;**21**(23):8173

[66] Li X, Sun J, Cheng J, Guo J. A blockchain-enabled intrusion detection system with machine learning in software-defined networking. EURASIP Journal on Wireless Communications and Networking. 2022;**2022**(1):105

[67] Akram N. Anwar S Rashid S. Farooq MO. Blockchain-based intrusion detection system for cloud computing. arXiv preprint arXiv:2201.04803. 2021

[68] Shafagh H, Burkhalter L, Hithnawi A, Duquennoy S. Towards Blockchain-based Auditable Storage and Sharing of IoT Data. In Proceedings of the 2017 ACM SIGSAC Conference on Computer and Communications Security, Dallas, TX, USA; 3 November 2017. pp. 45-50

[69] Al-Nemrat A, Benkhelifa E, Mahmood Z. Intrusion detection systems using blockchain technology: A review, issues, and challenges. In: 2021 IEEE 2nd International Conference on Emerging Trends in Engineering, Science and Sustainable Technology (ICETESST 2021), 7-8 November 2021; Dubai, UAE: IEEE; 2021. pp. 1-7

[70] Snapp SR, Brentano J, Dias GV, Goan TL, Heberlein LT, Ho C-l, et al. DIDS (Distributed Intrusion Detection System) - Motivation, architecture, and an early prototype. In: Proceedings of the 14th National Computer Security Conference (NCSC 1991), 14-16 October 1991; Baltimore, Maryland, USA: National Institute of Standards and Technology (NIST); 1991. pp. 167-176

[71] Snapp SR, Smaha SE, Teal DM, Grance T. The DIDS (Distributed Intrusion Detection System) prototype. In: USENIX Summer 1992 Technical Conference, 8-12 June 1992; San Antonio, Texas, USA: USENIX Association; 1992. pp. 1992

[72] Jaeger D, Sapegin A, Ussath M, Cheng F, Meinel C, Parallel and distributed normalization of security events for instant attack analysis. In: 2015 IEEE 34th International Performance Computing and Communications Conference (IPCCC 2015); 14-16 December 2015; Nanjing, China: IEEE; 2015. pp. 1-8

[73] Joseph Frederick Traub, Wasilkowski GW, and Henryk Woźniakowski. Information, Uncertainty, Complexity. Addison-Wesley, 1983.

[74] Steiner M, Tsudik G, Waidner M. Diffie-Hellman key distribution extended to group communication. In: Proceedings of the ACM Conference on Computer and Communications Security, New York: ACM; 1996, pp. 31-37

[75] Bercu S, Proïa F. A sarimax coupled modelling applied to individual load curves intraday forecasting. Journal of Applied Statistics. 2013;**40**(6):1333-1348

[76] Vagropoulos SI, Chouliaras GI, Kardakos EG, Simoglou CK, Bakirtzis AG. Comparison of SARIMAX, SARIMA, modified SARIMA, and

ANN-based models for short-term PV generation forecasting. In: 2016 IEEE International Energy Conference (ENERGYCON), IEEE. Piscataway, NJ: IEEE; 2016, pp. 1-6

[77] Tarsitano A, Amerise IL. Short-term load forecasting using a two-stage sarimax model. Energy. 2017;**133**: 108-114

[78] Choi T-M, Yong Y, Kin-Fan A. A hybrid sarima wavelet transform method for sales forecasting. Decision Support Systems. 2011;**51**(1):130-140

Chapter 2

Perspective Chapter: Blockchain-Based Data Access Control Framework in Cyber-Physical Systems

Agoye Olorunfemi David and Francisca Nonyelum Ogwueleka

Abstract

Cyber-physical systems (CPS) are extensively used in overseeing the critical infrastructure of diverse domains such as medical healthcare, energy, and power. These applications typically receive input data from sensors, assess the current state of the system, and subsequently, make pivotal decisions for the automatic control of the underlying infrastructure. Consequently, safeguarding the security and integrity of the system state data becomes imperative to guarantee the secure and reliable operation of CPS. Therefore, the need to establish a stringent and dependable access control mechanism for data integrity within cyber-physical systems is imperative to ensure the effective implementation of modern functionalities. This paper addresses the intricacies of designing a robust access control system for cyber-physical systems. Leveraging blockchain technology, we introduce a practical framework and demonstrate how it will contribute to establishing a secure, dependable, and controlled system for data access with integrity. The central concept advanced by this research involves the meticulous management of access rights and the preservation of privacy through the application of blockchain strategies. The analytical findings underscore a high level of protection, decentralization, and reliability inherent in the proposed solution, capitalizing on the advantages offered by blockchain.

Keywords: cyber-physical system, data access control, blockchain, data security, framework

1. Introduction

The advent of Industry 4.0 has given rise to the emergence of cyber-physical systems (CPSs), characterized by a synergy of cyber and physical components. In a typical CPS, cyber elements take charge of controlling the corresponding physical components or processes within a critical infrastructure. These cyber components derive input from sensor data to assess the current state of the physical elements. In response to this state estimation, the cyber components generate decisions, issuing commands to alter the state of the physical process. The current trajectory towards more affordable sensors, rapid communication networks, and improved data acquisition methodologies result in a substantial influx of data generated by diverse sensors and autonomous resources within a CPS. The acquired data is transmitted over the internet for subsequent data processing through cyber information sharing (CIS). The management of this voluminous data necessitates adept access management techniques, giving rise to challenges associated with system performance, security, reliability, scalability, and fault tolerance. Given that decisions within a CPS hinge on sensor input data, ensuring the security of this sensitive data becomes of utmost importance. Commonly, data from Cyber-Physical System (CPS) devices is transmitted through sensors and conveyed to external service providers using traditional data-sharing protocols [1]. Third-party service providers use machine learning and statistical analysis methods to enhance the quality of the data [2]. The advantages of receiving individualized, superior service must be weighed against the possible loss of personal data [3]. In recent times, blockchain has surfaced as an alternative avenue to augment security, embodying a relatively uncharted and less enticing prospect for malicious actors [3]. Blockchain technology demonstrates superior efficacy in validating both ownership and integrity and data, excelling in minimizing vulnerabilities and affording a robust encryption framework [4]. The imperative control of unauthorized systems' access to and utilization of infrastructure information and assets is pivotal in maintaining the security of said data [5]. By verifying users and only allowing access to those who meet the requirements for accessing secure areas of the network, rules of access control achieve this goal [6]. Access control limits the capability of unauthorized systems to view data, making sure that systems with permission can have access to sensitive system information [7]. Encrypting the data before transmitting it to the cloud servers is imperative. This precaution ensures that, in the event of other safeguards failing, potential attackers would be limited to accessing the encrypted data only [8]. Implementing encryption on transmitted data through the utilization of a secret key is a vital precaution to ensure data security and confidentiality [9]. Traditional encryption methods can be used, in which the originating systems of the data send the decryption key ahead of time to specific systems [10]. Symmetric encryption necessitates either the originating systems of the data and systems sharing the same key or reaching an agreement on a shared key to facilitate the decryption of the information [11]. Originating systems of the data are unable to predict how systems will access their data. As such, sensitive data must first be encrypted with a key that is known only to the starting systems, and then it must be re-encrypted using a key that is known only to the end systems (Guo [12]). Continuous online presence is needed to work well using this decrypt-and-encrypt system. However, scalability issues arise when dealing with an expanding number of data parameters, varying types of infrastructures, and systems, consequently escalating the complexity of the issue [13].

Blockchain integrated with cyber-physical systems (CPS) for effective access control has great potential to create an intelligent, efficient, and secure framework for the future. Through integrating advances in machine learning algorithms, edge computing, sensors, and actuators, CPS can capture massive volumes of data in real time from physical environments. The information produced can at this point be securely entered and confirmed on the blockchain ledger, making it an immutable and reliable source, thereby, guaranteeing the accuracy and reliability of the data transmitted throughout the framework. On the other hand, the integration of cyber-physical systems improves blockchain technology by broadening its applications and upgrading its scalability, resilience, and performance. Acting as a node in the blockchain network, CPS devices can execute smart contracts, validate transactions, establish consensus, and other functions. This distributed architecture reduces the dangers associated with single points of failure and increases the resilience of the network thereby enhancing the decentralization and fault tolerance of the blockchain. Through the complementary combination of blockchain and CPS, we are establishing the pathway for an intelligent future that is autonomous, sustainable, and interconnected. Blockchain-based data access control framework in CPS will enable secure and transparent data exchange and serve as an effective enabler to realize an intelligent future.

This paper makes the following key contributions:

- It designs a Blockchain-Based Access Control framework to improve Cyber-Physical Systems (CPS) overall data security.
- It presents a public key encryption method called attribute encryption, which lets users encrypt and decrypt messages according to particular user attributes.
- After the assessment, the proposed framework outperformed alternative models in terms of increased throughput, data confidentiality, lower latency, and computation time.

The remainder of the paper is organized as follows: Section 2 delves into the review of literature, Section 3 presents the Blockchain-Based Data Access Control Framework BDAC, Section 4 discusses the results, and Section 5 is the research paper conclusion.

2. Review of related studies

Kumar et al. [14] proposed the Interplanetary File System and Blockchain (IPFS- B) for improving secure distributed detection within the framework of image and video data security. The author used a perceptual hash (pHash) technique to find instances of media files being used without permission in various formats. The content's perceptual hash (pHash) is computed and checked against the values already saved in the blockchain before any content is added to the IPFS. Experimental images are sourced from Caltech 256 dataset. If the calculated pHash value closely resembles those previously recorded, the media undergoes scrutiny for potential tampering. The findings illustrate that blockchain offers the advantage of eliminating third-party involvement, preventing a single point of failure in the process. However, the IPFS-B model exhibits performance in comparison to alternative models.

Jia et al. [15] examined a federated learning data protection aggregation scheme (BFLDPAS) for the industrial Internet of Things (IIoT) that is enabled by blockchain. Differential privacy, homomorphic encryption-based distributed K-means clustering, homomorphic encryption-based distributed AdaBoost, and differential privacy-based distributed random forests are a few examples of methods that enable many layers of safety when sharing data and models. The authors ended with a thorough security analysis, and they skillfully combined the methods with federated learning and blockchain. The suggested aggregation scheme and operational mechanism performed well across the chosen indicators, as shown by the numerical results. Moreover, this study did not significantly improve the safe exchange and sharing of information.

Chadwick et al. [16] presented the use of a cloud-edge-based data security architecture (CEDSA) to exchange and examine cyber threat intelligence (CTI). The owner can choose a trust level and sanitization method that best suits the nature of the CTI data before releasing it for analysis. Plain text, pseudonymization/anonymization, and homomorphic encryption are a few examples of this. Furthermore, depending on how much faith an organization has in cloud service providers, the sanitization process may be assigned to either the cloud provider or edge device. To meet the strictest requirements for secure CTI information exchange, the authors investigated organizational methodology, cloud-edge infrastructures, and trust architecture. Finally, the authors confirmed the dependability of their infrastructure by summarizing the deployment and testing stages using four pilot projects. One drawback of the proposed architecture is that each shared data object that is meant to be analyzed has to follow the same standard data-sharing agreement policy that is contained within it.

Le Nguyen et al. [17] investigated the use of privacy-preserving blockchain technology (PPBT) for safe and dependable IoT data sharing. Secure ant colony optimization can be facilitated by applying multi-kernel support vector machine training techniques on partial views of Internet of Things (IoT) data from multiple sources. The multi-kernel SVM process was used by the authors to create a privacy barrier for ant colony optimization using Elliptic Curve Cryptography (ECC), which ensures accuracy and efficacy. IoT data was encoded and stored on distributed ledgers, and the research team used blockchain technology to build safe and reliable platforms for exchanging data between various data sources. The results of the security evaluation indicated that the variables in the proposed model were safe for data analysts to use, guaranteeing the privacy of critical information from every source. Additional simulation results confirmed the recommended model's superiority over alternative approaches. Notwithstanding, certain issues were observed, such as a downloaded file that was not functional and the false data that was kept in the system for covert persistence.

Yang [18] explored the use of blockchain and the proof-of-stake, proof-of-work, and secure hash (PoS-PoW-Hash) algorithms to manage business risks in internet data security. The algorithm was initially tested in a business risk simulation. After that, its users and the company's employees' opinions about the service were gathered. According to the test results, the sub-platform's design reduced the company's business risk by 5–10%, and staff members were generally satisfied with the setup. The algorithm's signature was simulated in realistic settings, demonstrating better performance than other approaches, much like the Source Management Routing Algorithm (SMRA) and Rough Set-based Attribute Reduction (RSAR) techniques. While this research offers medium-sized and small businesses a fresh method of thwarting potential threats, it also recognizes that using blockchain technology to manage internet data security and minimize risks within business processes is inefficient.

Latif et al. [7] presented a method for managing the security of data in cyber-physical systems that combines blockchain, software-defined networks (SDN), and artificial intelligence (AI). When data is being transmitted within the network, the system is intended to simultaneously manage energy efficiency and data security. To enhance overall security in this process, a blockchain approach was incorporated. Moreover, peer-to-peer communication, both public and private, was maintained through the use of Proof of Work (PoW). As a result, general data security and privacy were efficiently managed by the blockchain-enabled software-defined network. Nevertheless, when assessing the effectiveness of this architecture, the study ignored the resource constraints and energy consumption of Internet of Things devices.

Fazal et al. [19] suggested a decision support system intended to manage privacy issues when exchanging large amounts of data in a third-party setting. The authors performed a security analysis using patient health data from COVID-19 cases. First, the attributes were encrypted using the Blowfish algorithm, and the identity and quasi-attributes were obscured using pseudonymization. To improve overall data security and effectively decrease unauthorized activities, the encrypted data was later linked. It is imperative to acknowledge, though, that this study solely focused on privacy issues associated with contact tracing, rendering it inappropriate for situations requiring a comprehensive assurance of data security as well as privacy.

Kaushal et al. [20] analyzed medical applications using mobile computing technologies to control data privacy and confidentiality. Modern encryption techniques were integrated into their strategy to protect data from unauthorized access. To process the data and reduce irrelevant information, a normalization process was used. Then, feature dimensions were decreased using principal component analysis. Finally, to maximize overall security, kernel homomorphism was applied. In addition, the incorporation of Two-Fish encryption and spider monkey optimization improved data security, integrity, and confidentiality. The incapacity to track the well-being of patients in real time was a drawback of this approach, though.

Wenhua et al. [21] claimed that with the introduction of Health 5.0, the history of medical care is entering a new phase. They emphasized the features of blockchain as a technological solution, highlighting its tamper resistance, secure sharing, decentralization, and high privacy. They contend that this offers a novel viewpoint for resolving the present roadblocks in the development of Electronic Health Records (HER) security and privacy. Protecting patient health information from cyberattacks and maintaining privacy via authenticated access is regarded as one of the most important issues facing the healthcare sector. Although the advancement of healthcare is considered contingent upon blockchain security, the future course of blockchain security is expected to be significantly influenced by technological applications, expanded use cases, and monitoring frameworks.

El-Shafai et al. [22] suggested the use of the Genetic Encryption Algorithm (GEA) to authenticate data. Instead of starting with a single template, the GEA searches from a population of templates. The algorithm makes use of mathematical operators to create subsequent populations by leveraging the initial population. After that, crossover and mutation operations are used to create the final cancelable biometric data templates. The average Area Under the Receiver Operating Characteristic (AROC) value of 0.9998 for the suggested framework was impressive.

Thabit et al. [23] suggested enhancing cloud computing data security by utilizing a lightweight cryptographic algorithm. An essential requirement for the algorithm is a key of the same length (16 bytes or 128 bits) as the block size (16 bytes). By using Feistel architectural techniques and replacement permutation, the strategy increases the complexity of the encryption. This method uses logical operations such as XNOR, XOR, swapping, and shifting to realize Shannon's idea of dispersion and confusion. The length of the secret key and the number of turns can be freely changed using the proposed algorithm. When the proposed algorithm was tested against other widely used cryptographic systems in cloud computing, the test results demonstrated high security and significant improvements in cipher execution time.

S/N	Author(s) and year	Title of research	Outcome of research	Limitation of research
1	Kumar et al. [14]	A secured distributed detection system based on IPFS and blockchain for industrial image and video data security.	This research proposed the Interplanetary File System and Blockchain (IPFS- B) model aimed at improving secure distributed detection within the framework of image and video data security.	The IPFS-B model hashing algorithm inhibits performance in comparison to alternative models.
2.	Jia et al. [15]	Blockchain-enabled Federated Learning Data Protection Aggregation Scheme with Differential Privacy and Homomorphic Encryption in IIoT	The study devised a model of a federated learning data protection aggregation scheme (BFLDPAS) utilizing a combination of differential privacy and homomorphic encryption, tailored for the industrial Internet of Things (IIoT) enabled by blockchain. This enables multiple layers of data protection in both data sharing and model sharing.	The work showed better performance only in a few selected indicators such as accuracy and F1-score and did not significantly show an overall improvement in the safe exchange and sharing of information in IIoT.
3.	Chadwick et al. [16]	A Cloud-Edge based Data Security Architecture for Sharing and Analyzing Cyber Threat Information	The study presented an adaptable framework that uses a cloud-edge-based data security architecture (CEDSA) to exchange and examine cyber threat intelligence (CTI). The sharing infrastructure allows the data owner to choose a trust level and sanitization method that best suits the nature of the CTI data before releasing it for analysis.	A drawback of the proposed architecture is that each shared data object that is meant to be analyzed has to follow the same standard data-sharing agreement policy that is contained within it.
4.	Le Nguyen et al. [17]	Privacy Preserving Blockchain Technique to Achieve Secure and Reliable Sharing of IoT Data.	The work proposed the use of privacy-preserving blockchain technology (PPBT) for safe and dependable IoT data sharing by introducing a new approach, the Secure Ant Colony Optimization with Multi Kernel Support Vector Machine (ACOMKSVM) utilizing Elliptical Curve Cryptosystem (ECC), designed to ensure secure and dependable sharing of IoT data.	The proposed model's framework is limited by its reliance on a limited number of training algorithms and, therefore unable to adequately protect privacy in multiple components of the encrypted datasets.
5.	Latif et al. [7]	AI-empowered, blockchain and SDN integrated security architecture for IoT network of cyber physical systems.	The work presented a method for managing the security of data in cyber-physical systems that combines blockchain, software-defined networks (SDN), and artificial intelligence (AI).	The study did not factor in the resource constraints and energy consumption of Internet of Things devices when assessing the effectiveness of this architecture.

S/N	Author(s) and year	Title of research	Outcome of research	Limitation of research
6.	Fazal et al. [19]	Achieving data privacy for decision support systems in times of massive data sharing.	The study suggested a decision support system intended to manage privacy issues and improve overall data security when exchanging large amounts of data in a third-party setting.	This model proposed is inappropriate for situations requiring a comprehensive assurance of data security as well as privacy.
7	Kaushal et al. [20]	Using Mobile Computing to Provide a Smart and Secure Internet of Things (IoT) Framework for Medical Applications.	The study analyzed medical applications using mobile computing technologies to control data privacy and confidentiality.	The incapacity of the framework to provide real-time information was a drawback of this approach.
8	Thabit et al. [23]	A new lightweight cryptographic algorithm for enhancing data security in cloud computing.	The research suggested enhancing cloud computing data security by utilizing a lightweight cryptographic algorithm.	The algorithm is yet to be implemented in hardware to verify its capability to achieve high security and significant improvements in cipher execution time.

Table 1.
Summary of related, recent, and relevant studies reviewed.

According to the review, current models—such as BFLDPAS, CEDSA, and PPBT—face several difficulties when trying to maximize computation time, guarantee data confidentiality, achieve high throughput ratios, and minimize latency. To improve overall data security in Cyber-Physical Systems (CPS), this paper proposes a Blockchain-Based Data Access Control Framework (**Table 1**).

3. Methodology

In the traditional data-sharing space, Interoperability, security, and privacy are critical are very important. First, system state information that is necessary to ensure the safe and dependable operation of CPS is frequently included in CPS data, which needs to be protected.

As a result, the compromise of such information may have serious repercussions for the infrastructures in question. Second, the lack of a decentralized system for exchanging CPS data creates vulnerabilities that can be exploited by Distributed Denial of Service (DDoS) attacks and single points of failure. The security and resilience risks present in a centralized framework are best illustrated by these vulnerabilities. Furthermore, managing data access rights and enabling the safe exchange of this data presents a significant obstacle in the field of cybersecurity information sharing. An attribute-based encryption mechanism for cybersecurity information sharing was included in the study's introduction of the Blockchain-Based Data Access

Control Framework. By utilizing a blockchain platform, the system makes it easier to manage vulnerability and cybersecurity certification data. Blockchain protocols are acknowledged for their potential to revolutionize the field of information technology due to their remarkable attributes, such as decentralization and confidentiality preservation. Blockchain is the best architectural solution in a trustless environment, as it ensures secure execution.

Figure 1 shows the suggested structure of the proposed framework. Every IoT service in our design has its edge gateway. Every gateway at the edge of the network operates as a peer node linked to the blockchain of the consortium and connects to the cloud via fifth-generation wireless networks (5G). The gateway node participates in the consensus process as an orderer node once it satisfies the requirements. Interestingly, IoT devices are not included in our consortium blockchain architecture as peer nodes. Rather, they are connected to the edge gateway in their respective domains and exchange access control information using the lightweight Message Queuing Telemetry Transport (MQTT) protocol. The 5G base station enables the edge gateway to connect to 5G networks and the cloud with millisecond-level latency. This configuration makes it possible for edge gateways to effectively use cloud-based storage services, facilitating quick and accurate data reporting for remote monitoring. Certification authority (CA) is a prerequisite for edge gateways to join the consortium blockchain network. By utilizing 5G, edge gateways can gain access to cloud-based storage services, which reduces the blockchain's need for data storage. Moreover, they can offer unified application services connected to production and receive data from the edge gateway for remote monitoring.

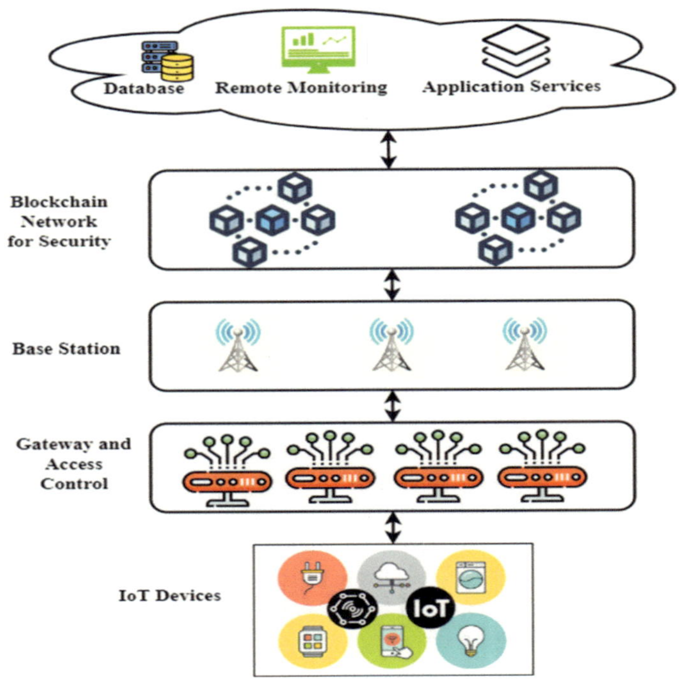

Figure 1.
Proposed blockchain framework.

3.1 Step 1: System initialization

Utilizing encryption algorithms to enable the conversion of plain text into encrypted text and vice versa is necessary to ensure data security during network transit. Sensitive data is typically protected from public view by encoding or encryption procedures. By encryption, the data is effectively "locked," meaning that only the owner or those with the right decryption key can access it. The content that was originally unencrypted is called plaintext, and the content that was encrypted using a secret key is called ciphertext. To achieve a higher level of security for data transmission between client applications and servers, the encryption algorithm parameter is essential. The attribute-based encryption scheme uses setup algorithms to build B from the corresponding bilinear mappings and the prime number orders of q bilinear groups H1, represented by h are $e: H_1 \times H_1 \rightarrow H_2$ and shown as G: 1 {0, 1} H. The attribute-based encryption scheme parameter is selected randomly $\beta \in Z_q$ and creates public keys using Eq. (1):

$$\text{h}\, PK_B = e(h, h)^b . MK_B = h^b \tag{1}$$

In Eq. (1), PK_B is represented as the public key, and the parameter selected by the key server $\alpha \in Z_q$ randomly generates the public and private keys.

$$PK_K = h^{\alpha} . MK_K = \alpha \tag{2}$$

In Eq. (2), PKK is the public key MK that is produced when the master key is used.

3.2 Step 2: Key generation

The key generation algorithms are implemented by the attribute-based encryption scheme and the key server, which then generates user keys with extra homomorphic encryptions. It then establishes the attribute-based encryption scheme establishes $S = Enc\ (PK_B, \beta)$, and directs it to key servers. The key servers choose a arbitrarily and generate $\delta \in Z_q$, create $U = (S \oplus Enc\ (PK_B, \delta)) \otimes \alpha$, and send it to the CPS infrastructure. Eq. (3) defines the attribute-based encryption scheme, which uses additional homomorphic encryption to decrypt U and obtain Y.

$$Y = Dec(MK_A, U) = (\beta + \delta)\alpha \tag{3}$$

The prime numbers β and ∈ Zq are selected at random by the attribute encryption mechanism. and the computing of $Z = h^{Y/}\tau$ is then forwarded by key servers. The key server calculates $M = Z^{1/}\alpha^2 = h^{(\beta + \alpha)/}\tau\alpha$ and forwards it to the CPS infrastructure. The CPS infrastructure uses τ to generate the user key WK_B = D = $M^T = h^{(\beta + \delta)/\alpha}$ and securely transmits it to the users. The key servers then execute the key generation programs, randomly choosing $\delta_i \cup Z_q$ for each attribute of users $\beta_i \in W$, generate and store attribute keys WK_K. User keys WKB and attribute keys WKK are used to create the user's attribute private key WK using Eq. (4):

$$WK_K = D_i = g^{\delta}G(i)^{\delta i}, D' = h^{\delta i}\ i \in W \tag{4}$$

Data security and confidentiality are guaranteed by encryption, which is applied to the collected data after key values are generated. In the section that follows, the specific encryption procedure is explained.

3.3 Step 3: Encryption

The ciphertexts CT are generated, the information N is encoded, the access policy tree T is defined, and the encoding algorithms are carried out by the data owners. First, data owners select $DK \in Z_q$ randomly and use DK to encode the data N by utilizing symmetric encryptions. Subsequently, they construct the access strategy tree T, describe $Bk_y - 1$degree polynomials p_y for every node y in the tree in B top-down way, and choose $w \in Z_q$ arbitrarily. For root nodes R of tree T, they describe $p_R(0) = w$. For other nodes y of tree T, they denote $p_y(0) = p_{parent}(index(y))$ and select the random variable to finish the description of p_y. Supposing that X represents the set of parameters respective to the leaf node in the access policy tree T, ciphertexts are generated by using Eqs. (5) and (6):

$$CT = T, E = WEnc_{DK}(N), C = DK{\cdot}e(h,h)^{\beta y}, C = h^{\alpha w} \tag{5}$$

$$C_x = h^{px(0)}, C = G(Attribute_x)^{px(0)} \tag{6}$$

In the decryption process, the user can only decode e(h, h)dw if the collection of attributes they own satisfies the access policy, as per Eq. (7). The attribute encryption mechanism uses arbitrary and unique attributes to generate a private attribute key for each user, ensuring diversity among the keys for all users. Collusive users can calculate e(h, h) dpy(0) from the corresponding node y, but they are unable to calculate e(h, h) dy from the same node y.

3.4 Step 4: Decryption

After obtaining the ciphertext from cloud service providers, the user requests decryption from the key server. Using attribute keys, the key servers run the model and decode the ciphertext. The procedure of decryption is defined by recursive algorithms, which describe recursive algorithms $DecryptNode\ (CT, WK_K, y)$, input ciphertexts CT, attribute keys WK_K, and nodes y in the access policy tree T. If y is a leaf node, express $j = attribute\ y$.

$$DecryptNode\ (CT, WK_{K,y}) = \frac{e(H_j, C_y)}{e(D_j, C_y)} = \frac{e(D^{\delta}, G(j)^{\delta j}, h^{py(0)})}{e(h^{\delta}G(j)^{py(0)})} = e(h,h)\ \delta_{py}(0) \tag{7}$$

Following Eq. (7) in the decryption process, the user is capable of decoding e(h, h)dw only if the access policy is satisfied by the collection of attributes they own. To ensure diversity among the private attribute keys for all users, the attribute encryption mechanism generates the private attribute key for each user using arbitrary and unique attributes. If collusive users can compute e(h, h) dpy(0) from the corresponding node y but cannot calculate e(h, h) dy, from the respective node y but cannot calculate e(h, h)dy, they also cannot decrypt DK. The CIS process of CPS is illustrated in **Figure 2**.

Figure 2 illustrates the CIS of the CPS model, tackling the difficult issues of allowing authorized access control and effective data sharing in the networks. The blockchain model is easily combined with cybersecurity information-sharing and access control mechanisms of CPS to address issues with conventional policies. Blockchain thus ensures data integrity, fairness, authenticity, security, and distribution while addressing several important concerns. Data sharing and access control management are crucial tasks for smart contracts. This and other distributed ledger technologies improve data security and privacy by making transactions more dependable, transparent, and easily verifiable. This gives data owners more authority to manage their information more effectively. The blockchain system distributes membership keys and logs the data's users and owners. When a user requests access to data, the system uses the user's login information to create a new encryption key, which is then sent to the proxy server. Then, the blockchain is informed of the rules and limitations regarding who can access and use the data. Before allowing access, a data user's identity is carefully checked.

The trusted authority initiates the initial setup to set up a master key and the system's default settings. After that, users' keys are dynamically generated in real-time by the KeyGen method. After that, the data system uses the encryption algorithm to produce the ciphertext. The metadata is stored using blockchain., and cloud providers are in charge of ciphertext management. Our architecture increases availability by

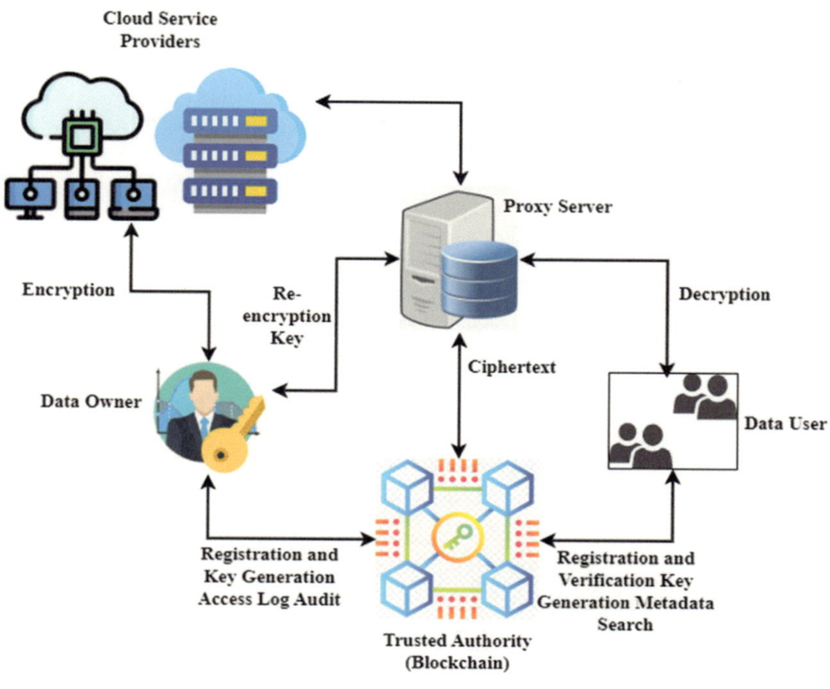

Figure 2.
Cybersecurity information sharing (CIS) of the CPS model.

strengthening content delivery's resistance to packet losses through the use of data caches in the forwarding process. Furthermore, an information-centric network's multipoint delivery system guarantees effective use of storage and bandwidth. Furthermore, since the content is no longer unique, bandwidth usage drops as the number of viewers rises.

The flowchart for access right authorization is shown in **Figure 3**. A virtual identity that serves as information reflecting the right of access could be created by linking it to permissions. Thus, a key component in avoiding forgeries is the capacity to authenticate oneself. Domain owners respond to a user's request for access by creating a capability token based on a predefined access control strategy. They then execute transactions to make updates to the smart contracts' token data. Identity-related elements are arranged via smart contract capability pools, which allow for consistency and verification across blockchain network nodes. Before allowing service providers to grant access to the subject, they must first obtain the capability token from smart contracts using the subject's address.

Next, we will consider the local access control strategy. As long as local service providers apply suitable access validation, smart objects can actively participate in decision-making regarding access control. Thanks to this feature, controlling access to CPS can be done flexibly and comprehensively. Our method implements the capability delegation mechanism by correctly configuring a delegation set inside the identification capability. After receiving an update transaction for tokens from the user, the smart contract will verify the delegation right by closely reviewing the list of delegations. The time has come.

Figure 4 depicts the blockchain-based key management system. Among the operations covered are initialization registration, access record, access query, key updates, leaving a node, and rescinding access. The topology, which is shared by all security access managers inside the same deployment domain, serves as the basis for validating access query transactions. When introducing someone to the blockchain,

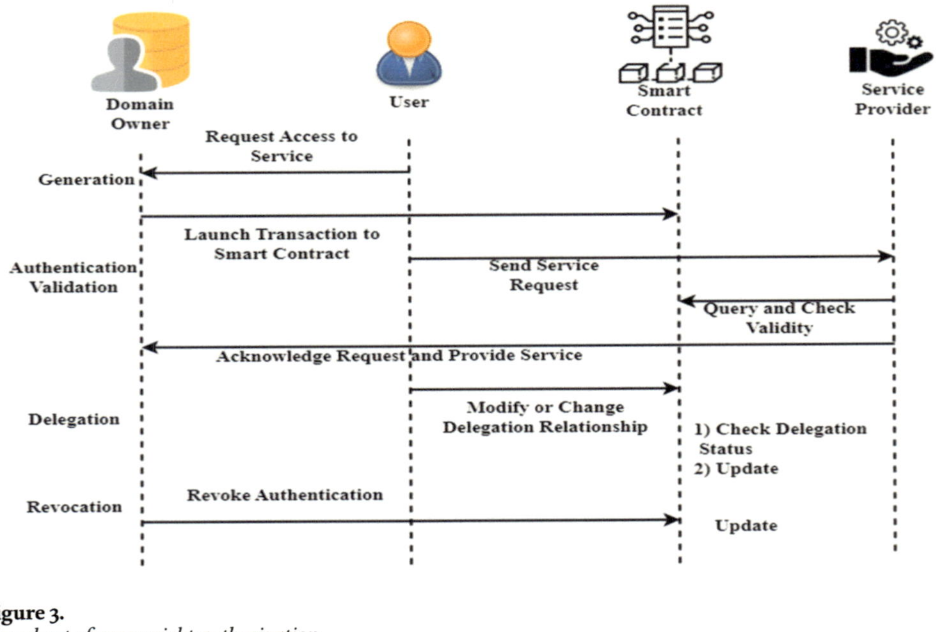

Figure 3.
Flowchart of access right authorization.

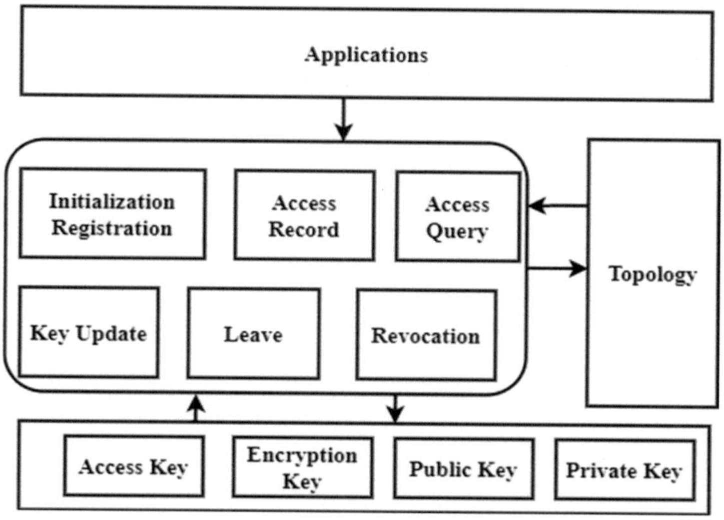

Figure 4.
Blockchain-assisted key management.

they should apply for initialization registration first. The user entry needs to define the deployment tuple, endorsed node, and encrypted access keys (for auditing). Next, to obtain permission to access the designated node, the individual has to start an access query transaction with the security access managers. Security access managers have full access to all authorized node data across all devices once the blockchain is operational. This capability allows them to more precisely identify and confirm the legitimacy of access transactions. It is the subject's choice to use or not use any access that they are granted to an object during the key's lifetime. As a result, the object's access operation needs to be recorded in the access record transaction along with the subject's access signature. This phase usually signifies the end of the access cycle. Users must then send a key update transaction with the key details to security access managers.

4. Results and discussion

The deployment of distributed access control and the safe interchange of data from CPS devices is illustrated. The NS2 simulation tool was used to put the developed blockchain-based secure access control system into practice. An Intel i3 CPU with 2GB RAM and the Ubuntu operating system were used in the implementation. An i7-4510U processor with 8GB of RAM was used for the secure data transaction process. The gradual integration of data-sharing technologies into different industries has been facilitated by their advancements. Secure transactions have a major impact on data effectiveness. However, there is insufficient tracking of digital data usage in traditional data-sharing architectures. Furthermore, CPS owners might be reluctant to divulge their information. The present research presents a data-sharing approach that utilizes blockchain technology to tackle security and control issues that are common in traditional centralized data sharing and management. This study also assessed the safety and usability of the model. The study presented a blockchain-based data-sharing paradigm and demonstrated its high efficiency, security, manageability, and practicality.

Parameter	Description
Block size	1 MB
Transmission range	300 m
Message size	1.5 GB
Total number of nodes	Random (10,000–30,000)
Number of blocks	Random (100–250)
Security protocols	AP, CKP
Traffic type	Constant Bit Rate
Timestamp	128 bit

Table 2.
Simulation parameters.

Based on the framework, this model makes use of blockchain technology to provide decentralized access to information security. Moreover, the extensive database is methodically encrypted, which serves as the foundation of the entire architecture and a security measure against data content leaks. With distributed storage serving as the foundation. Presenting a solution to problems like the vulnerability of a single point of failure in a centralized system. Simulation parameters, delineating security specifications, are detailed in **Table 2**.

4.1 Data confidentiality ratio (%)

Blockchain offers a reliable and effective data exchange platform. By classifying users based on label data, the suggested approach improves the level of detail in data-sharing services and guarantees strong data security. Applying steps 1–4 in the suggested section—which include initialization, identity authentication, signature and verification, and data transfer—calculates data confidentiality and ensures a safe and effective data exchange. The detection server is the main part of the information-sharing system. In this setup, all client-label data is gathered and analyzed by a central server, which then uses cosine similarity to identify communities and stores them on a blockchain. Users can collaborate on shared data and access shared analytics more easily with the help of the blockchain client. The detection server is the main part of the information-sharing system. In this setup, all client-label data is gathered and analyzed by a central server, which then uses cosine similarity to identify communities and stores them on a blockchain. Users can collaborate on shared data and access shared analytics more easily with the help of the blockchain client.

In **Figure 5**, the framework presented achieved a high level of confidentiality, with a ratio of 97.54% compared to other methods. This success can be attributed to the effective generation of public and private keys, which helped encrypt the original data. Additionally, the implementation of access control mechanisms played a crucial role in maintaining data access restrictions.

4.2 Throughput ratio (%)

Here, throughput is expressed in megabits, kilobits, or bits per second and is calculated by dividing the file size by the processing time. The speed at which data can be transferred between two points is known as network throughput. Network

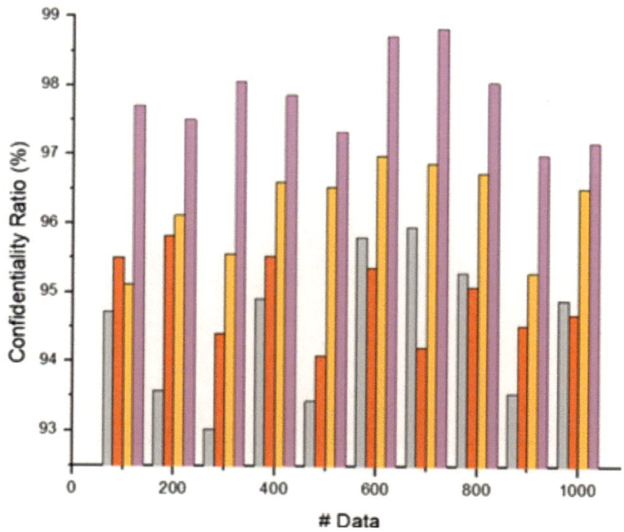

Figure 5.
Data confidentiality ratio.

speed is usually measured in megabits or gigabits, which are units of measurement for the amount of data transferred per second. The throughput analysis took into account input parameters like speed and data volume. Evaluating the effectiveness of securely transmitting information to the end user was justified by the throughput metric. Notably, even though attribute-based encryption is an expensive cryptographic primitive, it has not been able to meet the demanding throughput requirements of time-series Internet of Things data in a commercial setting. By utilizing a large degree of decentralization, the suggested method successfully avoided the problems related to a single point of failure. First, the shared data storage devices and blockchain technology form the basis of this data exchange method's framework. Integrity protection and the decentralized, distributed architecture of blockchain make sure that the failure of a single node does not jeopardize the integrity of the entire system. Second, this paradigm makes it easier for different attribute management authorities to coordinate. The system becomes more resilient as a result of the roles being divided among various attribute authorities, thereby enhancing its ability to prevent unauthorized actions from disrupting services. Additionally, this research has purposefully separated attribute management from the data owner, in contrast to situations where the owner supervises attribute administration. With this method, the data owner is limited to the position of a data manager and cannot perform any user-managed tasks. This limitation avoids data unavailability that might result from the data owner's slow response time. The impressive throughput ratio of 98.2 percent was attained by the model that was presented. This demonstrates the efficacy and efficiency of the framework in enabling safe and rapid data throughput, as shown in **Figure 6**.

4.3 Efficiency ratio (%)

The blockchain network's efficiency is an important factor that includes latency, throughput, and scalability. This includes the proportion of all data items transmitted

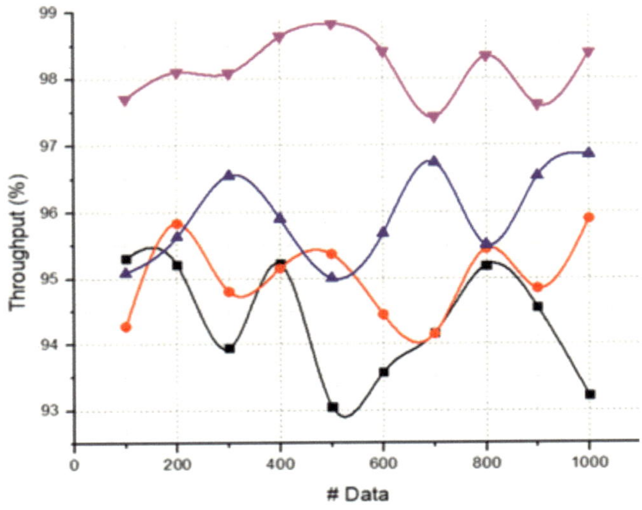

Figure 6.
Throughput ratio.

by third parties to the total amount of data transmitted securely. Online data transfer has many benefits, not the least of which is timeliness. On the other hand, as the amount of information available online increases, so does the need for safe data sharing and storage practices. This emphasizes how important strong blockchain frameworks are to meeting these changing needs. Conventional data transmission methods face challenges from the modern technological landscape's demands for security and privacy. The suggested system presents itself as a viable path forward for the development of next-generation data-sharing technologies by utilizing the intrinsic decentralization, audibility, and tamper-proof characteristics of blockchain technology. A safe and effective method of exchanging data is provided by integrating blockchain technology with data sharing, which simplifies the procedure into a few clicks. The method detection algorithm divides users into data-sharing communities according to how similar their labels are to one another. The degree of data sharing was determined in large part by evaluating the community detection results based on the degree of sharing. By reducing the amount of shared data queries, this method effectively improves data sharing efficiency. The results of the experiments confirmed the effectiveness and security of the proposed data exchange strategy among clients. The ACE-BC model achieved an impressive efficiency ratio of 97.4%, as depicted in **Figure** 7.

4.4 Latency ratio

Network latency has been a major source of concern because it is the total of all possible delays that a packet may experience during secure data transmission. To reduce latency, this study suggested a distributed key-generation framework that is integrated with cloud computing and supported by blockchain technology. To attain domain access, several blockchains operating in the cloud were also implemented. Cloud managers, which supervise multiple blockchains, each consisting of different blockchains within its deployment domain, were introduced to fulfill the low-latency and high-scalability requirements of Internet of Things scenarios. The numerical

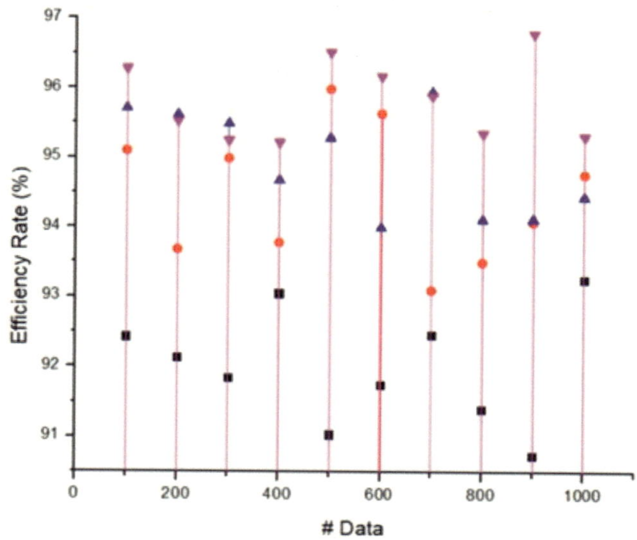

Figure 7.
Efficiency ratio.

results showed that the efficiency of the system was largely dependent on network latency. For IoT scenarios, it was therefore beneficial to use blockchain technology on the cloud, closer to the terminal devices. When deployed on security access managers, the suggested blockchain for key generation enabled low-latency key generation for user entries in comparable deployment domains. As a result, the ACE-BC model obtained a 10.9 percent reduction in latency. In **Figure 8**, the latency ratio is shown.

4.5 Computation time

The computation times needed for different encryption algorithms during user operations were assessed in this study. It was found that blockchain operations took

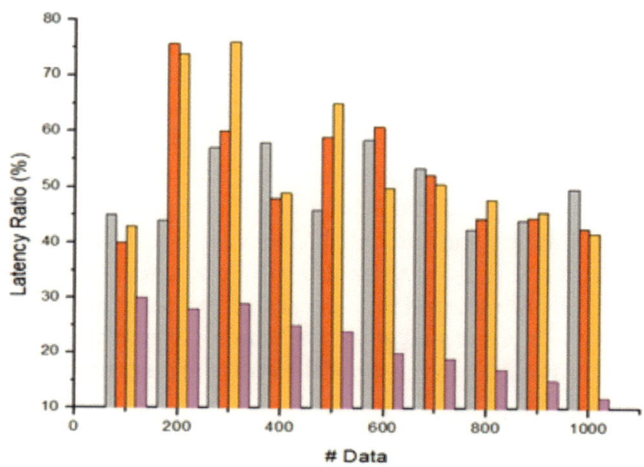

Figure 8.
Latency ratio.

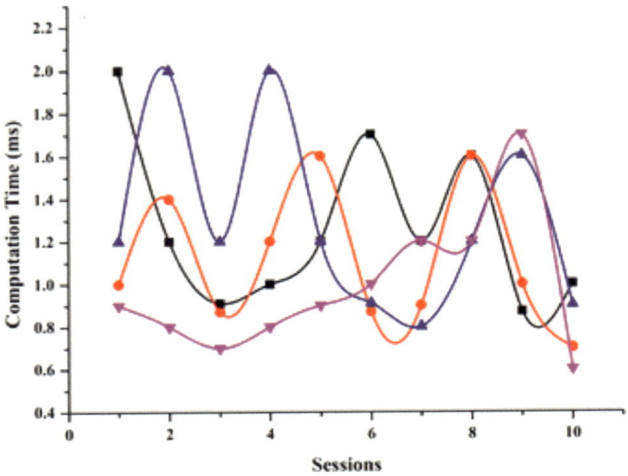

Figure 9.
Computation time.

up a sizable amount of the total time. This protocol had computation times that were independent of data size since data access keys were distributed on blockchains. But most of each user's operational time was spent on blockchain operations, since fair behavior required verification of both the sender and the recipient. In the blockchain operations, the receiver in particular took 0.6 ms to figure out his data access key. We can see the computation time in **Figure 9**.

In comparison to previous methods, such as BFLDPAS [15], CEDSA [16], and PPBT [17], the suggested framework performed better in terms of throughput ratio, data confidentiality, efficiency ratio, computation time, and latency.

5. Conclusions and future works

The paper presents a framework to enhance CPS's overall data security. Many systems are implementing data storage and exchange technologies as a result of their advancements. Nevertheless, there are no easy ways to track the amount of digital data used in the conventional data-sharing architecture. The study focused on issues related to traditional data-sharing, where major issues include the infrastructure system's unwillingness to share and the difficulty of tracking digital data usage. To address security and control concerns, a centralized approach for data sharing and administration utilizing blockchain technology was proposed. In the study, the model's security and viability were assessed. The study presented a blockchain-based data-sharing paradigm and illustrated its effectiveness, safety, and efficiency. The framework served as the foundation for a decentralized encrypted data storage and access system when it was combined with blockchain. To guard against the loss of sensitive data and maintain the integrity of the entire infrastructure, real-time database encryption was put in place. The experimental findings showed that, in comparison to other well-established models, the suggested framework greatly enhanced some performance measures.

These improvements included a lower latency rate (10.9 percent), better efficiency ratio (97.4 percent), higher throughput ratio (98.2 percent), and increased data confidentiality ratio (97.54 percent). The main goal of the operational concept was to overcome the drawbacks of centralized servers and single points of failure by using distributed storage. In the future, further functionalities like policy hiding and ciphertext search could be added based on the current attribute-based encryption to meet more specific access control needs.

Author details

Agoye Olorunfemi David* and Francisca Nonyelum Ogwueleka
Computer Science Department, University of Abuja, Nigeria

*Address all correspondence to: olorunfemi.agoye@gmail.com

References

[1] Oks SJ, Jalowski M, Lechner M, et al. Cyber-physical systems in the context of industry 4.0: A review, categorization and outlook. Information Systems Frontiers. 2022. DOI: 10.1007/s10796-022-10252-x

[2] Si H, Sun C, Li Y, Qiao H, Shi L. IoT information sharing security mechanism based on blockchain technology. Future Generation Computer Systems. 2019;**101**:1028-1040. DOI: 10.1016/j.future.2019.07.036

[3] Jiang Y, Liu X, Kang K, Wang Z, Zhong RY, Huang GQ. Blockchain-enabled cyber-physical smart modular integrated construction. Computers in Industry. 2021;**133**:103553. DOI: 10.1016/j.compind.2021.103553

[4] Kumari A, Sukharamwala UCC, Tanwar S, Raboaca MS, Alqahtani FH, Tolba A, et al. Blockchain-based peer-to-peer transactive energy management scheme for smart grid. System. 2022;**22**(13):4826-4826. DOI: 10.3390/s22134826

[5] Lee D, Lee SH, Masoud N, Krishnan MS, Li VC. Integrated digital twin and blockchain framework to support accountable information sharing in construction projects. Automation in Construction. 2021;**127**:103688. DOI: 10.1016/j.autcon.2021.103688

[6] Dwivedi SK, Amin R, Vollala S. Blockchain based secured information sharing protocol in supply chain management system with key distribution mechanism. Journal of Information Security and Applications. 2020;**54**:102554. DOI: 10.1016/j.jisa.2020.102554

[7] Latif SA, Wen FBX, Iwendi C, Wang LF, Mohsin SM, Han Z, et al. AI-empowered, blockchain and SDN integrated security architecture for IoT network of cyber physical systems. Computer Communications. 2022;**181**:274-283. DOI: 10.1016/j.comcom.2021.09.029

[8] Yang X, Zhang C. Blockchain-based multiple authorities attribute-based encryption for EHR access control scheme. Applied Sciences. 2022;**12**(21):10812. DOI: 10.3390/app122110812

[9] Yu K, Tan L, Aloqaily M, Yang H, Jararweh Y. Blockchain-enhanced data sharing with traceable and direct revocation in IIoT. IEEE Transactions on Industrial Informatics. 2021;**17**(11):7669-7678. DOI: 10.1109/tii.2021.3049141

[10] Xu Z, Zhang S, Han H, Dong X, Zhang Z, Wang H, et al. Blockchain-aided searchable encryption-based two-way attribute access control research. Security and Communication Networks. 2022;**2022**:1-13. DOI: 10.1155/2022/2410455

[11] Li M, Yu S, Zheng Y, Ren K, Lou W. Scalable and secure sharing of personal health records in cloud computing using attribute-based encryption. IEEE Transactions on Parallel and Distributed Systems. 2013;**24**(1):131-143. DOI: 10.1109/tpds.2012.97

[12] Kaiyang G, Han Y, Riming W, Kai L. CD-ABSE: Attribute-based searchable encryption scheme supporting cross-domain sharing on Blockchain. Wireless Communications and Mobile Computing. 2022;**2022**:1-15. DOI: 10.1155/2022/6719302

[13] Fan Y, Lin X, Liang W, Wang J, Tan G, Lei X, et al. TraceChain: A blockchain-based scheme to protect data confidentiality and traceability. Software: Practice and Experience. 2022;**52**(1): 115-129. DOI: 10.1002/spe.2753

[14] Kumar R, Tripathi R, Marchang N, Srivastava G, Gadekallu TR, Xiong NN. A secured distributed detection system based on IPFS and blockchain for industrial image and video data security. Journal of Parallel and Distributed Computing. 2021;**152**:128-143. DOI: 10.1016/j.jpdc.2021.02.022

[15] Jia B, Zhang X, Liu J, Zhang Y, Huang K, Liang Y. Blockchain-enabled federated learning data protection aggregation scheme with differential privacy and homomorphic encryption in IIoT. IEEE Transactions on Industrial Informatics. Jun 2022;**18**(6):4049-4058. DOI: 10.1109/TII.2021.3085a960

[16] Chadwick DW, Fan W, Costantino G, de Lemos R, Di Cerbo F, Herwono I, et al. A cloud-edge based data security architecture for sharing and analysing cyber threat information. Future Generation Computer Systems. 2020;**102**:710-722. DOI: 10.1016/j.future.2019.06.026

[17] Le Nguyen B, Laxmi Lydia E, Elhoseny M, Pustokhina V, et al. Privacy preserving blockchain technique to achieve secure and reliable sharing of IoT data. Computers, Materials & Continua. 2020;**65**(1):87-107. DOI: 10.32604/cmc.2020.011599

[18] Yang B. Prevention of business risks of internet information security platforms based on Blockchain technology. Computational Intelligence and Neuroscience. 2022;**2022**:1-10. DOI: 10.1155/2022/7671810

[19] Fazal R, Shah MA, Khattak HA, et al. Achieving data privacy for decision support systems in times of massive data sharing. Cluster Computing. 2022;**25**:3037-3049. DOI: 10.1007/s10586-021-03514-x

[20] Kaushal RK, Bhardwaj R, Kumar N, Aljohani AA, Gupta SK, Singh P, et al. Using Mobile computing to provide a smart and secure internet of things (IoT) framework for medical applications. Wireless Communications and Mobile Computing. 2022;**2022**:1-13. DOI: 10.1155/2022/8741357

[21] Wenhua Z, Qamar F, Abdali T-AN, Hassan R, Jafri STA, Nguyen QN. Blockchain technology: Security issues, healthcare applications, challenges and future trends. Electronics. 2023;**12**(3):546. DOI: 10.3390/electronics12030546

[22] El-Shafai W, Mohamed FAHE, Elkamchouchi HMA, Abd-Elnaby M, Elshafee A. Efficient and secure Cancelable biometric authentication framework based on genetic encryption algorithm. IEEE Access. 2021;**9**:77675-77692. DOI: 10.1109/access.2021.3082940

[23] Thabit F, Alhomdy APS, Al-Ahdal AHA, Jagtap PDS. A new lightweight cryptographic algorithm for enhancing data security in cloud computing. Global Transitions Proceedings. 2021;**2**(1):91-99. DOI: 10.1016/j.gltp.2021.01.013

Section 2

Blockchain and Cryptography

Chapter 3

Blockchain Mining: Understanding Its Difficulty in Terms of Hashing Algorithm Efficiency

Carlos Roberto Martinez Martinez

Abstract

This study systematically evaluates the performance of the hashing algorithms SHA-2 and SHA-3 (in both 256-bit and 512-bit variants), as well as MD5, in generating and verifying a thousand-block chain to understand the computational costs associated with blockchain mining. Java-specific source code was developed to simulate key aspects of a blockchain back-end environment, focusing on block creation and validation. The five distinct hashing algorithm configurations were tested at varying levels of complexity, with performance measured by the duration of each test. The study reveals that SHA-3, despite producing stronger hash values, is slower than MD5 and SHA-2. An optimal balance between security and calculation time was achieved at a four-character complexity level. While higher complexity levels enhance security, they significantly reduce performance, deeming them suitable for systems with lower data processing needs. These findings can guide small and medium-sized businesses in understanding the computational costs of employing blockchain technologies.

Keywords: cryptography, SHA-2, SHA-3, MD5, proof of work, computational costs

1. Introduction

Blockchain technology, transcending its initial role in cryptocurrencies, is now emerging as a versatile agent of change in the modern digital age. Its decentralized, transparent, and immutable characteristics are expected to significantly influence numerous sectors. For instance, blockchain technology has been proposed to be implemented in African nations to increase voter trust and reduce electoral violence [1]. Other possible applications are: facilitating data exchange, medication administration, biomedical research, remote patient monitoring, health data analytics, and log management [2]. Furthermore, recent studies highlight that smart contracts, based on blockchain programming interfaces, have the potential to transform several established industries, including healthcare, energy, and banking [3].

The present study examines the computational requirements imposed on blockchain systems by extensive mining activities while also providing important insights to alleviate their respective workloads. It thoroughly evaluates the algorithms of Message-Digest version 5 (MD5), as well as Secure Hash Algorithm versions 2 (SHA-2) and 3 (SHA-3), in both their 256-bit and 512-bit forms. The focus is on assessing the effectiveness of these algorithms in generating and validating blockchains. The primary goal of this research is to achieve a balance between hash strength, which directly impacts system security, and computing time, which significantly affects overall performance.

2. Theoretical framework

The core of the blockchain mining process is the calculation of the hash value for each block, but this requires significant computational power and direct and indirect costs of these technologies. The complexity of designing a balanced solution has led to the development of a number of specialized technologies, such as a proposed decentralized agent-oriented modeling (DAOM) framework [4] for designing and developing blockchain-decentralized applications to facilitate secure and efficient interorganizational collaborations. Additionally, there are proposals for the implementation of Bloom filters on GPUs, utilizing special frameworks to enhance hashing performance [5]. However, utilizing trustworthy digest algorithms to calculate hash values is fundamental for maintaining the integrity of the network, its security and efficiency. In this context, the National Institute of Standards and Technology (NIST) of the USA recommends the SHA hashing algorithms, including the SHA-2 family and SHA-3 in their 224, 256, 384, and 512-bit modalities [6]. These algorithms have been subjected to extensive scrutiny and cryptographic analysis, validating their security for a variety of applications. The previous SHA-1 algorithm was deemed insufficient and was removed from the Secure Hash Standard in March 2023 [6].

The Java programming language, known for its platform independence, robustness, and extensive ecosystem, is widely used to develop and test blockchain-related algorithms. Numerous blockchain platforms, frameworks, and libraries, such as Ethereum, Hyperledger Fabric, and Corda, provide Java SDKs and automation support for creating blockchain back-end applications [7]. Regarding the hashing process, the *MessageDigest* class from the *java.security* library supports various algorithms, including MD5, which is based on the RFC 1321 standard [8]. The information to be hashed with this algorithm is initially padded so that its length conforms to a 448 modulus of 512. Padding consists of appending a single '1' bit, followed by '0' bits, until the desired length is reached. A 64-bit representation of the original message length is subsequently appended. If the length is greater than 264 bits, only the lowest 64 bits are considered. The resulting 512-bit message is split into 32-bit words. A four-word buffer (A, B, C, and D) is initialized with specific hexadecimal values to compute the message digest. Subsequent cycles of transformations on the buffer and message words generate the final message digest. Despite MD5 being considered as insecure in recent years [9], its high performance in blockchain mining continues to attract interest, as evidenced by [10].

SHA-2 is implemented in Java in compliance with the standard outlined in [6]. According to the official documentation of the programming language [11], there are two primary configurations: 256-bit and 512-bit, and all other possible bit lengths are just variations of these. Both configurations consist of the text being split into eight 32-bit words. To prepare these strings for processing, a single '1' bit is appended, followed by 'k' zero bits. The value of 'k' is chosen so that the entire length of the message is a multiple of 512 bits minus 64. Then, a 64-bit block representing the original binary length is appended. The then-padded message is parsed into multiple 512-bit segments. Each block is subdivided into 32-bit words (for SHA-256) or 64-bit words (for SHA-512), depending on the algorithm. Then, a main loop is executed on each word performing calculations with constants, rotations, and shifts of quantities. The entire procedure returns the final hash value.

SHA-3 is a family of cryptographic hash functions derived from the Keccak algorithm [12], which utilizes mathematical permutations on the width of the strings. The number of internal transformation iterations, or rounds, allow transformations on a state array of bits. This process enables the conversion of binary strings into state arrays and vice versa, following certain predefined rules. In addition, SHA-3 uses a framework known as Sponge construction, which uses a function on fixed-length strings, a rate parameter, and a padding rule in order to processes a series of input blocks and then integrate them with the internal state of the hash function through XOR operations. This design makes SHA-3 a robust and versatile cryptographic instrument.

In a comparative analysis of various cryptographic algorithms, Gupta et al. [13] stated that while MD5 offers speed due to its relatively simpler calculations, it falls short in providing robust security against collision attacks. Collision resistance is a characteristic of cryptographic hash functions that makes it extremely difficult to find two different inputs that result in the same output. MD5 is considered less collision resistant than the SHA family because of vulnerabilities that make it easier to find two distinct inputs that produce the same hash value [14]. This vulnerability compromises the security of systems that depend on MD5 for data integrity or authentication. SHA-2 and SHA-3 are meant to provide much stronger collision resistance, making them better suited for protecting digital data and communications across various applications [15].

SHA-2, specifically its 256- and 512-bit variants, demonstrated significant resistance against cryptographic attacks [16] because of its more complex hash calculations. However, the enhanced security offered by SHA-2 comes at the cost of computational speed, especially when dealing with large datasets. Similarly, Chandran and Manuel [17] noted that SHA-3, the successor to SHA-2, provides even stronger security features but with increased demands on computational efficiency. Despite this limitation, the authors emphasized the resistance of SHA-3 to known cryptographic vulnerabilities, making it a preferable choice for applications requiring high-security measures. However, these findings contrast with those of Sailaja and Vucha [18], who indicated that the performance and security of hashing algorithms depend mostly on the nature and volume of the data being processed. In the latter study, SHA-3 was found to be more efficient than SHA-2 for smaller datasets, while SHA-2 outperformed SHA-3 with larger data volumes. For similar reasons, Quist-Aphetsi and Blankson [19] proposed a hybrid approach, suggesting the combined use of MD5 and SHA-2 of 256 bit for a balance between security and computational efficiency, mitigating the vulnerabilities associated with MD5 and the performance drawbacks of SHA-2.

The choice between these hashing algorithms should therefore hinge on the specific needs of the application regarding security and performance.

Table 1 scrutinizes 10 recent studies, each delivering insights into the efficacy of hashing algorithms within the realm of blockchain mining. Despite the consistent approach to hashing algorithms, their computational costs, and their impact on blockchain mining across these studies, the current research distinguishes itself by specifically concentrating on the exhaustive evaluation of the MD5, SHA-2, and SHA-3 algorithms in the particular context of blockchain mining, utilizing the Java

Year, study	Approach	Comparative analysis with present article
2023, [20]	Using the Modified Merkle Hash Tree algorithm as a foundation, this study investigated a framework for identity management in decentralized IoT blockchain networks. Multiple encryption techniques and hash functions were included, such as RIPEMD, Whirlpool, Tiger, Gost, Shake, SHA1, and SHA2 in 256, 384, and 512 bits. The study indicated that a combination of the SHA3 function and AES-128 encryption reduced execution time by 36% compared to other combinations in regards of identity threat protection and network protection.	The study does not specify the software platform used for conducting the test, thereby eliminating the possibility of reproducibility. Moreover, the performance results are obtained by first encrypting each block and then calculating the hash value using a cross-combination of algorithms instead of directly evaluating the mining process efficiency itself.
2022, [21]	Given the vulnerabilities of blockchain systems to quantum attacks, the study explored the performance of various post-quantum signature algorithms, such as the ECDSA, Dilithium, and Falcon, in a blockchain environment. The study identified that the main weakness is related more to the large sizes of the keys than to the signatures produced by cryptographic methods.	Post-quantum algorithms and hashing algorithms are distinct in purpose and design. Post-quantum algorithms are designed to secure information against the potential capabilities of quantum computers, which are not yet commonly used in current blockchain applications.
2022, [22]	This article introduces ALDER, a method developed to augment the efficiency of blockchain systems by utilizing multiplexed execution of the consensus protocol. It enacts a two-phase strategy: a reduction phase that utilizes a voting mechanism to achieve consensus on a specific block hash and a binary Byzantine agreement phase that finalizes consensus anchored on hash values. Alongside these phases, ALDER integrates cryptographic hashing into the construction of macroblocks, thereby enhancing throughput and reducing latency.	Although the ALDER method uses cryptographic hashing to construct macroblocks, it does not evaluate the relative efficacy compared to other available hashing algorithms.
2022, [23]	The article contrasted the performance of SHA-256 and BLAKE2b in a Proof of Work (PoW) architecture, specifically in a Bitcoin-like mining scenario. It addressed the need for efficient hash algorithms in blockchain applications, considering power consumption and environmental concerns. The results indicated that BLAKE2b was faster for single plaintext hashing, while SHA-256 outperformed in PoW architectures.	The article focused solely on two hashing algorithms: SHA-2 in 256-bit mode and BLAKE2b. Additionally, Python was used for developing the blockchain framework, as it possesses several commendable characteristics. However, this language is frequently outperformed by Java in large-scale back-end operations.
2022, [24]	It offers performance indicators, trade-offs, trends, drawbacks, and proposed solutions for blockchain consensus algorithms in decentralized architectures. The study assesses performance metrics, including fairness for smaller clients, and discusses the potential influence of quantum computation on blockchain technology.	An algorithm was developed for evaluating SHA-2 in 256-bit mode, taking precedence over other potentially more efficient algorithms. The findings are presented predominantly through qualitative assessments rather than quantitative measurements.
2021, [25]	Using queuing models, this study analyzes Bitcoin's transaction confirmation time, revealing a non-work conserving mechanism that may exclude lower-fee transactions. It also specifies a nonhomogeneous Poisson process as an appropriate model for simulating block generation, providing accurate estimates for transaction confirmation time, particularly for larger block sizes.	The study used one single hashing technique. The performance analysis of the blockchain is primarily based on the implementation of independent Bernoulli trials for hashing calculations, recommending the creation of mini pools consisting of multiple nodes for enhanced performance.

Year, study	Approach	Comparative analysis with present article
2020, [26]	The study systematically evaluates blockchain efficacy using theoretical analysis, a literature review, and performance experiments using frameworks such as Blockbench, DAGbench, and Hyperledger Caliper. It also tested the performance of several Distributed Layer Technologies (DLTs), such as HLF, Ethereum Geth, Parity, and Quorum, among others. The survey identifies bottlenecks of those technologies and outlines future directions for blockchain system optimization research.	This study is comprehensive and offers significant comparisons among various Blockchain frameworks and DLTs. However, it lacks quantitative evidence about blockchain mining performance.
2019, [27]	This study assesses the efficacy of hash calculation in the Parity and Multichain blockchain frameworks by evaluating transaction validation time, transaction mining time, transaction-seek time, and block-seek time. The results indicate that Multichain outperformed Parity in the evaluated metrics. However, it should be noted that Multichain only supports transactions for asset exchange between pairs. On the other hand, Parity requires more time for computations but offers support for complex transactions, including the execution of smart contracts.	The study presented results on transaction-mining time for the evaluated frameworks and explored the efficiency of storing and retrieving blocks from the blockchain. However, it did not provide specific details about the mining strategy employed or the efficiency of the hashing algorithms used in the frameworks.
2018, [28]	The study examines the use of a blockchain proof-of-work mechanism and SHA3-256 cryptographic hashing to enhance the security of mobile commerce. This paper demonstrates how these blockchain techniques can be adapted for mobile platforms, providing effective security solutions for future m-commerce.	It is not specified which programming platforms were used to develop the described blockchain framework, limiting the insight into technology performance. Only the performance of SHA3-256 was evaluated.
2016, [29]	This study presents a new framework for quantitatively analyzing security and performance in proof-of-work blockchains, considering real-world factors. The framework enabled optimal comparison of performance and security trade-offs in various blockchain scenarios, including configuration of the block size, generation intervals, and propagation mechanisms.	The security evaluation of the software was based solely on Markov Decision Processes (MDP). The results focused on measuring the mining power of hypothetical adversaries to analyze competition in "selfish mining" techniques, rather than evaluating the computational performance of various ciphering algorithms

Table 1.
Comparative analysis of the literature on blockchain mining performance.

programming language as a back-end software platform. This refocusing of the surveyed studies is highlighted to underscore the relevance of the present research.

The balance between security and performance in blockchain technology was based on the technical methods used to maintain network integrity and operational effectiveness. Pillai et al. [30] were investigated regarding the trade-offs related to blockchain interoperability, where the aim of smooth transactions between various blockchain systems might lead to increased complexity that could compromise security and performance; therefore, a modular approach to interoperability was suggested, utilizing dedicated protocols to fulfill security and performance needs for secure and efficient cross-chain interactions, without overly burdening the participating blockchains. Also, Gervais et al. [31] offered a technical examination of how Proof of Work (PoW) techniques, which aim to protect blockchain by demanding computationally difficult tasks for block validation, naturally restricted transaction throughput and raised latency. To address this trade-off, they proposed using other consensus mechanisms like Proof of Stake (PoS) or hybrid models that combine different consensus techniques to enhance both security and performance while reducing computational complexity. In a more recent trend, Dinh and Thai [32] indicated that AI enhanced blockchain by optimizing decision-making across security, performance, and governance. It automated parameter adjustments for improved efficiency and introduced advanced mechanisms for data confidentiality. Machine learning algorithms within blockchain could detect and neutralize threats, ensuring component isolation during attacks. These measures could contribute to enhancing security and reducing the computational costs of hashing.

3. Methodology

In this study, a systematic approach was adopted to evaluate the performance of MD5, SHA-2, and SHA-3 (the two latter in 256-bit and 512-bit variants) in the generation and verification of a thousand-block chain. The testing environment utilized Ubuntu Linux version 22.04 as a virtual machine [33], equipped with a 1.8 GHz processor and 4 GB of RAM. The software was developed using Java Development Kit (JDK) version 18 and served both as a blockchain framework and a testing application, providing a controlled environment for comparing the performance of the hashing algorithms. The framework simulated basic aspects of a blockchain network, such as block creation, transaction processing, and blockchain validation, ensuring repeatable and consistent performance measurements and serializable network transmission capabilities [34]. A procedure was used to generate and populate the blocks [35], filled with hypothetical monetary transactions. The configurations of each hashing algorithm were tested four times at six different levels of complexity: from one to six characters used in the hash value as proof-of-work. Therefore, in this study, the mining process executed to verify a hash value with a substring of two zeros (*'00'*) was named Complexity Level #2, or simply *"C-2,"* and so on. The highest level of complexity evaluated, consisting of six zeros (*'000000'*), was named *"C-6"*.

The performance was determined based on the duration of each test, which was recorded in seconds [36] by the same software that conducted the tests. After the mining process, blockchain validation consisted of a routine that recalculated each block hash and verified the integrity of the nonce values and precedent hash in the chain, also recording performance data such as time, CPU, and memory load. While Linux memory caching and sharing subsystems can distort actual usage, *'meminfo'* command provided a general load estimate.

After conducting the tests, an inflection point in mining complexity was identified, where increased nonce calculation iterations began to significantly extend computational time, thereby negatively impacting performance. This point marked a threshold beyond which further increases in complexity no longer yielded proportional security benefits, as the additional security gains did not justify the heightened calculation time. This criterion was used to determine the most appropriate level of complexity for practical applications in regular real-life organizations.

4. Development of testing software

In the developed source code, each block represented a class instance with six attributes and a non-limited list for storing transaction objects. Only the most basic information was included in the declaration of the Block and Transaction classes to reduce the possibility of creating unnecessary bottlenecks while calculating the hashes in order to focus mostly on the performance of the algorithms. The pseudocode is as follows:

```
Class Block
Declare integer id
Declare integer nonce
Declare long timeStamp
Declare string hash
Declare string previousHash
Declare List of Transaction objects, named lTransactions
EndClass
Class Transaction
Declare integer id
Declare long timeStamp
Declare string sender
Declare string receiver
Declare double amount
EndClass
```

The *BlockChain* class was designed to manage the blockchain's business logic, holding all blocks in a dynamically allocated structure. Upon initialization as *BCManager*, the class required inputs for the mining complexity level, a character for the proof of work, and the hashing algorithm's name. The genesis block was created initially, and the number of iterations (*nonces*) needed to meet the complexity requirements was recorded. For demonstration, a loop was executed to create and add a predetermined number of blocks, each with a sample transaction. After mining each block, the cumulative number of iterations required was updated, serving as a key metric for evaluating the hashing algorithm's efficiency. The Java code was:

```
this.BCManager = new BlockChain(pComplexity, "0",
pHashingAlgName);
this.BCManager.createGenesis();
this.iterationCount=this.BCManager.getBlock(0).getNonce();
for(int i=0; i<RequestedBlocks; i++)
{
BCManager.createBlock();
BCManager.getLastBlock().setTransaction("Wallet_ID_1",
100.8,   "Wallet_ID_2");
this.iterationCount +=BCManager .mineBlock();
}
```

The *BCManager* class contained a function called createBlock that was responsible for appending a new block to the blockchain. The method entailed obtaining the hash of the most recent block in the blockchain to serve as the previous hash for the new block. Subsequently, the new block was initialized with its index set to the current size of the blockchain and its prior hash set to that of the last block. In the Block class, a method named setTransaction was created to add a new transaction to a block at the same time. The method utilized the sender's identity, transaction amount, and receiver's identity as inputs to generate a new transaction object. This object included the aforementioned details and an index based on the current number of transactions in the block. Subsequently, the transaction was appended to the block's transaction list. The hashing process was executed inside of *BCManager.mineBlock()*, so the last block was mined. The method made use of the plain String version of every block, generated by the *toString()* method. Then, using a MessageDigest object configured with the provided parametrized hash method, the String was converted into a byte array. This conversion was done according to a specific encryption method. The byte array was then converted into a readable hexadecimal string, as presented in the following Java code snippet:

```
MessageDigest digest =
MessageDigest.getInstance(hashMethod.toString());
byte[] hash = digest.digest(Block.toString().getBytes("UTF-8"));
StringBuffer hexadecimalString = new StringBuffer();
for (int i = 0; i < hash.length; i++)
{
String hexadecimal = Integer.toHexString(0xff & hash[i]);
if (hexadecimal.length()==1) hexadecimalString.append('0');
hexadecimalString.append(hexadecimal);
}
return hexadecimalString.toString();
```

The mining method was coded inside *BCManager*, and no business logic was provided within the block objects. The method created a hash value from the plaintext, composed of the String representation of each attribute in a block, plus a nonce, until achieving the desired proof of work, as specified in *PoW_String*. The complexity level was indicated by the variable *complexity_Str*. The blockchain management object, *BCManager*, provided access to the last block available for mining. It also recorded the nonce and calculated hash in a manner consistent with the fundamental rules of blockchain. The code is presented below:

```
String str= BCManager.getLastBlock().toString();
int nonce=0;
String sHash="";
while(true)
{
sHash=this.generateHash(str+Integer.toString(nonce));
if (sHash.subSequence(0, complexity_Str).equals(PoW_String))
{
BCManager.getLastBlock().register(nonce, sHash);
break;
}
nonce++;
}
return nonce;
```

After block generation, a validation procedure was performed on each mined block to confirm the integrity of the blockchain. This procedure was also part of the managing class and involved the recalculation of every hash using the previously stored nonce and then comparing against the stored hash. If both hashes matched, the proof of work was considered valid; if not, the blockchain was deemed compromised. The code snippet is presented below. The full source code is available in the repository [37].

```
String sHash= BCManager.generateHash(Block.toString()+
Block.getNonceString());
return sHash.equals(BCManager.getBlock(blockID).getHash());
```

5. Results and discussion

Each algorithm configuration produced different lengths of hashes, as shown in **Table 2**. MD5 created the smallest hashes, which were also the easiest to calculate in terms of computational resources. Hashing algorithms operating in the 256-bit modality returned hashes of 64 bytes, while those in the 512-bit mode returned hashes of 128 bytes. Both SHA2 and SHA3 in 512-bit mode showed more security potential, as they were more computationally challenging.

Table 3 illustrates the maximum average random access memory (RAM) used during the creation of the test blockchain. With increasing complexity, RAM usage also increased. Notably, "C-5" and "C-6" levels required extensive resources, implying substantial computational costs for real-life applications. Such expenses could be justified only in high-revenue businesses that prioritize extreme security demands over cost.

Figure 1 illustrates the exponential memory usage increase with rising complexity levels. These results suggest that enhancing server RAM capacity becomes necessary when hardening the proof-of-work method for security purposes. After generating the test blockchain, a separate revalidation was performed, which involved recreating the hash of every block using its converted plain String and nonce value. This process was significantly lighter than the intensive mining required for new blocks during the initial blockchain construction. **Figure 2** reveals that verification times for complexity levels C-2 through C-5 are relatively consistent but markedly increases for C-6 across all algorithms. In a real-world implementation, enhancing the CPU and

Hashing method	Resulting length (Bytes)
MD5	32
SHA2-256 bits	64
SHA2-512 bits	128
SHA3-256 bits	64
SHA3-512 bits	128

Table 2.
Byte length of the calculated hash values.

Complexity level	RAM peak (mega bytes)
C-2	21.9
C-3	52.3
C-4	251.9
C-5	538.7
C-6	1474.56

Table 3.
Maximum memory usage while mining.

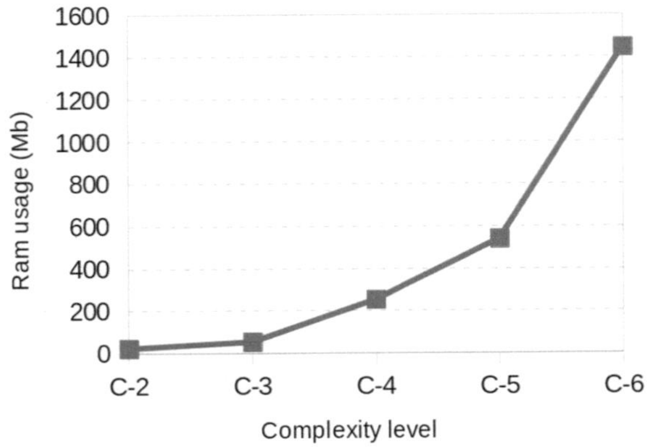

Figure 1.
Peak memory usage during processing for each complexity level.

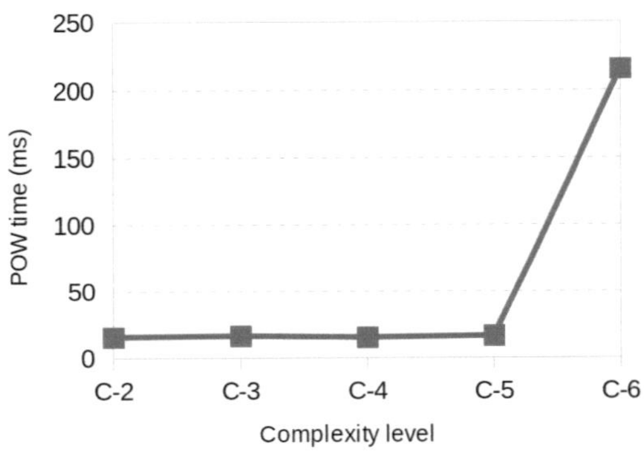

Figure 2.
Proof of work (PoW) calculation time for each complexity level.

RAM of a multicore server, together with utilizing Java's concurrency utilities such as the Fork/Join framework and the Executor framework, greatly improves blockchain efficiency and security. These Java solutions utilize multicore processors to accelerate the blockchain mining process and data management chores, hence decreasing the time required to solve cryptographic challenges. Upgraded RAM guarantees efficient processing of extensive datasets and intricate procedures. These enhancements utilize the capabilities of Java for parallel processing capabilities to speed up the performance of complex proof-of-work tasks, thus improving speed and scalability efficiently.

While generating the test blockchain, the process with C-2 proved to be the fastest, and therefore the least secure, needing about 250,000 iterations and up to 5 ms of processing for each block (**Table 4**). The process with C-3 required approximately 4 million iterations, with block mining times ranging from 13 to 52 ms (**Table 5**), offering improved security. For C-4, over 60 million iterations were necessary, resulting in mining times from 183 to 838 ms per block (**Table 6**). With C-5, security further improved, requiring nearly a billion iterations for the test and mining times from 2.5 to 17.5 seconds per block. In the case of SHA3-256 (**Table 7**), the most secure encryption method tested, generating a thousand-block test took more than 4 hours. However, it is notable that the mining times varied significantly depending on the

Method	Iterations	PoW (ms)	Mining time per block (ms)
MD5	259,060	17	2
SHA2-256	235,921	13	3
SHA2-512	254,267	13	3
SHA3-256	242,535	14	3
SHA3-512	263,058	20	5

Table 4.
Mining test results, using complexity level of 2 characters (C-2).

Method	Iterations	PoW (ms)	Mining time per block (ms)
MD5	4,242,809	13	13
SHA2-256	4,163,061	17	30
SHA2-512	4,217,957	16	26
SHA3-256	3,979,857	14	32
SHA3-512	4,081,028	21	52

Table 5.
Mining test results, using complexity level of 3 characters (C-3).

Method	Iterations	PoW (ms)	Mining time per block (ms)
MD5	67,948,703	12	183
SHA2-256	65,845,949	16	443
SHA2-512	67,982,908	12	347
SHA3-256	65,054,242	14	476
SHA3-512	66,335,940	21	838

Table 6.
Mining test results, using complexity level of 4 characters (C-4).

Method	Iterations	PoW (ms)	Mining time per block (ms)
MD5	995,404,013	10	2456
SHA2-256	1,019,771,696	13	5673
SHA2-512	1,033,485,474	13	5931
SHA3-256	1,012,483,152	17	9711
SHA3-512	1,055,056,190	28	17,480

Table 7.
Mining test results, using complexity level of 5 characters (C-5).

hashing method used. Lastly, for C-6 (**Table 8**), the tests were considerably more time-consuming, requiring more than 10 billion iterations and several minutes per block. Specifically, the time to generate a single block ranged from 2.5 seconds using MD5 to 175 seconds using SHA3-512. Consequently, the creation of a thousand blocks under C-6 complexity varied significantly depending on the hashing algorithm: for

Method	Iterations	PoW (ms)	Mining time per block (ms)
MD5	12,329,239,600	124	36,154
SHA2-256	13,764,806,500	175	90,388
SHA2-512	11,346,805,800	143	66,695
SHA3-256	15,032,843,700	252	137,983
SHA3-512	14,349,920,600	381	248,370

Table 8.
Mining test results, using complexity level of 6 characters (C-6).

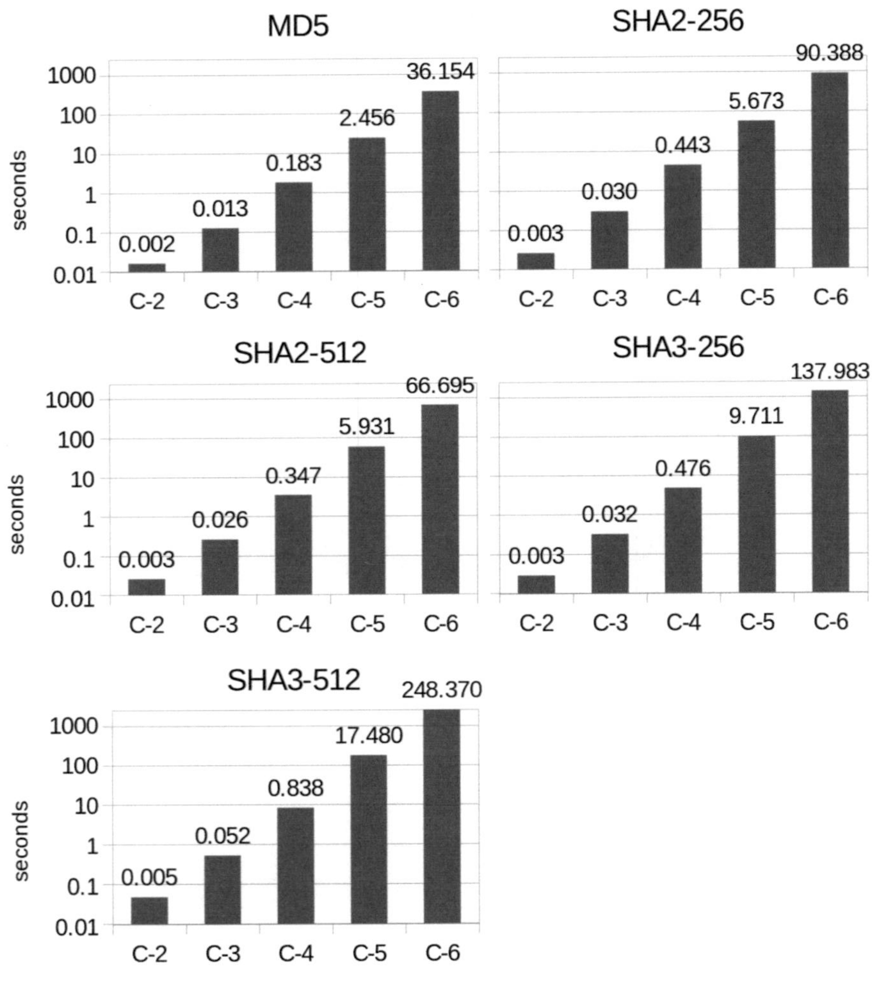

Figure 3.
Block mining time versus level of complexity (in logarithmic scale).

MD5, it took approximately 42 minutes, while for SHA3-512, it extended to over 48 hours, demonstrating a substantial increase in both time and computational effort.

Figure 3 depicts the average elapsed time for processing various complexity levels using five different methods. The simplest level, C-2, showed the shortest processing time, while C-6 had the longest, indicating an exponential increase in processing load with each additional character in the proof of work. MD5, the simplest algorithm, was notably faster at C-5. In contrast, the more robust SHA3-256 required significantly more resources, especially from C-5 onward. SHA2-256 maintained similar efficiency up to C-4, compared to SHA2-512 and SHA3-256, while SHA3-512 was only slightly slower. When considering the cost of complexity, measured by the average number of iterations needed for a new block, MD5 and SHA2-256 were the most efficient at C-5. However, SHA-512, SHA3-256, and SHA3-512 showed peak efficiency at C-4. Despite MD5 and SHA2–256's higher efficiency at more complex levels, C-5 demanded substantially more iterations than C-4, suggesting that C-4 is a more optimal balance of security and resource use.

Validation of the test blockchain was achieved by executing a new proof of work to recalculate the hash of every block in a single process. Results depicted in **Figure 4** revealed that MD5, SHA2-256, SHA2-512, and SHA3-256 performed similarly, with low validation costs for C-2, C-3, and C-4. However, C-5 and especially C-6 had high computation costs and were much slower, affirming C-4 as the most cost-effective

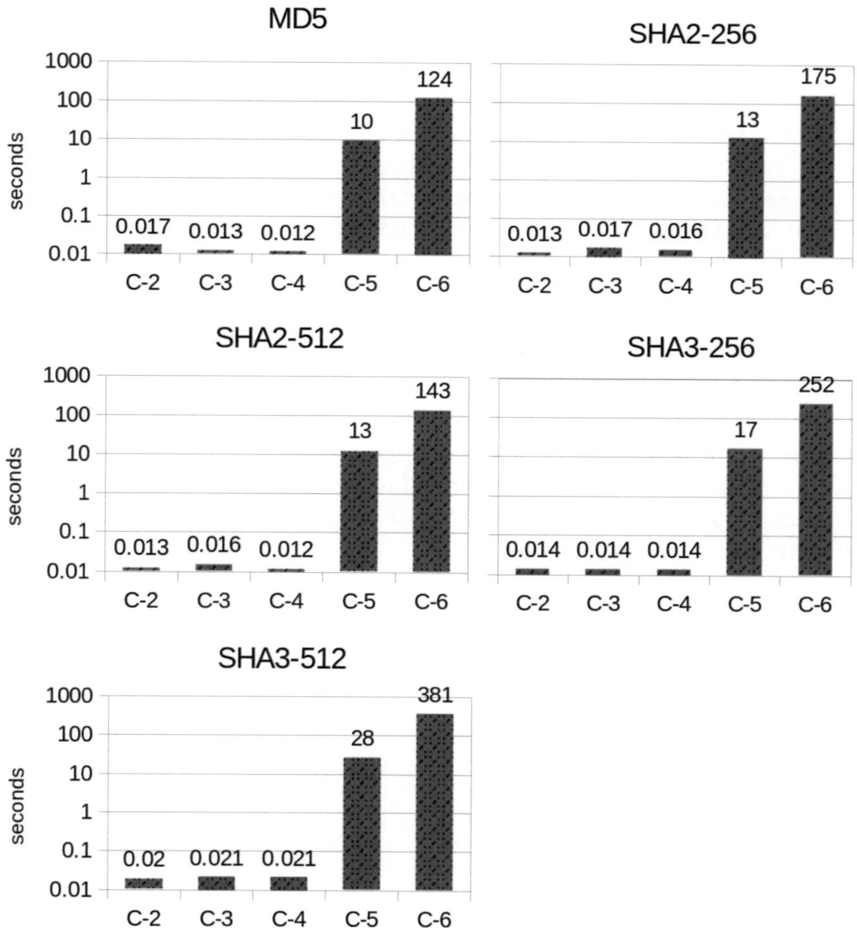

Figure 4.
Elapsed time of Proof of Work (PoW) versus level of complexity in the test blockchain (in logarithmic scale).

option. In the case of MD5, the time duration for C-5 was 833.3 times longer than for C-4, and for C-6, it was 12.4 times longer than C-5. This suggests that the most substantial inflection point is reached starting from C-5. Similarly, for SHA2-256, the duration for C-5 was 812.5 times longer than for C-4, and for C-6, it was 13.5 times longer than C-5. In the case of SHA2-512, the increase was even more pronounced: C-5 took 1083.3 times longer than C-4, and C-6 took 11.0 times longer than C-5. The pattern for SHA3-256 was comparable, with C-5 taking 1214.3 times longer than C-4 and C-6 taking 14.8 times longer than C-5. For SHA3-512, the increase was the most significant: C-5 took 1333.3 times longer than C-4, and C-6 took 13.6 times longer than C-5.

Given that the mining process consists of finding a specific hash value through repetitive iterations, the average number of iterations for each algorithm was calculated against each level of complexity. The results of this respective test, illustrated in **Table 9**, show that MD5, which produces the shortest byte length in hash values, executed more iterations for hash calculations per second. This suggests that while MD5 is less secure, it is the fastest in terms of operations per second. At complexity level C-4, SHA2-256 and SHA3-256 yielded a similar number of iterations per second; however, SHA3-256 demonstrated a reduction in operation count starting from C-5. In comparison, at C-5, SHA2-512 generated approximately 2.5 times more iterations. This study offers a novel perspective on the comparative performance of MD5, SHA-2, and SHA-3 hashing algorithms against varying levels of mining complexity in a Java-based blockchain framework. The results highlight the trade-off between security and computational efficiency, with the four-character complexity level providing an optimal balance for the aforementioned algorithms. Small and medium-sized enterprises seeking to understand the computational costs associated with blockchain technologies will find these findings particularly useful. The selection of a hashing algorithm and complexity level should be tailored to the specific requirements of the system, balancing security needs with performance capabilities. Additionally, investigating the impact of data size and hardware specifications on hashing algorithm performance would be valuable. As the field of cryptography continues to evolve, ongoing research is essential to keep pace with technological advancements and to deepen our understanding of blockchain technologies. Excluding MD5, SHA2-256 proved to be the most efficient in single hashing operations at C-5 compared to the other algorithms at C-4, although it exhibited noticeably less robustness in hash calculation. Across all evaluated complexity levels, SHA2-512, SHA3-256, and SHA3-512 outperformed in the aforementioned order.

Considering these findings for the implementation of a new blockchain system in an actual organizational setting, the computational capacity required for executing

Complexity	MD5	SHA2-256	SHA2-512	SHA3-256	SHA3-512
C-2	160,608	91,442	97,720	82,327	54,964
C-3	332,665	139,485	161,936	122,631	78,507
C-4	370,676	148,637	195,916	136,562	79,170
C-5	405,329	179,762	174,251	104,263	60,359
C-6	341,025	152,285	170,131	108,947	57,776

Table 9.
Hash calculations per second.

complexity levels of two to four characters is similar. Therefore, as C-4 provides the best level of security, it emerges as the most suitable option. It is evident in this case that all hashing algorithms showed a similar trend. However, if a more demanding proof of work is required, increasing the complexity level to five characters, a significant expansion in computational capacity is necessary, and even more so for six characters. However, the incremental demand from five to six characters is approximately just over 10 times, which might imply that scaling between these levels is somewhat more manageable, but it remains substantially costly compared to performing a four-character hash as proof of work.

Every test carried out for this study was done on blocks of 250 bytes. With C-4 being determined to be the most appropriate option for most applications, several block sizes were evaluated at this complexity level (**Figure 5**). Although the MD5 algorithm was the fastest—completing a 250-byte block in 2456 ms and a 1 MB block in 23,378 ms—it is only suitable for non-sensitive applications due to well-documented security flaws. The mining time for SHA2-256 and SHA2-512 increased significantly from 250-byte blocks to 1 MB blocks, although SHA2-256 performed better overall, finishing at 54,455 ms for the larger blocks as opposed to SHA2-512's 67,320 ms. This demonstrated that, among the SHA2 family, SHA2-256 was a more effective choice, particularly for greater data processing requirements. The highest mining times were reported by SHA3 algorithms, which provided increased security. SHA3-512, for example, reached 132,162 ms for a 1 MB block, highlighting its computational intensity. These findings shed light on the trade-off between security and performance that usually exists in cryptographic processes. A balance between the quick but unreliable MD5 and the safe but slow SHA3 versions was offered by SHA2-256.

The results about the efficiency of different hashing algorithms are generally applicable to Proof of Work (PoW) and Proof of Stake (PoS) systems in a broad range of blockchain applications. Although PoS presents a model in which the stakes of validators are important for transaction validation, it does not necessarily outperform PoW [38]. While PoS emphasizes less on energy usage and instead offers possible advances in network governance and decentralization, PoW is well known for its computation-based security capabilities. Blockchain framework architecture is significantly impacted by hashing algorithm efficiency, as demonstrated by Ethereum, Hyperledger Fabric, and Corda. Ethereum made the switch to proof-of-stake (PoS) in an effort to increase security and scalability through more effective consensus. The

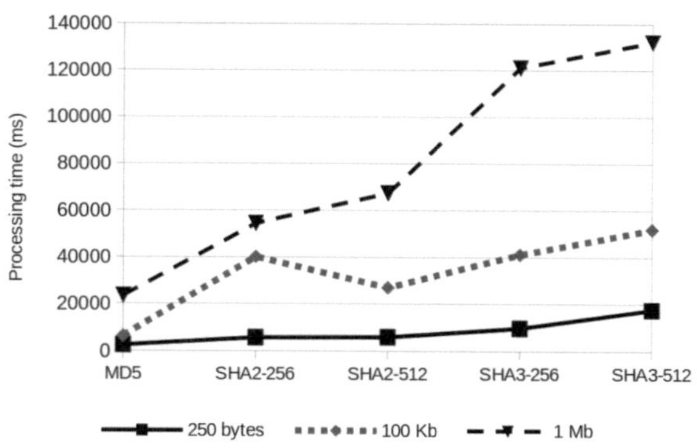

Figure 5.
Mining times for blocks of different sizes, by algorithm.

adaptability of Hyperledger Fabric's consensus processes highlights how effective hashing may improve transaction privacy and productivity for businesses [39]. With an emphasis on the financial sector, Corda emphasizes how crucial it is to select effective hashing algorithms in order to guarantee privacy and finality [7]. When combined, these frameworks show how hashing efficiency plays a key role in maximizing the security, performance, and adaptability of blockchain applications.

While this study examines the efficiency of various mining configurations, energy consumption can be inferred by analyzing their computational expenses and effectiveness. Higher complexity levels result in more computational work and longer processing durations, indicating a likelihood of increased energy usage. Differences in algorithm performance suggest variations in energy efficiency, where certain algorithms may operate more quickly yet potentially consume higher amounts of energy. These findings underscore the importance of considering the environmental effects of hashing algorithms and mining operations for sustainable computing in blockchain technology.

In the blockchain industry, the effectiveness and safety of mining activities are greatly impacted by the selected hashing algorithm and its level of complexity. Public blockchains, benefiting from decentralization and open access over the Internet, find a balanced solution in choosing an algorithm such as SHA2-256 with a complexity level of C-4. This level guarantees efficient transaction processing essential for user interaction while maintaining high security standards. Private blockchains, limited to certain businesses, can focus on security rather than speed. SHA3-256 is preferred for complexity levels C-4 or C-5 because of its strong security characteristics. Private networks can benefit from improved security without incurring excessive computational costs due to their lower computational requirements. Therefore, carefully choosing hashing algorithms and their complexity levels is crucial for enhancing the efficiency of blockchain networks based on their specific needs and operational environments.

In the dynamic realm of blockchain technology, the integration of newer but promising hashing algorithms presents significant advantages. BLAKE3 [40] offers enhanced security through its resistance to modern cryptographic attacks, while KangarooTwelve [41] boasts improved collision resistance and computational efficiency. Argon2 prioritizes memory hardness, making it ideal for password hashing and key derivation functions. Additionally, RandomX introduces a novel approach by leveraging random code execution [42], which enhances resistance to ASIC mining and promotes a more equitable distribution of mining rewards. By adopting these cutting-edge algorithms, blockchain systems can bolster their security, efficiency, and resilience in the face of evolving threats and technological advancements.

6. Conclusion and future work

This study offers a novel perspective on the comparative performance of MD5, SHA-2, and SHA-3 hashing algorithms against varying levels of mining complexity in a Java-based blockchain framework. The results highlight the trade-off between security and computational efficiency, with the four-character complexity level providing an optimal balance for the aforementioned algorithms. Small and medium-sized enterprises seeking to understand the computational costs associated with blockchain technologies will find these findings particularly useful. The selection of a hashing algorithm and complexity level should be tailored to the specific requirements of the system, balancing security needs with performance capabilities. Future research could further explore these dynamics in emerging programming environments, new hashing algorithms, and blockchain networks. Additionally, investigating the impact of data size and hardware specifications on hashing algorithm performance would be valuable. As the field of cryptography continues to evolve, ongoing research is essential to keep pace with technological advancements and to deepen our understanding of blockchain technologies.

Future works should also include testing the hashing efficiency of blockchain systems using different block sizes. While smaller blocks could jeopardize security, larger blocks might lead to increased computing overhead and longer mining times. Optimizing security and performance requires an understanding of this relationship.

Conflict of interest

The author declares no conflict of interest.

Appendices and nomenclature

MD5	Message-Digest algorithm version 5
SHA2-256	Secure Hash Algorithm version 2, with a 256-bit length
SHA2-512	Secure Hash Algorithm version 2, with a 512-bit length
SHA3-256	Secure Hash Algorithm version 3, with a 256-bit length
SHA3-512	Secure Hash Algorithm version 4, with a 512-bit length
PoW	Proof of Work process
C-2	complexity level of 2 characters in a hash string
C-3	complexity level of 3 characters in a hash string
C-4	complexity level of 4 characters in a hash string
C-5	complexity level of 5 characters in a hash string
C-6	complexity level of 6 characters in a hash string

Author details

Carlos Roberto Martinez Martinez
Faculty of Engineering and Architecture, Catholic University of El Salvador, El Salvador, Central America

*Address all correspondence to: carlos.martinez@catolica.edu.sv

References

[1] Alam M, Yusuf MO, Sani NA. Blockchain technology for electoral process in Africa: A short review. International Journal of Information Technology. 2020;**12**:861-867. DOI: 10.6028/NIST.FIPS.202

[2] Ghosh PK, Chakraborty A, Hasan M, Rashid K, Siddique AH. Blockchain application in healthcare systems: A review. Systems. 2023;**11**(1):38. DOI: 10.3390/systems11010038

[3] Khan SN, Loukil F, Ghedira-Guegan C, et al. Blockchain smart contracts: Applications, challenges, and future trends. Peer-to-Peer Networking and Applications. 2021;**14**:2901-2925. DOI: 10.1007/s12083-021-01127-0

[4] Udokwu C, Brandtner P, Norta A, et al. Implementation and evaluation of the DAOM framework and support tool for designing blockchain decentralized applications. International Journal of Information Technology. 2021;**13**:2245-2263. DOI: 10.1007/s41870-021-00816-6

[5] Bhat R, Thilak RK, Vaibhav RP. Hunting the pertinency of hash and bloom filter combinations on GPU for fast pattern matching. International Journal of Information Technology. 2022;**14**:2667-2679. DOI: 10.1007/s41870-022-00964-3

[6] Dang QH. Secure Hash Standard. Gaithersburg, MD: Federal Inf. Process. Stds. (NIST FIPS), National Institute of Standards and Technology; 2015. DOI: 10.6028/NIST.FIPS.180-4

[7] Saraf C, Sabadra S. Blockchain platforms: A compendium. In: 2018 IEEE International Conference on Innovative Research and Development (ICIRD); Bangkok, Thailand. 2018. pp. 1-6. DOI: 10.1109/ICIRD.2018.8376323

[8] Rivest RL. The MD5 message-digest algorithm. In: RFC 1321. Internet Engineering Task Force; 1992. Available from: https://www.rfc-editor.org/info/rfc1321

[9] Zhang Y, Kabir MMA, Xiao Y, Yao D, Meng N. Automatic detection of Java cryptographic API misuses: Are we there yet? IEEE Transactions on Software Engineering. 2022;**49**(1):288-303. DOI: 10.1109/TSE.2022.3150302

[10] Sosu RNA, Quist-Aphetsi K, Nana L. A decentralized cryptographic blockchain approach for health information system. In: 2019 International Conference on Computing, Computational Modelling and Applications (ICCMA); Cape Coast, Ghana. 2019. pp. 120-1204. DOI: 10.1109/ICCMA.2019.00027

[11] Java Cryptography Architecture. In: Standard Algorithm Name Documentation for JDK 8. Oracle, 1993-2023. Available from: https://docs.oracle.com/javase/8/docs/technotes/guides/security/StandardNames.html [Accessed: June 13, 2023]

[12] Dworkin MJ. SHA-3 Standard: Permutation-Based Hash and Extendable-Output Functions. Gaithersburg, MD: Federal Inf. Process. Stds. (NIST FIPS), National Institute of Standards and Technology; 2015. DOI: 10.6028/NIST.FIPS.202

[13] Gupta S, Goyal N, Aggarwal K. A review of comparative study of MD5 and SSH security algorithm.

International Journal of Computer Applications. 2014;**104**(14):1-2. DOI: 10.5120/18267-9305

[14] Stevens M, Bursztein E, Karpman P, Albertini A, Markov Y. The first collision for full SHA-1. In: Katz J, Shacham H, editors. Advances in Cryptology – CRYPTO 2017, Lecture Notes in Computer Science. Vol. 10401. Cham: Springer; 2017. DOI: 10.1007/978-3-319-63688-7_19

[15] Leurent G. Practical key-recovery attack against APOP, an MD5-based challenge-response authentication. International Journal of Applied Cryptography. 2008;**1**(1):32-46. DOI: 10.1504/IJACT.2008.017049

[16] Debnath S, Chattopadhyay A, Dutta S. Brief review on journey of secured hash algorithms. In: 2017 4th International Conference on Opto-Electronics and Applied Optics (Optronix); Kolkata, India. 2017. pp. 1-5. DOI: 10.1109/OPTRONIX.2017.8349971

[17] Chandran NR, Manuel EM. Performance analysis of modified SHA-3. Procedia Technology, ScienceDirect. 2016;**24**:904-910. DOI: 10.1016/j.protcy.2016.05.168

[18] Sailaja P, Vucha M. High speed architecture for KECCACK secure hash function. International Journal of Computer Applications. 2016;**139**(9):19-24. DOI: 10.5120/ijca2016909237

[19] Quist-Aphetsi K, Blankson H. A hybrid data logging system using cryptographic hash blocks based on SHA-256 and MD5 for water treatment plant and distribution line. In: 2019 International Conference on Cyber Security and Internet of Things (ICSIoT); Accra, Ghana. IEEE; 2019. pp. 15-18. DOI: 10.1109/ICSIoT47925.2019.00009

[20] Kairaldeen AR, Abdullah NF, Abu-Samah A, Nordin R. Peer-to-peer user identity verification time optimization in IoT blockchain network. Sensors. 2023;**23**(4):2106. DOI: 10.3390/s23042106

[21] Yokubov B, Gan L. A performance comparison of post-quantum algorithms in blockchain. The Journal of the British Blockchain Association. 2022;**6**(1):1-3. DOI: 10.31585/jbba-6-1-(1)2023

[22] Korkmaz K, Bruneau-Queyreix J, Ben Mokhtar S, Réveillère L. ALDER: Unlocking blockchain performance by multiplexing consensus protocols. In: 2022 IEEE 21st International Symposium on Network Computing and Applications (NCA); Boston, MA, USA. IEEE; 2022. pp. 9-18. DOI: 10.1109/NCA57778.2022.10013556

[23] Özcan MM, Ayaz BA, Karagöz MM, Yolaçan E. Performance evaluation of SHA-256 and BLAKE2b in proof of work architecture. Eskişehir Türk Dünyası Uygulama ve Araştırma Merkezi Bilişim Dergisi. 2022;**3**(2):60-65. DOI: 10.53608/estudambilisim.1086400

[24] Merrad Y et al. Blockchain: Consensus algorithm key performance indicators, trade-offs, current trends, common drawbacks, and novel solution proposals. Mathematics. 2022;**10**(15):2754. DOI: 10.3390/math10152754

[25] Kasahara S. Performance modeling of bitcoin blockchain: Mining mechanism and transaction-confirmation process. IEICE Transactions on Communications. 2021;**104**(12):1455-1464. DOI: 10.1587/transcom.2021ITI0003

[26] Fan C, Ghaemi S, Khazaei H, Musilek P. Performance evaluation of blockchain systems: A systematic survey. IEEE Access. 2020;**8**:126927-126950. DOI: 10.1109/ACCESS.2020.3006078

[27] Oliveira MT et al. Towards a performance evaluation of private blockchain frameworks using a realistic workload. In: 2019 22nd Conference on Innovation in Clouds, Internet and Networks and Workshops (ICIN); Paris, France. IEEE Xplore; 2019. pp. 180-187. DOI: 10.1109/ICIN.2019.8685888

[28] Suankaewmanee K, Hoang DT, Niyato D, Sawadsitang S, Wang P, Han Z. Performance analysis and application of mobile blockchain. In: 2018 International Conference on Computing, Networking and Communications (ICNC); Maui, HI, USA. IEEE Xplore; 2018. pp. 642-646. DOI: 10.1109/ICCNC.2018.8390265

[29] Gervais A, Karame GO, Wüst K, Glykantzis V, Ritzdorf H, Capkun S. On the security and performance of proof of work blockchains. In: Proceedings of the 2016 ACM SIGSAC Conference on Computer and Communications Security. New York, USA: Association for Computing Machinery (ACM), Digital Library; 2016. pp. 3-16. DOI: 10.1145/2976749.2978341

[30] Pillai B, Hóu Z, Biswas K, Bui V, Muthukkumarasamy V. Blockchain interoperability: Performance and security trade-offs. In: SenSys '22: Proceedings of the 20th ACM Conference on Embedded Networked Sensor Systems. New York, USA: Association for Computing Machinery (ACM), Digital Library; 2022. DOI: 10.1145/3560905.3568176

[31] Gervais A, Karame GO, Wüst K, Glykantzis V, Ritzdorf H, Capkun S. On the security and performance of proof of work blockchains. In: Proceedings of the 2016 ACM SIGSAC Conference on Computer and Communications Security (CCS '16). New York, USA: Association for Computing Machinery (ACM), Digital Library; 2016. DOI: 10.1145/2976749.2978341

[32] Dinh TTA, Thai MT. AI and blockchain: A disruptive integration. IEEE Computer. 2018;**51**(9):48-53. DOI: 10.1109/MC.2018.3620965

[33] Ramazhamba PT, Venter HS. Using distributed ledger technology for digital forensic investigation purposes on tendering projects. International Journal of Information Technology. 2023;**15**:1255-1274. DOI: 10.1007/s41870-023-01215-9

[34] Ismailisufi A, Popović T, Gligorić N, Radonjic S, Šandi S. A private blockchain implementation using multichain open source platform. In: 2020 24th International Conference on Information Technology (IT), Zabljak, Montenegro. IEEE; 2020. pp. 1-4. DOI: 10.1109/IT48810.2020.9070689

[35] Birim M, Ari HE, Karaarslan E. GoHammer blockchain performance test tool. Journal of Emerging Computer Technologies. 2021;**1**(2):31-33

[36] Ampel B, Patton M, Chen H. Performance modeling of hyperledger sawtooth blockchain. In: 2019 IEEE International Conference on Intelligence and Security Informatics (ISI), Shenzhen, China. IEEE; 2019. pp. 59-61. DOI: 10.1109/ISI.2019.8823238

[37] Martínez Martínez CR. Blockchain Mining Performance Test Results. GitHub Repository. Available from: https://github.com/carlos-rmm/mining

[38] Košt'ál K, Krupa T, Gembec M, Vereš I, Ries M, Kotuliak I. On Transition between PoW and PoS. In: 2018 International Symposium ELMAR; Zadar, Croatia. IEEE Xplore; 2018. pp. 207-210. DOI: 10.23919/ELMAR.2018.8534642

[39] Thakkar P, Nathan S, Viswanathan B. Performance

benchmarking and optimizing hyperledger fabric blockchain platform. In: 2018 IEEE 26th International Symposium on Modeling, Analysis, and Simulation of Computer and Telecommunication Systems (MASCOTS), Milwaukee, WI, USA. IEEE Xplore; 2018. pp. 264-276. DOI: 10.1109/MASCOTS.2018.00034

[40] Kahri F, Bouallegue B, Machhout M, Tourki R. An FPGA implementation of the SHA-3: The BLAKE hash function. In: 10th International Multi-Conferences on Systems, Signals & Devices 2013 (SSD13), Hammamet, Tunisia. IEEE Xplore; 2013. pp. 1-5. DOI: 10.1109/SSD.2013.6564030

[41] Bertoni G, Daemen J, Peeters M, Van Assche G, Van Keer R, Viguier B. Kangaroo twelve: Fast hashing based on keccak-p. In: Applied Cryptography and Network Security: 16th International Conference, ACNS 2018, Leuven, Belgium, July 2-4, 2018, Proceedings. Vol. 16. Springer International Publishing; 2018. pp. 400-418. DOI: 10.1007/978-3-319-93387-0_21

[42] Ünsal E, Örnek HK, Taşdemir Ş. A review of hashing algorithms in cryptocurrency. Proceedings of the International Conference on Frontiers in Academic Research. 2023;**1**:544-550

Chapter 4

Perspective Chapter: Reexamining Coase's Transaction Costs Paradigm in the Context of Blockchain Technology and Smart Contracts

Nasser Arshadi

Abstract

This paper introduces blockchain-based smart contracts and Decentralized Autonomous Organizations (DAOs) as compelling alternatives to conventional corporate structures. Coase's pioneering work in the 1930s posited that the decision to organize transactions within a firm hinges on whether it is more cost-effective than executing them in the open marketplace. However, if these transactions can be conducted more efficiently in the marketplace without the need for a traditional firm, that becomes the preferred approach. The advent of blockchain-based smart contracts, along with the adoption of numerous self-executing smart contracts, has the potential to significantly reduce the dependence on traditional firms. Coase's theorem was contingent on the magnitude of transaction costs, and if smart contracts can substantially diminish these costs, facilitating the emergence of DAOs, the original rationale for forming a firm may no longer apply when considering the blockchain paradigm.

Keywords: Coase, transaction costs, markets vs. firms, blockchain, smart contracts, decentralized autonomous organizations (DAOs), tokenization

1. Introduction

Coase's seminal contributions, spanning from 1937 to 1988 [1–4], posited that the formation of firms, including public corporations, could be attributed to their role in minimizing transaction costs. Coase, along with other scholars, argued that specific transactions might be more efficiently handled within a firm rather than through market mechanisms, primarily due to the presence of substantial transaction costs. Conversely, transactions with lower costs in a market setting tended to gravitate toward market-based interactions.

However, the advent of blockchain technology, smart contracts, and Decentralized Autonomous Organizations (DAOs) challenges the traditional paradigm proposed by Coase. Blockchain technology serves as the enabler of smart contracts, while a collective assembly of such contracts, known as a DAO, can effectively replicate the fundamental characteristics of what Coase defines as a firm, with the primary objective of reducing transaction costs. The intriguing proposition arises when we consider the potential for significantly lowering transaction costs without relying on the conventional firm structure. This has the potential to undermine the longstanding economic rationale for the existence of firms.

This chapter aims to provide a comprehensive analysis of the relationship between blockchain technology and the formation of firms and corporations, with a focus on transaction costs. The methodological framework employed emphasizes a conceptual approach, facilitating a thorough exploration of key concepts and theories.

Section 2 details the methodological approach utilized in structuring the chapter, highlighting the conceptual nature of the discussion. Section 3 delves into the origins of public corporations and elucidates the theoretical foundation underpinning their formation, drawing from Coase's theorem.

Subsequently, Section 4 introduces blockchain technology and its potential impact on the formation of firms and corporations, particularly regarding transaction costs. This section also investigates the evolution of blockchain and its integration with the internet, including discussions on Web 1–3, smart contracts, and DAOs.

Section 5 explores strategies for improving corporate efficiency through the adoption of blockchain, smart contracts, and DAOs, showcasing their diverse applications across various industries.

Finally, Section 6 presents the conclusions drawn from the chapter's findings, summarizing key insights and identifying both limitations and avenues for future research. By critically examining the influence of blockchain technology on organizational structures and transaction costs, this chapter contributes to the ongoing discourse on the evolution of corporate governance and efficiency in the digital era.

2. Methodology

This chapter provides a conceptual analysis of how blockchain technology, smart contracts, and DAOs can impact the decision-making process regarding internal functions within a firm or their outsourcing to the market. While Coase's work and subsequent research have been primarily conceptual, blockchain's theoretical foundations lie in computer science, mathematics, and cryptography. Blockchain draws upon these disciplines, relying on concepts such as distributed systems, data structures, algorithms, cryptography, game theory, and probability theory.

The decentralized nature of blockchain networks requires a deep understanding of computer networking protocols, consensus mechanisms, and peer-to-peer communication. Mathematics plays a crucial role in ensuring the security and integrity of blockchain systems, with cryptographic hash functions and elliptic curve cryptography being key components. Cryptography is fundamental to blockchain security, employing techniques like asymmetric encryption, digital signatures, and hash functions to safeguard transactions and authenticate network participants. However, there are currently insufficient empirical data to directly assess the effectiveness of blockchain, smart contracts, and DAOs in reducing transaction costs and their potential superiority over traditional organizational structures. Hence, this chapter focuses on discussing the conceptual implications of blockchain for reducing transaction costs and shaping decision-making processes within firms.

3. The public corporation

3.1 Origins of the public corporation

The inception of public corporations traces its roots to as far back as 1600 when the British East India Company issued stocks to shareholders, marking a seminal juncture in the evolution of corporate organization [5]. Across the centuries, corporations have assumed a pivotal role in the global economy, particularly during eras characterized by industrialization, globalization, and technological progress.

While the number of publicly traded companies has experienced a significant decline over the past three decades, their economic significance remains undiminished. In the United States, the total number of publicly traded companies reached its zenith at 8090 in 1996 [6]. However, since that peak, there has been a consistent decrease in the count of publicly traded companies. As of 2023, only 3700 publicly traded companies remain in the U.S. market [7].

Several factors have played a pivotal role in the decline in the number of publicly traded companies. These influential factors encompass firms facing delisting due to financial turmoil, a notable shift in the strategy of startups, which now prefer acquisition by established companies over opting for initial public offerings (IPOs), the prevailing trend of larger corporations acquiring their smaller counterparts, and the rising prominence of private equity firms. Private equity firms, in particular, have gained substantial influence by offering significant financial support to privately held enterprises, thereby enabling these companies to continue operating outside the realm of publicly traded markets. This evolution has profoundly altered the dynamics of corporate financing and market participation.

Another change in the landscape of corporations today is the extent to which aspects of production are outsourced. For example, Apple Inc. outsources the manufacturing of its products such as iPhone, iPads, and MacBooks to third-party manufacturers in China and elsewhere in Asia. It retains design, software development, and marketing in-house to tightly control its intellectual property. Similarly, Nike outsources the manufacturing of its athletic shoes and apparel to contract manufacturers in Asia, while retaining design and marketing of its products in-house.

This ongoing transformation in the landscape of public corporations reflects the ever-evolving dynamics of the business world and highlights the adaptability of corporate structures in response to changing economic conditions. While these changes reflect ever-evolving features of the modern corporation, they align with Coase's earlier insights into the economics of firms, where companies make decisions regarding outsourcing and in-house production based on transaction costs. Companies may choose to outsource certain aspects of their production when it is more cost-effective to do so, considering factors like coordination costs, information costs, and enforcement costs.

3.2 The economics of corporate formation

Firms, including public corporations, have evolved with the aim of reducing transaction costs. Coase, along with other scholars, contended that transactions incurring substantial coordination costs tend to be more cost-effective when conducted within a firm, whereas tasks with lower coordination costs can be efficiently managed through market mechanisms. These transaction costs encompass "search and information costs, bargaining and decision costs, and policing and enforcement costs" [8].

Williamson [9, 10] further elaborated on this paradigm by introducing asset specificity, uncertainty, and frequency as key factors influencing the choice between market and firm-based transactions.

Asset specificity refers to the ease of redeploying an asset for alternative purposes. For instance, general-purpose buildings exhibit low specificity, while highly specialized labor is highly specific. Uncertainty arises from external changes or opportunistic behavior. The frequency of transactions also plays a significant role; infrequent transactions are better suited for markets, while frequent ones are more efficiently organized within firms. In cases where assets are highly specific, transactions are frequent, and uncertainty is substantial, firm integration becomes the preferred governance structure. Conversely, when assets have low specificity, uncertainties are minimal, and transactions are infrequent, market governance is the most economical choice.

Transaction costs influence not only how economic activities are organized within firms but also decisions to outsource certain tasks. Outsourcing is driven by economies of scale and the need to mitigate intrafirm incentive conflicts. Outsourcing tasks, such as data processing, payroll management, and manufacturing to external vendors, can provide economies of scale and agility. Additionally, divisions within firms with incentive issues may be outsourced to alleviate conflicts. Ultimately, a firm's boundaries are defined by internalizing transactions when combined production and transaction costs are lower than market procurement costs.

Jensen and Meckling [11] extended this line of thought, introducing agency costs as pivotal in determining a firm's ownership structure. While ownership integration reduces market contracting costs, it engenders incentive conflicts between owners (stockholders and bondholders) and managers. Ownership structures typically encompass proprietorships, partnerships, and corporations. Interestingly, Jensen and Meckling defined firms as a nexus of "contracts" among various parties to the firm, including stockholders, bondholders, and management, with the goal of reducing agency costs (i.e., transaction costs). As we will discuss later in this conversation, DAOs also offer a solution based on smart "contracts" among parties to an enterprise.

Proprietorships involve single ownership and management, minimizing capital requirements, expertise, and uncertainty, with no owner-manager conflicts. Basic partnerships provide greater capital but dissolve when a partner exits. Professional partnerships, such as those in accounting or law, leverage mutual monitoring to mitigate incentive conflicts. Corporations offer solutions to capital and skill-set challenges, providing limited liability to investors.

Corporate types include open corporations with publicly traded stocks, privately held corporations with nontraded securities, mutual corporations, and not-for-profit corporations. Corporate governance addresses management incentive issues through boards of directors, who monitor and make decisions regarding projects, management appointments, and compensation. However, board effectiveness can vary due to potential conflicts of interest [12, 13].

In cases where boards fail to address management incentives, declining stock prices can make a corporation an attractive takeover target, leading to management replacement and increased efficiencies. The labor market also plays a role, as subpar performance may negatively affect managers' future career prospects. Reputational capital built over time can mitigate incentive problems [14].

Information asymmetry problems can be alleviated through signaling mechanisms. Positive news about a project can facilitate debt issuance or increased dividends, signaling confidence and mitigating incentive problems among shareholders [15].

4. Corporation in the realm of blockchain

Blockchain technology originated in 2008 as the foundational infrastructure for the groundbreaking cryptocurrency known as Bitcoin. Subsequent developments led to adaptations of the Bitcoin blockchain to serve various purposes. Notably, in 2014, the Ethereum blockchain emerged with a broader mission, enabling the exchange of assets that extended beyond the realm of cryptocurrencies.

In the following subsections, we will delve into the genesis of blockchain technology and explore its relevance to functions that have traditionally fallen within the purview of corporations.

4.1 Blockchain and the internet

Blockchain is a software system equipped with protocols for executing transactions and securely storing data. Within the blockchain network, transaction data between peers are recorded on member computers, often referred to as nodes. To fully grasp the evolution of blockchain, which operates within the realm of the internet, it's valuable to briefly trace the technological advancements that led to the modern internet.

The inception of the internet can be traced back to the late 1950s when the Advanced Research Projects Agency (ARPA), a division of the U.S. Department of Defense, embarked on a mission to create a decentralized computing system aimed at facilitating communication among multiple computers. This ambitious endeavor culminated in the late 1960s with the establishment of the Advanced Research Project Agency Network (ARPANET), marking a significant milestone in the interconnection of computing nodes.

In 1972, ARPA's name was changed to the Defense Advanced Research Projects Agency (DARPA), broadening its mission to encompass both national security and nondefense objectives. Presently, DARPA focuses on project outsourcing to scientists and engineers in academic institutions and the private sector, maintaining a relatively small in-house staff.

In 1989, a pivotal moment in the history of the internet occurred with the invention of the World Wide Web (WWW) by British scientist Tim Berners-Lee. Originally conceived to streamline automated information-sharing among scientists, Berners-Lee also introduced the world's first web browser, a groundbreaking development that paved the way for the diverse range of browsers we rely on today. These web browsers are sophisticated software applications that empower users to access, retrieve, and view internet-based documents seamlessly. Over time, a host of notable browsers emerged, including Chrome, Explorer, Firefox, Safari, Opera, and Edge, each contributing to the evolution of web browsing.

It's essential to differentiate between the internet and the Web. The Web provides user-friendly access to online data through hyperlinks and websites, while the internet constitutes the underlying network of computers and servers on which the Web operates. The term "internet" was formally adopted in 1983, signifying the interconnection of multiple networks. Although the internet's inception dates back to 1969, it did not reach full maturity until the early 1990s.

In 1990, Tim Berners-Lee and colleagues introduced the Web to the public, marking the inception of Web 1.0. This phase offered a readable protocol where information was posted, and user interactions with websites were limited. Notable applications of Web 1.0 included Amazon in 1994 and eBay in 1995. Web 2.0 emerged in 1999, introducing the writable phase of the Web, enabling users to both read and contribute to websites. This era encouraged user interaction and featured platforms like Facebook and YouTube, where users could post content and engage with others.

Web 3.0 represents the next evolutionary stage, allowing not only reading and writing but also executing commands. For instance, users can now interact with virtual assistants like Alexa, Siri, or ChatGPT, which utilize artificial intelligence (AI) to understand spoken language, search the Web, and provide responses in natural language. Web 3.0 also offers personalized responses based on individual users' previous searches and interests.

Intertwined with artificial intelligence and linked to the semantic Web, Web 3.0 comprehends the entirety of search queries, moving beyond keyword-based searches prevalent in Web 2.0. In contrast to Web 2.0, Web 3.0 tailors user experiences and securely stores data on a decentralized platform. This decentralization is pivotal, as it mitigates the risks associated with centralized intermediaries like Facebook, X, and TikTok where personal data can be compromised if mishandled or hacked. In Web 3.0, blockchain technology plays a central role, granting data ownership to users and ensuring data confidentiality through its public ledger.

4.2 Asymmetric cryptography and hashing

Blockchain technology introduces a peer-to-peer transaction protocol that incorporates validation, timestamping, and the secure archival of records within a decentralized ledger. This revolutionary protocol operates independently of intermediaries, facilitating transactions between parties, even when they lack prior familiarity or trust in one another. This trust-independent system relies on encryption protocols that harness the power of cryptography and hashing to verify asset ownership and establish consensus prior to recording data. These data are permanently etched onto a distributed ledger, commonly known as a blockchain, eliminating the need for centralized intermediary repositories.

The historical origins of cryptography trace back to centuries, initially serving as a means to securely transfer information, often in military contexts. Modern cryptography as we know it began taking shape in 1945, with further developments stemming from government research laboratories and university studies [16–19]. Cryptography encompasses two main categories: symmetric and asymmetric.

In symmetric cryptography, the same key serves both for encryption and decryption. The security of the encrypted message relies on safeguarding this key, as its compromise could lead to unauthorized access and exposure of the message's contents. On the other hand, asymmetric cryptography employs a pair of keys—a public key for encryption and a private key for decryption. A prime example of this is the Pretty Good Privacy (PGP) software, which enables a sender to encrypt a message using the recipient's public key, while the recipient utilizes their private key for decryption. This approach ensures secure and anonymous information exchange, such as whistleblowers securely sharing confidential government information with news outlets.

In asymmetric cryptography, both the sender and receiver generate a key pair using cryptographic software. This pair includes a public key, which is accessible through a shared directory, and a private key, known exclusively to the key's owner.

Hashing is a crucial process that transforms data of varying lengths into a fixed set of alphanumeric characters. It plays a pivotal role in bolstering the security of blockchain transactions. Among the various types of hash functions, cryptographic hash functions stand out due to their deterministic, one-way, pseudorandom, and collision-resistant nature. Deterministic implies that a specific dataset consistently produces the same hash value. One-way signifies that it's impossible to reverse the hash function to retrieve the original data. Pseudorandom indicates that the hash value is unpredictable based solely on the initial data. Collision resistance ensures that even slight alterations in the input data yield significantly different hash values [20].

The integration of asymmetric cryptography and hashing strengthens security within the blockchain domain, facilitating the creation and verification of digital signatures. To further clarify this concept, **Figure 1** demonstrates a secure protocol for transferring messages or assets using cryptographic hash functions. Let us imagine Alice wants to send the message "Transferring Bitcoin" to Bob. Initially, Alice encrypts the message using Bob's public key, which is accessible via a shared directory. Upon receiving the encrypted message, Bob decrypts it with his private key to access its content. However, at this stage, it's impossible to verify if Alice is truly the sender. To address this trust issue, Alice generates a digital signature by computing the hash value of the message and encrypting it with her private key before transmitting it over the network. (Reminder: Encryption with a public key requires decryption with the corresponding private key, and vice versa.) Bob then decrypts the message using Alice's public key to uncover its hash value. He also computes the hash value of the decrypted message he previously received. If these hash values match, it confirms Alice as the sender. Conversely, if the sender is different, the hash values would diverge, indicating otherwise. The combination of hashing and asymmetric cryptography enables a secure information exchange with identity verification. This protocol eliminates the need for prior trust, as identity confirmation is achieved through a digital signature.

4.3 Smart contracts

Smart contracts embody computer protocols that autonomously validate, execute, and enforce transactions based on predefined agreements among parties, all without the need for central intermediaries. When the specified conditions are met, the smart contract seamlessly executes the transaction and fulfills its intended function.

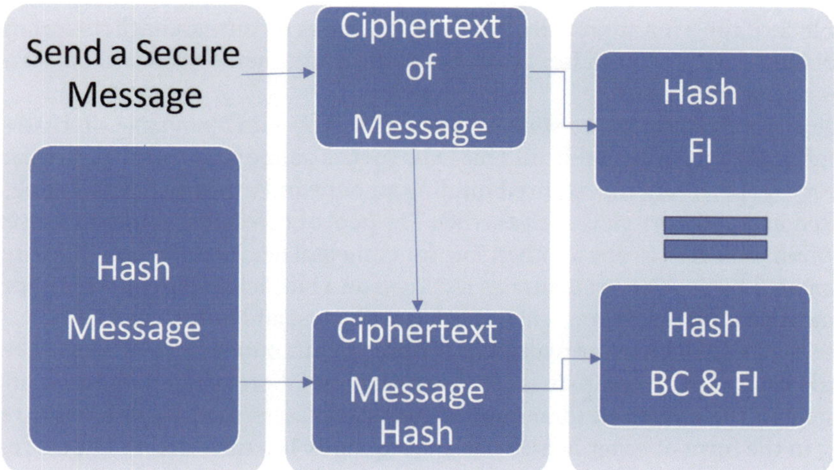

Figure 1.
A secure protocol for transferring messages.

Conversely, if the conditions remain unmet, the smart contract is promptly canceled, and the funds are promptly returned.

The concept of smart contracts, along with the associated terminology, can be traced back to the year 1994, credited to the pioneering work of computer scientist and cryptographer Nick Szabo [21]. A classic real-world analogy that helps understand smart contracts is a vending machine. In this analogy, a preprogrammed code dictates the prices of snacks within the vending machine. When an individual deposits the exact amount of money required, the machine dispenses the selected snack. However, if the deposited funds fall short, the machine promptly returns the money without delivering the snack. On the other hand, if the deposited amount exceeds the snack's price, the machine releases the snack and returns the surplus money.

The advent of the Ethereum blockchain in 2014 ushered in a more advanced era for smart contracts. In this evolution, smart contracts transformed into software agents that operate seamlessly on the blockchain. By residing on the blockchain, smart contracts inherit similar attributes such as enhanced security, rapid execution, and pinpoint accuracy.

Introducing artificial intelligence into the realm of smart contracts opens up new horizons, allowing iterative interpretation of contract intentions. This integration involves processes like reasoning and learning through cognitive computing. Machine learning within AI serves as a feedback loop, enabling the continuous refinement of the operational and implementation layers of smart contracts, elevating them from a simple if-then protocol to a sophisticated what-if rule [22].

Ethereum has been at the forefront of providing infrastructure for smart contracts, with its native currency, ether, emerging as the preferred medium of exchange in most smart contract scenarios. While smart contracts can be deployed within single transactions to enhance efficiency, security, and speed, their most profound impact lies in empowering Decentralized Autonomous Organizations (DAOs), marking a significant leap in the evolution of digital governance and automation.

4.4 Decentralized autonomous organizations (DAOs)

DAOs, or Decentralized Autonomous Organizations, operate by executing smart contracts, wherein all business and administrative rules are encoded and deployed onto a blockchain. This approach effectively mitigates incentive conflicts among stakeholders, with profound implications for the traditional organizational structures of firms and corporations.

To illustrate the concept, consider a DAO that serves as an innovative alternative to a conventional venture capital firm. This DAO invites online investors to participate in projects by specifying the required funding amount and investment timeframe, all conducted in cryptocurrency, such as ether. The pool of investors comprises a diverse group, often unrelated to one another. The fundamental decision-making processes are automated through smart contracts recorded on a blockchain. Investors are granted economic rights, participation rights, governance rights, and utility rights [23].

Once the DAO secures the necessary funding, it announces its readiness to review proposals from startup companies. The investing members evaluate these submissions and cast their votes on their merit. Proposals that garner a majority vote receive funding in the form of ether, which can subsequently be converted to fiat currency through cryptocurrency exchanges. It's noteworthy that investors who find themselves dissatisfied with the venture retain redemption rights, allowing them to sell their tokens back to the DAO.

This pioneering method of financing startups and entrepreneurial endeavors goes beyond the conventional venture capital framework. It democratizes the accessibility of investment prospects, allowing a wider range of individuals to engage in funding decisions and reap rewards from prosperous initiatives. Furthermore, the transparency and unchangeable nature of blockchain technology establish confidence and responsibility within the DAO, diminishing the necessity for intermediaries and cultivating a more streamlined and just investment environment.

4.5 DAOs: mitigating transaction costs and the need for firm formation

As explored in this paper, the formation of a firm historically revolves around minimizing transaction costs associated with various aspects of business operations, such as information acquisition, coordination, and supervision. Transactions that are more cost-effective when executed in the open market tend to stay outside the boundaries of a firm. Conversely, functions whose central management within a firm reduces overall transaction costs are typically incorporated into the organization. However, the emergence of blockchain technology, smart contracts, and DAOs has the potential to challenge the transaction cost advantage of many functions traditionally coordinated within a firm, thereby ushering in a paradigm shift in corporate function coordination.

The DAOs provide notable advantages in corporate governance compared to traditional systems, encompassing heightened transparency, amplified member engagement, and diminished monitoring expenses [23]. A primary advantage of DAOs lies in their innate transparency in decision-making procedures, curbing the possibilities of opportunistic conduct, inaccuracies, and fraudulent activities. Furthermore, DAOs broaden the spectrum of member participation, facilitating direct involvement determined by the extent of invested capital. The digital realm further diminishes the expenses associated with organizing and executing frequent voting sessions. Investment and financial determinations within DAO platforms are contingent on member votes, thus alleviating opportunistic conduct among stakeholders.

The earliest-known DAO, named "The DAO," was established in 2016 with the ambitious goal of raising capital from a broad range of credit investors within a short period and subsequently investing in startup companies—an innovative digital counterpart to a traditional venture capital firm. The DAO successfully amassed the equivalent of $150 million in ether. However, a vulnerability in the code allowed a hacker to access the system and pilfer a substantial sum [24]. To address this issue, the Ethereum Foundation executed an unprecedented hard fork in its architecture, revising the original code and nullifying the hacked transfer. This incident led to a hiatus in the creation of DAOs for over 2 years. Since 2019, several new DAOs have emerged, raising substantial funds and engaging in multiple investments.

Revisiting our earlier examination of publicly traded corporations, we emphasized the existence of incentive conflicts among stockholders, managers, bondholders, and both new and existing shareholders. As elucidated by Jensen and Meckling [11], a firm can be regarded as a nexus of contracts involving stockholders, bondholders, and management. The smart contracts that form the foundation of DAOs epitomize a digital mode of contract execution on a blockchain. These smart contracts adeptly alleviate incentive conflicts among contracting parties within a corporation, particularly those stemming from opportunistic behavior in post-agreement activities. The predefined parameters within the code leave no room for post-agreement renegotiation. For example, members collectively vote on investment and financing determinations, thus alleviating conflicts between management and stockholders. Similarly, members evaluate investment proposals exclusively based on their merit, effectively eliminating conflicts among stockholders and bondholders. Additionally, the smart-contract code eradicates issues of information asymmetry, consequently addressing conflicts between new and existing shareholders.

Examples of DAOs have continued to proliferate, each serving a unique purpose. Governance DAOs are stepping in to replace transactions that were previously handled by venture capital firms by facilitating decentralized decision-making. Non-Fungible Tokens (NFTs) are enabling the acquisition, management, and monetization of digital assets in novel ways. Philanthropic DAOs are emphasizing charitable activities through the collection of funds and their distribution to causes decided upon by the contributors. These examples showcase the versatility and transformative potential of DAOs in various domains of economic and social activity.

5. Advanced strategies for enhancing corporate efficiency using blockchain technology beyond DAOs

Blockchain technology not only offers an intriguing alternative to conventional corporations through the use of smart contracts among diverse stakeholders but also introduces additional pathways to bolster enterprise efficiency, transparency, and scalability. In the subsequent sections, we will delve into several examples of these opportunities that surpass what DAOs can offer, demonstrating how blockchain's reduction of transaction costs challenges the persuasiveness of Coase's theorem regarding firm formation.

5.1 Example 1: stock market trading

Settlement and reconciliation are pivotal functions in the stock market, crucial for instilling investor confidence, minimizing errors, and deterring fraud. In the traditional system, trades occur on established exchanges such as New York Stock Exchange (NYSE) or National Association of Securities Dealers Automated Quotations (NASDAQ), involving negotiations between buyers and sellers regarding share prices and quantities. Following trade execution, brokerage firms, representing the involved parties, confirm trade details, including price and quantity, to their clients. Subsequently, trade information is transmitted to central clearinghouses like the National Securities Clearing Corporation (NSCC), where it undergoes meticulous matching for accuracy. Once matched, the clearinghouse facilitates the transfer of ownership and funds between buyers and sellers through their brokerage accounts. Reconciliation necessitates brokerage firms to compare their records with the clearinghouses to ensure precise recording of trade details, ownership changes, and fund transfers. Custodial banks verify ownership shifts, with the Depository Trust & Clearing Corporation (DTCC) playing a pivotal role in settlement and reconciliation, addressing discrepancies.

Blockchain technology harbors the potential to profoundly reshape the cost landscape in the realm of stock market transaction verification. Transactions documented on a blockchain exhibit transparency and immutability, obviating the necessity for a multitude of intermediaries and protracted reconciliation processes. Moreover, blockchain facilitates rapid trade execution and settlement, vastly surpassing the conventional T + 2 settlement timeframe. The integration of smart contracts into the blockchain automates a significant portion of trading operations, guaranteeing error-free results and data integrity, consequently diminishing the demand for extensive verification protocols.

To address the "last mile problem," which relates to the final stages of a process, such as the actual execution of a trade, blockchain's smart contracts can be deployed to automate trading functions with remarkable precision and security. This approach caters to individual traders, institutional traders, and corporations as clients, ushering in technological advancements through blockchain adoption, thereby enhancing and partially supplanting the existing value chain.

This comprehensive approach harnesses blockchain's capabilities to enhance efficiency, trim costs, and heighten security in stock market transactions, ultimately benefiting traders, investors, and all participants in the market. The reduction in transaction costs brought about by blockchain technology challenges the persuasive power of Coase's theorem regarding firm formation.

5.2 Example 2: coinbase

Coinbase operates as a cryptocurrency exchange offering a comprehensive range of services, with a particular focus on addressing the challenges associated with the "last mile problem" in the realm of cryptocurrency transactions. Coinbase boasts a diverse set of functions, including:

1. Brokerage Services: Serving as a broker, Coinbase facilitates the buying and selling of various cryptocurrencies, enabling traders to place orders and convert fiat currencies into the required cryptocurrencies during trade execution.

2. Exchange Operations: Coinbase functions as an exchange, executing transactions between buyers and sellers, thereby fostering liquidity and ensuring efficient transactions among participants.

3. Settlement and Clearing Services: Beyond trade execution, Coinbase handles settlement and clearing processes. This involves finalizing transactions, verifying trade accuracy, and resolving any discrepancies that may arise.

Through the integration of blockchain technology and smart contracts, Coinbase pioneers innovative solutions to confront these challenges:

1. Tokenization of Fiat Currencies: Coinbase leverages blockchain and smart contracts to tokenize traditional fiat currencies. This transformative process represents conventional money as digital tokens on the blockchain, enhancing the efficiency and security of cross-party transactions.

2. Secure Exchanges: Capitalizing on blockchain's inherent security features and the self-executing logic of smart contracts, Coinbase ensures highly secure and tamper-resistant exchanges between parties.

3. Cost-Effective Transactions: Coinbase's integration of blockchain technology streamlines processes, potentially reducing the dependence on intermediaries and associated costs within the transaction flow.

4. Elimination of Intermediaries: By consolidating roles traditionally held by various intermediaries, such as brokers, exchanges, and custodial banks, Coinbase simplifies the transaction process within its platform.

This strategic approach harnesses the capabilities of blockchain to enhance efficiency, trim costs, and optimize the transaction experience for users. The reduction in transaction costs facilitated by blockchain technology challenges the convincing power of Coase's theorem concerning the formation of firms.

5.3 Example 3: harmony music

Harmony Music, a fictional firm, offers a mobile app enabling customers to search for songs, create and share playlists, and provides two subscription models: one with advertising and a premium option without advertisements. If Harmony considers introducing a digital token named "Harmony coin" using blockchain technology, let us explore the potential advantages, including reduced transaction costs, expanded monetized product lines, token utilization, rewarded activities, redemption mechanisms, and the inherent risks associated with this initiative.

5.3.1 Benefits of harmony music

1. Enhanced User Engagement: By incentivizing users to interact with music content, discover new artists, and engage in music-related events, Harmony Music can stimulate increased user activity and interaction, thereby elevating overall engagement on the platform.

2. Community Growth and Referrals: Rewarding users for referring friends and family to join the platform can foster community growth, potentially expanding the user base through word-of-mouth marketing.

3. Monetization of Engagement: Harmony Music can monetize user engagement, transforming active users into valuable contributors to the platform's ecosystem.

5.3.2 Utilization of harmony coin on the platform

1. Service Acquisition: Users could employ Harmony coin to access premium features, exclusive content, ad-free experiences, and other premium services, enhancing the value proposition of paid subscriptions.

2. Event Participation: The coin could enable users to participate in music events, concerts, and virtual meetups, bridging the gap between digital and real-world music experiences.

3. Artist Engagement: Harmony coin might facilitate direct interactions between users and artists, allowing users to support their favorite artists and access personalized content.

4. Cryptocurrency Exchange Listing: Listing Harmony coin on cryptocurrency exchanges would provide users with the opportunity to trade and sell the tokens, potentially attracting cryptocurrency enthusiasts.

5.3.3 Rewarded activities and redemption: To incentivize desired behaviors, harmony music could reward the following activities

1. Listening Diversity: Users could earn tokens by exploring a diverse range of artists and genres, promoting musical discovery.

2. Playlist Creation and Sharing: Incentivizing the creation and sharing of playlists could contribute to user-generated content and engagement.

3. Referrals: Users who successfully refer new members to the platform could earn tokens, promoting user growth.

4. Event Participation: Active participation in virtual or physical music events could be rewarded, encouraging user involvement.

Tokens earned through these activities could be redeemed for premium subscriptions, event tickets, exclusive content, merchandise, or even converted to other cryptocurrencies through crypto exchanges.

5.3.4 Risks

1. Security Concerns: Tokenization introduces cybersecurity risks, including hacking, data breaches, and fraud. Implementing robust security measures and conducting regular audits are essential to mitigate these risks.

2. Regulatory Compliance: The legal and regulatory status of the token could pose challenges. Ensuring compliance with relevant financial and data protection regulations is crucial.

3. User Experience: Poorly executed token implementation could lead to a complicated user experience. The platform must ensure that using and redeeming tokens remains intuitive.

4. Market Volatility: If Harmony coin is traded on cryptocurrency exchanges, its value could be subject to market volatility, potentially impacting user perceptions and engagement.

The introduction of Harmony coin as a digital token holds the potential to enhance user engagement, promote community growth, and create new revenue streams for Harmony Music. Notably, the reduction in transaction costs facilitated by blockchain technology challenges the convincing power of Coase's theorem regarding firm formation. Careful consideration of security, regulatory compliance, and user experience is vital to fully realize the benefits of this tokenization initiative.

5.4 Example 4: social media and content platforms

Platforms like Steemit leverage blockchain technology to incentivize content creation and sharing. Users are rewarded based on the engagement their content generates, fostering a community-driven approach to content creation and distribution. By directly rewarding users for their contributions, these platforms democratize content creation and incentivize quality content production.

5.5 Example 5: nonprofits and collectives

The DAOs are utilized for nonprofit causes and collective initiatives, where organizations are governed by smart contracts and tokens. For instance, DAOstack provides a platform for creating DAOs dedicated to charitable and community development projects. Participants can transparently govern these initiatives and allocate resources based on community preferences, reducing overhead costs and improving accountability.

5.6 Example 6: large manufacturing and retail businesses

Companies like Boeing and Walmart are exploring blockchain and DAOs to enhance efficiency, reduce transaction costs, and outsource functions previously conducted within firms. Boeing may utilize blockchain to improve supply chain transparency and traceability, ensuring the authenticity of parts and compliance with regulations. Meanwhile, Walmart has partnered with IBM to track food supply chains, authenticate products, and automate payments to suppliers using smart contracts. By leveraging blockchain technology, both companies streamline operations, reduce costs, and deliver value to customers while mitigating transaction costs through the automation and transparency afforded by blockchain and smart contracts.

6. Conclusions

The conventional concept of a firm, traditionally seen as a means to reduce transaction costs and establish contractual relationships among stockholders, bondholders, and management, encounters a significant challenge with the emergence of smart contracts central to Decentralized Autonomous Organizations (DAOs). In traditional corporations, conflicts of interest among contracting parties often arise from opportunistic behavior in post-transaction activities. However, DAOs, governed by immutable code, proactively prevent such behavior by stipulating agreements in advance, thus eliminating opportunities for *post hoc* alterations. This proactive approach effectively resolves conflicts between stockholders and managers, stockholders and bondholders, as well as between new and old shareholders.

The adoption of blockchain technology, smart contracts, and DAOs has the potential to question Coase's argument for organizing transactions within a firm based on the reduction of transaction costs. The rise of DAOs, supported by the precision of smart contracts, represents a significant evolution in corporate governance and coordination. This transformation carries substantial implications for the conventional model of firms, as blockchain's capacity to reduce transaction costs fundamentally challenges the essence of the Coasean firm.

Despite demonstrating potential to revolutionize traditional organizational structures and reduce transaction costs, DAOs face significant challenges. While offering alternatives in organizing functions within a firm, there are limitations to their implementation. Blockchain's inherent transaction costs, coupled with complexities in its technology and protocols, present obstacles to widespread adoption. Additionally, scalability, interoperability, and regulatory compliance issues pose further challenges for blockchain and DAO implementation.

When compared to legacy systems, blockchain and DAOs provide immutable records and trustless transactions, yet they may lack the efficiency and flexibility of centralized counterparts. Established frameworks for legal compliance and dispute resolution in legacy systems also present hurdles for DAOs to overcome.

Looking ahead, future research endeavors should concentrate on addressing these limitations and enhancing the functionality of blockchain and DAOs. Areas of exploration include scalability improvements, interoperability enhancements, governance model development, and synergies with emerging technologies like AI, Internet of Things (IoT), and Decentralized Finance (DeFi).

In conclusion, while blockchain and DAOs hold promise for disrupting various industries, including venture capital, realizing their full potential necessitates concerted efforts to address challenges and innovate solutions. Only through continuous refinement and adaptation can the vision of a decentralized future be realized. Regulatory unknowns, among other factors, also play a role in shaping the future trajectory of blockchain and DAO adoption.

Author details

Nasser Arshadi
Department of Finance and Legal Studies, University of Missouri, St. Louis, MO, USA

*Address all correspondence to: arshadi@umsl.edu

References

[1] Coase R. The nature of the firm. Econometrica. 1937;**16**:386-405

[2] Coase R. The problem of social cost. The Journal of Law and Economics. 1960;**3**:1-44

[3] Coase R. The new institutional economics. Journal of Institutional and Theoretical Economics. 1984;**140**:229-231

[4] Coase R. The Firm, the Market, and the Law. Chicago (IL): The University of Chicago Press; 1998

[5] Micklethwair J, Wooldridge A. The Company. New York (NY): Modern Library Chronicles; 2005

[6] World Bank. Number of publicly traded U.S. stocks; c1975-2019. Available from: https://data.worldbank.org/indicator/CM.MKT.LDOM.NO?locations=US [Accessed: March 15, 2023]

[7] CNN Business, America has lost half of its public companies since the 1990s. Available from: https://edition.cnn.com/2023/06/09/investing/premarket-stocks-trading/index.html

[8] Dahlman C. The problem of externality. The Journal of Law and Economics. 1979;**22**(1):141-162

[9] Williamson O. Markets and Hierarchies: Analysis and Antitrust Implications. Glencoe, IL: Free Press; 1975

[10] Williamson O. The Economic Institutions of Capitalism. Glencoe, IL: Free Press; 1985

[11] Jensen M, Meckling W. Theory of the firm: Managerial behavior, agency costs, and ownership structure. Journal of Financial Economics. 1976;**3**(4):305-360

[12] Fama E, Jensen M. Separation of ownership and control. The Journal of Law and Economics. 1983a;**26**(2):301-325

[13] Fama E, Jensen M. Agency problems and residual claims. The Journal of Law and Economics. 1983b;**26**(2):327-349

[14] Arshadi N. Blockchain, corporate structure, and financial intermediation. Technology and Innovation. 2023;**23**:1-22

[15] Ross S. The determination of financial structure: The incentive signaling approach. Bell Journal of Economics. 1977;**8**(1):23-40

[16] Shannon CE. A mathematical theory of communication. Bell System Technical Journal. 1948;**27**:379-423

[17] Diffie W, Hellman M. New directions in cryptography. IEEE Transactions on Information Theory. 1976;**22**(6):644-654

[18] Merkle R. A Certified digital signature. In: The Proceedings of the Advances in Cryptology — CRYPTO '89 Conference. New York: Springer-Verlag; 1989. pp. 218-238

[19] Damgard I. A design principle for hash functions. In: Advances in Cryptology – CRYPTO'89 Proceeding. New York: Springer-Verlag; 1989. pp. 416-427

[20] Drescher D. Blockchain Basics. Frankfurt am Main, Germany: Apress; 2017

[21] Szabo N. Smart contracts. Extropy #. 1996;**16**. Available from:

https://www.fon.hum.uva.nl/rob/Courses/InformationInSpeech/CDROM/Literature/LOTwinterschool2006/szabo.best.vwh.net/smart_contracts_2.htm [Accessed: January 24, 2022]

[22] Wang S, Ouyang L, Yuan Y. Blockchain-enabled smart contracts: Architecture, applications, and future trends. IEEE Transactions on Systems. 2019;**49**(11):2266-2277

[23] Wright A. The rise of decentralized autonomous organizations: Opportunities and challenges. Stranford Journal of Blockchain Law & Policy. 2021;**4**(2). Available from: https://stanford-jblp.pubpub.org/pub/rise-of-daos/release/1 [Accessed: January 24, 2022]

[24] Lacity M. Blockchain Foundations for the Internet of Value. Fayetteville (AR): The University of Arkansas Press; 2020

Chapter 5

Perspective Chapter: Stable Coins Backed by Real-World Assets – The Best of both Worlds

Paul Meeusen and Yulin Liu

Abstract

Stable coins can bring stability in volatile crypto markets and during uncertain times. To examine their well-functioning, we assess the degree to which they fulfill the three main functions of a currency: means of payment, unit of account, and store of value. The true benefits of digital money will only materialize when living up to the key principles of peer-to-peer, trustless, and cryptographically secured electronic cash, as proposed in the original bitcoin whitepaper. We conclude that tokenized real-world assets, such as gold, can form an attractive reserve for stable coins. By combining the convenience, portability, and security enabled by blockchain technology with the proven reserve value of gold, it brings the best of both worlds.

Keywords: stable coins, tokenization, real-world assets, financial stability, decentralized finance

1. Introduction

Over the past decade, the benefits of decentralized systems, the innovation of smart contracts, and blockchain technology have become obvious across different industries and user segments. However, recent volatility and turbulence in crypto markets have instilled fear and uncertainty. The sharp value depletion of cryptocurrencies over the past 2 years has further diminished confidence, as almost all top 30 cryptocurrencies have lost between 60 and 95% of their value. It coincided with fraudulent actions by prominent "trusted parties", who turned out to be bad actors. Rather than being isolated events, bad conduct has manifested itself across the industry, including exchanges, market makers, decentralized finance platforms, intermediaries, and even protocols.

Faced with such turbulence, anything or anyone bringing stability seems like a god's gift. Does this lead us to "stable coins"[1]?

Stable coins are digital currencies that combine the innovation of blockchain technology with the stability, guarantee, and simplicity of traditional currencies. They are

[1] Although often written as one word, we adhere to a strict grammatical use of two separate words: stable coins.

a subset of crypto assets, which, under MiCA[2] regulation, are defined as "a digital representation of value or rights which may be transferred and stored electronically, using distributed ledger technology or similar technology". Stable coins minimize volatility by being pegged to a stable asset or a group of assets, often reserve-backed currencies like the US dollar or other commodities such as gold. Under the same MiCA regulation, they are "E-money tokens" whose main purpose is to be used as a means of exchange and that purports to maintain a stable value by being denominated in (units of) a fiat currency. The term "fiat" is a Latin word meaning "it shall be". Thus, fiat currencies have no utility, nor value other than the one that a government maintains.

As the term suggests, stable coins are stable, meaning that they are worth exactly as much as the real-world commodity or currency to which they are pegged, which reduces volatility. The most known examples are USDT and USDC, which are pegged to the US Dollar. Like the traditional banking system, where electronic money circulates and is backed by real deposits on bank accounts, stable coins need institutions who guarantee and transparently report the proof of reserves that back up the digital money that is issued on-chain. Tether and Circle play that role for USDT and USDC, respectively. For every "real" dollar deposited with them, they will issue (or "mint") a digital twin version minus a fee. Converting the digital twin back into a "real" dollar triggers the reverse process.

The market appreciates the features of stable coins, the "24/7" accessibility, efficiency to scale, lower transaction cost, and programmability of running on the blockchain, combined with the stability and trust that comes with a regular currency. They provide the cash leg for crypto traders as evidenced by the fact that the largest trading pairs of leading cryptocurrencies are with stable coins.

However, is this value proposition really living up to the vision of providing peer-to-peer digital money transfer without dependency on a central trusted party? To examine this, we consider the key functions of a currency: means of payment, unit of account, and store of value.

2. Methodology

The chapter employs an analytical and evaluative methodology to examine the functions and potential of stable coins backed by real-world assets. The absence of primary qualitative research methods such as interviews, observations, or case studies—typically associated with qualitative research—is noted. Instead, the authors engage in a multi-faceted analysis utilizing theoretical and conceptual evaluations. This approach encompasses:

Comparative analysis: Various stable coin types are contrasted to evaluate their risks and their adherence to the functions of currency, thereby assessing their stability and efficacy.

Risk assessment: Idiosyncratic and systematic risks associated with different stable coin models are assessed, drawing on financial data and historical events.

Market analysis: Market dynamics, including adoption rates and performance metrics of stable coins, are compared to those of traditional currencies.

---

[2] Markets in Crypto-Assets Regulation (MiCA), published by European Securities and Markets Authority (see Ref. [1]).

Regulatory analysis: The chapter engages with the regulatory landscape impacting stable coins, with specific attention given to regulations such as the Markets in Crypto-Assets Regulation (MiCA).

Economic analysis: The chapter presents an economic perspective, appraising stable coins concerning inflation, purchasing power, and their role within the broader monetary system.

Conceptual discussion: The proposition of stable coins backed by real-world assets, such as gold, is advanced, with a discourse on the prospective advantages of this approach.

The study conducts a macroeconomic analysis of stable coins, applying established economic theory to dissect their role concerning the tripartite functions of currency: as a medium of exchange, a unit of account, and a store of value. It identifies and explicates the discrepancies between contemporary stable coins and the decentralized, trustless, and cryptographically secure vision of digital cash initially outlined in Satoshi Nakamoto's Bitcoin whitepaper [2]. The research forwards a conceptual framework for the evolution of stable coins backed by real-world assets. It details a systematic procedure encompassing tokenization, fractionalization, fungibility, collateralization, and decentralization, culminating in the creation of a stable coin underpinned by real-world assets, with gold serving as a paradigmatic example.

3. Means of payment

This is arguably the strongest feature of stable coins. Most business transactions or asset transfers require a cash settlement in a generally accepted or "fiat" currency. Fiscal and accounting policies require or prefer that business transactions and assets are settled and valued in regular currencies. Most goods and services in the global economy are still being paid for with fiat currency. Bitcoin is increasingly accepted as a means of payment or legal tender, by regulators, tax authorities, merchants, and businesses. However, most parties tend to mainly hold their cash and cash equivalents in regular "fiat" currencies. Since a stable coin is like a mirror image or proxy of such regular currency, for example USD or EUR, it is much easier to use in regular commercial transactions or employee remuneration, and to process in accounting and financial reporting.

Since stable coin payments run on the blockchain, they have multiple advantages compared to the normal banking system. Transactions are not limited to banking hours and can be executed 24/7, in a quite rapid and cost-efficient manner. They are also programmable by linking them to smart contracts that can be transparently monitored on-chain. The recipient can always redeem the stable coin to its fiat equivalent, guaranteed by a proof of the reserves of the issuing institution, such as Tether for USDT and Circle for USDC. Since their introduction, there have been no significant shortfalls in reserves of these currencies. With a few short-lived exceptions, their market value has been equal to 1 USD. Admittedly, the governance and regulation of such institutions can significantly differ, for example in the way they are regulated or the extent to which they transparently publish audited proof of reserves[3].

However, stable coins are far from a perfect means of payment. To fully deliver on the promise of efficient, truly peer-to-peer digital money, much can be improved to

[3] Transparency reports published by Tether [3] and Circle [4].

further reduce cost, latency, and complexity. Sending money globally is not yet as straightforward and cost-effective as sending secure email or short messages. It highly depends on the medium of exchange used for the transfer, as well as on the blockchain network that the stable coin lives on. To make progress in "banking the unbanked", the security and convenience is insufficient. It clearly manifests itself in today's retail payment world and the deficiency will become even more apparent as the future of payments evolves. Beyond micropayments of workers sending small amounts to family overseas or donations to charity programs or victims of war, the world will move to streaming payments, where online consumption of audio, video, and games will require "on-the-go" micropayments, by the minute or even second for usage, tipping, or rewards. The high fees (including "gas fee") and high latency (in part caused by network congestion) of current stable coin transactions limit the ability to handle such processes, further burdened by additional fees depending on the exchange or platform used. Bitcoin shares similar constraints. Workarounds (such as Bitcoin Lightning) have been introduced but still do not offer the convenience to become mainstream. They are a good current fix but are clearly not built for the future.

A final consideration is foreign exchange (fx). The current offering of stable coins is almost exclusively in USD, without a strong multi-currency offering. This is essential for the young generation of internet native users. They have learned to avoid the high fx fees imposed by financial institutions, especially in Europe, and fled to alternative providers such as Revolut and Wise. Unlike regular banking or credit card providers, they provide users with fair fx rates closer to the mid-market spot rate. For wholesale transactions, the introduction of the SEPA regime has made payments frictionless within the EURO banking zone, meaning quasi free and instantaneous.

These improvements in cross-border payments have largely solved the international money problem for both retail and commercial users. Hence, for non-crypto specialists, there is an insufficient incentive to leave the traditional banking world in favor of stable coins. Launching EURO denominated stable coins has so far seen minimal adoption. As of November 2023, more than 1 year after its introduction, Circle's EURO Coin (EURC) represented only 0,2% of USDC: EURC had 51.5 million reserves, compared to USDC 24.2 billion. European regulation, such as MiCA, might present some compliance hurdles, but it cannot be the only reason for this large gap. Unlike the stable coin world, in the real economy, the USD is the most used currency for international trade, but it does not have a 99% dominance. To date, stable coins have not yet offered an attractive alternative in the non-USD economy.

In commercial banking, stable coins have yet to enter most operational treasury systems. While many vendors offer the option to pay in a fiat or stable coin—mostly limited to USD—banking, treasury, and accounting systems are seldom equipped to properly handle stable coin payment rails. Reconciling stable coin banking transactions with accounting books and records remains largely patchwork.

4. Unit of account

This function of a currency is obvious but easily overlooked. Every expression of monetary value needs a unit: prices of a product, value of an asset, or financial strength of a company. People make consumption, business, or investment decisions, by applying comparative, profit, or return calculations. This obviously requires a unit of account. Historically, the currency world has been much more diverse. Going back in history, we will find that local cities, regions, provinces all had their own currency.

Even in a small country like Switzerland, with its robust Swiss franc, not so long-ago, municipalities or cantons had their own currency. In the last 30 years, Europe's currency landscape has been much simplified with the introduction of the EURO. Consumers and businesses now enjoy this simplicity as they travel and do business around Europe. It is unlikely that they want to revert to more diverse currencies. The promise of peer-to-peer bitcoin payments is attractive but the notion of having to pay a restaurant bill with 0.002 BTC is quite impractical. Some systems are even unable to handle more than 2 decimal places behind the comma. We will neither see companies publish their financial statements nor citizens report their tax return in bitcoin, ethereum, or a stable coin of other denomination than their domestic currency. Certain authorities, such as the small canton of Zug in Switzerland, allow citizens to pay taxes in bitcoin. However, since the authorities do not want to hold any crypto exposure, the Swiss Franc tax liability is simply settled in bitcoin at the prevailing spot market price.

Hence, this explains an advantage of stable coins. They are expressed in an underlying currency that people recognize and find easy to report, so that it conveniently co-exists with regular fiat currencies. Expressed in the accountant's terminology: people and especially businesses see a strong relationship between the currency they do business in ("functional currency") and the one they use to publish their financial statements ("reporting currency").

All combined, the adoption of stable coins has therefore strongly benefited from the simplicity to account for it in a unit that is commonly used. However, adoption could grow much further, if more stable coins would be available in addition to the USD.

Countries where the local currency devalues so rapidly and prices inflate exponentially have a different challenge. Their citizens have lost trust in their domestic currency and rather prefer an alternative currency. That, however, is primarily motivated by a desire to store and safeguard value, which brings us to the final function of a currency.

5. Store of value

Keeping the value of financial assets intact requires a way to store them securely and to preserve their real economic value, relative to the chosen market benchmark and protected against inflation and fluctuation of economic cycles. Since the 1970s, currency rates have been permitted to "float" in the global foreign exchange markets relative to other fiat currencies. Trust in scarcity of an asset backing up the currency was replaced by trust in the economic stewardship of national monetary authorities. Hence, let us examine how stable coins can become stable stores of value.

Stability is a challenge for most stable coins, which are USD pegged, as they represent both idiosyncratic as well as systematic risks.

The fiat-backed stable coin is, in essence, an IOU ("I owe you"), where users transfer fiat currency to a centralized institution and receive stable coins as digital receipts. These stable coins represent claims on the corresponding fiat deposits held by the institution, effectively tokenizing the fiat currency.

A primary risk associated with fiat-backed stable coins is counterparty risk, as the issuance of stable coins is controlled by a centralized institution. There is a possibility that the issuer may print excessive stable coins or abscond with the underlying bank deposit. Additionally, third-party risk arises from the potential default of banks or the freezing/confiscation of funds by governmental authorities. An illustration of this is when USDC was detached from its peg to USD due to the imminent risk of banking default at Silicon Valley Bank in March of 2023, a custodian bank used by Circle. Following that event, USDC saw a significant decrease in volume, down 62% from Q1 to Q3 2023[4].

To maintain the functionality and reliability of fiat-backed stable coins, users must place trust in both the issuer and the custodian banking institution. To address these risks and improve transparency, various fees are incurred, ultimately borne by users. These fees cover expenses such as auditors, custodian banks, financial firms, regulators, and legal services.

Alternatively, users have the option to collateralize their crypto assets in a smart contract (i.e., an autonomous bank on the blockchain). Through this method, stable coins (i.e., crypto fiat loans) are generated automatically against the collateralized assets. Given the volatile nature of crypto collateral, stable coins are over-collateralized to mitigate potential price swings. This decentralized approach reduces reliance on traditional banks, simplifies administrative processes, and eliminates the need for middleman fees. Users can easily create stable coins at any time simply by utilizing their idle crypto assets. Unlike fiat-backed stable coins, crypto-backed stable coins offer decentralization, transparency, and traceability. Users' collateral remains locked within the smart contract, and the issuance and verification of stable coins can be publicly tracked. Furthermore, the liquidation of crypto-backed stable coins is instantaneous, allowing users to withdraw their crypto assets within seconds by returning the stable coins to the smart contract. However, inherent risks exist, such as the stability of the underlying crypto collateral. If its value plummets rapidly, the stable coin may become under-collateralized and liquidated. Additionally, a cascade effect can occur when a collateral price drop leads to under-collateralization of certain stable coin loans. The smart contract automatically triggers collateral liquidation to repurchase the stable coins, causing a fire sale that further drives down the collateral's price. This situation can trigger a chain reaction of non-performing loans and result in a crash of the underlying collateral. To mitigate these risks, it is advisable to diversify the crypto collateral by adopting multiple assets. It is important to note that the system is also vulnerable to hacks, if the code governing the locked crypto assets is not well-written, leading to the near impossibility of collateral recourse.

Algorithmic stable coins, though still in the early stages of development, also face numerous challenges. One notable example is Basecoin, which employs bond sales to contract the money supply. Stable coin holders can exchange their stable coins for bonds, entitling them to receive future stable coins as the monetary expansion progresses. The bond buyers effectively sell their stable coins to the system, gaining more stable coins over time. During periods of money contraction or black swan events, users may lose confidence in the stable coin. This can trigger a death spiral in which the bond prices rapidly decline due to increased risk perception. Consequently, the system needs to issue more bonds to purchase stable coins, further reducing bond prices. This death spiraling effect can eventually render the bonds worthless, destabilizing the stable coin. The stability mechanism employed by algorithmic stable coins is vulnerable and cannot withstand prolonged periods of reduced demand for the stable coin. Additionally, a rumor-triggered drop in bond prices can lead to fragility in market sentiment and, subsequently, stability. Nevertheless, algorithmic stable coins represent an ambitious design that paves the way for future stable coin

4 See 2023 Development of USDC market capitalization [5].

innovations. Notably, they differ from fiat-backed and crypto-backed stable coins as they do not rely on collateral. Instead, these coins create a new crypto asset—bonds—to maintain price stability. By shifting volatility to the bond tokens, the system attempts to uphold stability of its stable coin. However, the lack of endorsement for these bonds poses a significant concern, akin to building a stable coin on an unbacked asset—resembling a foundation built on sand.

Despite the idiosyncratic risks associated with each type of stable coin, it is essential to consider a systematic risk that is often overlooked: the fiat currency, especially the USD, to which most stable coins are pegged. This risk stems from the continuous loss of purchasing power, as major central banks target a 2% annual inflation rate. For example, over the past 30 years, the USD has experienced a steady erosion of purchasing power. Inflation has consumed more than 50% of the value of USD[5].

The USD is supported by the US National Debt, which has been growing at a substantial and concerning rate. Pegging a stable coin to the inherently unstable nature of government-issued IOUs is deemed impractical and untenable.

Also relative to GDP (Gross domestic product), the US budget deficit has been steadily increasing over the last 20 years. In that time frame, sharp deficit increases have strongly correlated to recessions, for example, by the dot com bubble (2000) and financial crisis (2008). Even when considering the pandemic impact as an exceptional one-off event, the evolution of the last 24 months is not encouraging for the USD as a store of value[6].

This is further worsened by concerns from recent developments in the US economy and its state of over indebtedness. The housing market is substantially down as homeowners do not want to roll over their mortgages into new rates as high as 8%. Banks have piled up assets with low interest rates, while the Fed has increased rates 22-fold in a year's time. The weakest US banks went into bankruptcy in April of 2023, but a slow bleeding is still going on among many others. Credit default swaps have been steadily increasing. As of June 2023, subprime debt made up 21% of the $1.58 trillion in outstanding auto loans, the second-largest kind of consumer debt after mortgages and 77% higher than its 2013 level, according to the Federal Reserve Bank of New York[7].

US companies' earnings are also going down as they lose pricing power, combined with consumers losing purchasing power.

In the event of a hypothetical scenario where the United States defaults on its debt and experiences a significant depreciation in the value of the USD, like the occurrences witnessed with the Argentine Peso and the Turkish Lira, concerns arise regarding the potential impact on individuals who hold cryptocurrencies and choose to store their assets in USD-pegged stable coins. It prompts a critical examination of whether these individuals have effectively assessed and prepared for the associated systemic risk in such scenario. Also, in the current environment, when holding USD cash reserves, the available high yield on USD placements in the normal money

---

[5] See Consumer Price Index for All Urban Consumers: Development of Purchasing Power of the Consumer Dollar in U.S. City average [6].

[6] See the Evolution of U.S. Federal Budget Deficit/Surplus [7].

[7] See Federal Reserve Bank of New York, Center for Microeconomic Data, Household Debt and Credit Report [8].

Stable coin categories	Idiosyncratic risks	Systematic risk
Fiat-backed	Centralization of bank deposit	(Hyper)inflation of fiat currencies
Crypto-backed	Liquidation risk[a]	(Hyper)inflation of fiat currencies
Algorithmic	Lack of collateral	(Hyper)inflation of fiat currencies

[a]*The liquidation risk is due to the volatile price of the crypto assets.*

Table 1.
Categories of fiat-pegged stable coins and their risks.

market appears more attractive than relying on decentralized finance (DeFi) platforms with yield or reward.

Table 1 adeptly encapsulates the principal idiosyncratic and systematic risks that are encountered by the three distinct classifications of stable coins. This table delineates the potential vulnerabilities and uncertainties inherent in these stable coin variants, thereby providing valuable insight for risk assessment and management purposes.

All combined, this places substantial doubt on USD denominated stable coins to provide a sustainable store of value. It was recently evidenced by several US credit ratings being lowered[8].

6. A better alternative: Real-world assets

Scarcity drives value preservation over time, which can be embedded in real-world assets. Examples are precious metals, like gold, which are limited in supply, unlike fiat money which governments keep printing. This may, for example, explain the recent interest in gold-backed stable coins. Gold is a precious metal considered as a trusted store of value. It has always been deeply connected with humanity and desired as it is timeless, corrosion-resistant, and highly malleable. Historically, it has been associated with wealth and prestige. Its price volatility is low and uncorrelated to traditional market trends, which is particularly appreciated during times of uncertainty. Its value has grown throughout the years with its purchasing power becoming stronger as compared to the USD. There are different ways to buy and possess gold. However, traditional options have disadvantages and constraints, such as lack of transferability, that can be addressed by the symbiosis with novel blockchain technologies.

Gold as a stable coin reserve combines all the convenience and ease of digital use of stable coins with a store of value that is backed by a scarce real-world asset, rather than a promise to pay from governments and their central banks. This is particularly appreciated during times of uncertainty.

From an investor's perspective, a clear disadvantage of gold is that it is a non-productive asset. Unlike, for example, a piece of land that produces crops, gold is mainly held in storage, except when used for jewelry and by artisans. When, however, gold can be used as a reserve to back up a stable coin with all the same functionality of digital money, as we know it today, it offers unique possibilities and potentially brings the "best of both worlds".

To enable the creation of a gold stable coin, some essential challenges must be overcome: *tokenization, fractionalization, fungibility, collateralization,* and *decentralization*. This needs to be done in a sequential and carefully orchestrated way. It should

[8] See Fitch and S&P US rating downgrades in 2023 [9] and [10].

also be governed by a decentralized autonomous governance system, as both control and profit—if any—of this monetary circuit should belong to a community that owns the currency, much in the "peer-to-peer" spirit of the original bitcoin whitepaper.

Tokenization – Minting a token produces a digital certificate of ownership of gold. The certificate points to a unique underlying gold bar, including various informational attributes valuable to the owner, such as provenance, purity, and storage custodian. These data might be quite rich, including high resolution images, and therefore require blockchain protocols with powerful and efficient data storage capability. The token is non-fungible, as every gold bar is unique with an individual serial number. Owners can effectively redeem the physical asset, which prevents the custodian from misusing or embezzling the gold bars. However, being non-fungible implies being non-fractional. To function as a payment vehicle, it would need to be fractionalized.

Fractionalization and *fungibility* – Gold assets, in above non-fungible token (NFT) form, can be swapped for a gold-backed stable coin, by using a fixed weight to token rate, for example, 1 gram of gold to mint 100 "gold tokens". The minting process is administered and guaranteed by a smart contract. This generates fractionalized gold tokens, which can function as any cryptocurrency. As an illustration, at current prices, such a "gold token" would be worth approximately 0.64 USD.

Collateralization – A final step to create a fiat-pegged stable coin would be to use the above "gold token" as collateral and peg it to a fiat currency, such as, for example, the US dollar. This provides a stable coin denominated in USD, the most used currency for international trade, backed by physical gold via gold tokens by way of using it as collateral. It, therefore, creates a gold-backed and fiat-pegged stable coin. It would require a sophisticated collateralization mechanism, adjusting for market prices and collateralization requirements.

Decentralization – To function in a truly trustless, decentralized, and autonomous manner, the above steps need to be governed by a decentralized and autonomous nervous system, rather than central trusted parties or intermediaries. This allows a community of participants to vote and decide on the well-functioning of the entire "token economics". As mentioned earlier, should any fees or rewards be created, they would also belong to the community, which functions as a decentralized autonomous organization (DAO).

The use of gold tokens as collateral within the realm of DeFi carries significant advantages. The inherent stability of the gold token's value, which is pegged to the real-time spot price of gold, contrasts favorably with the volatility often associated with cryptocurrencies like Ether. Consequently, this characteristic notably diminishes the risk of liquidation. Additionally, beyond its price stability, the gold token acts as a hedge against inflation, conferring it with enhanced resilience as a collateral option for the creation of stable coins. Notably, when compared to fiat-pegged stable coins, which are supported by reserves and bank deposits that historically have experienced depreciation in purchasing power, the price of gold has demonstrated a threefold increase over the past 20 years, reinforcing the appeal of gold tokens as a robust choice for collateralization in the DeFi landscape.

The above example, taking gold as a "real-world asset", is only one illustration of blockchain technology using digital authentication of the underlying asset in a tamper proof manner. Not only does it provide collateral certainty, but it also informs the owner of relevant ESG[9] features of the asset, directly certified by the smart contract,

[9] Environmental, Social, and Governance (ESG) features relevant to gold include proof of mining with respect to environmental and human rights considerations.

rather than relying on a third-party reporting mechanism. Such a certificate is different from a paper certificate that relies on intermediaries, like banks, to hold custody of the asset, resulting in frictional costs and counterparty risk. This on-chain traceability can provide a proof of location of storage in a stable jurisdiction in a reliable and well insured way, fully remote from the bankruptcy of any financial intermediary. Holding a digital, on-chain certificate, like an NFT, also facilitates easier redemption or trading in the secondary market, hence providing liquidity to the investor, with low frictional costs. This offers a stable asset, a strong store of value, owned in a self-sovereign way, yet with high transferability.

7. Conclusion

If well orchestrated and governed, in the way that is described above, we propose that a gold stable coin can offer a strong currency alternative. Different to other gold investment products, a gold-backed stable coin uses blockchain technology that strongly reduces the otherwise necessary trust in intermediaries and is therefore much more efficient, transportable, transparent, and thus more secure. Altogether, this tokenization combines the advantages of an efficient and highly secure store of value with a high portability and liquidity. The choices of a gold token and a gold-backed USD stable coin and the ability to quickly and easily move between them combine the benefits of unit of account and reduction of day to day volatility.

The key assertions made by the bitcoin whitepaper, which proposed to avoid relying on a trusted third party, prevent double-spending and doing this by relying on cryptographic proof provided by an on-chain network of nodes apply well to tokenization of "real-world" tangible assets. Much of the well-functioning of a currency can be improved when backed by real-world assets.

This will be an evolution. It took some time for email to replace the fax machines. We now have the technology and the governance mechanism to renew the old payment system rails. That is exactly what well-designed stable coins can do.

Acknowledgements

The authors express their gratitude to the editor, Dr. Luyao Zhang, for her invaluable and perceptive comments. Additionally, Yulin extends appreciation to Mr. Gian Bochsler for his inspiration in the development of the gold-backed stable coin. Paul extends his gratitute to his colleagues at the DFINITY Foundation for their ground breaking work in establishing the technology that enables the innovation of digital assets.

Author details

Paul Meeusen[1] and Yulin Liu[2,3]*

1 Dfinity Foundation, Zurich, Switzerland

2 Bochsler Consulting, Neuchatel, Switzerland

3 SciEcon CIC, London, UK

*Address all correspondence to: yulin@bochslerfinance.com

References

[1] Eurepean Securities and Markets Authority. 2023. Available from: https://www.esma.europa.eu/esmas-activities/digital-finance-and-innovation/markets-crypto-assets-regulation-mica [Accessed: November 21, 2023]

[2] Bitcoin Whitepaper. 2008. Available from: https://bitcoin.org/bitcoin.pdf [Accessed: November 28, 2023]

[3] Tether Transparency. 2023. Available from: https://tether.to/en/transparency/#usdt [Accessed: November 28, 2023]

[4] Circle Transparency. 2023. Available from: https://www.circle.com/en/transparency [Accessed: November 28, 2023]

[5] Coinmarketcap. 2023. Available from: https://coinmarketcap.com/currencies/usd-coin/ [Accessed: November 28, 2023]

[6] CPI. 2023. Available from: https://fred.stlouisfed.org/series/CUUR0000SA0R [Accessed: November 28, 2023]

[7] Evolution of U.S. Federal Budget Deficit/Surplus. Available from: https://ark-invest.com/podcast/economic-indicators-with-cathie-wood-podcast/ [Accessed: November 28, 2023]

[8] New York Federal Reserve. Available from: https://www.newyorkfed.org/microeconomics/hhdc [Accessed: November 28, 2023]

[9] Fitch. 2023. Available from: https://www.fitchratings.com/research/sovereigns/fitch-downgrades-united-states-long-term-ratings\-to-aa-from-aaa-outlook-stable-01-08-2023 [Accessed: November 28, 2023]

[10] House Budget Committee Democrats [Internet]. House Budget Committee Democrats. Available from: https://budget.house.gov/

Section 3

Blockchain in Emerging Applications (IoT, Web3, Energy)

Chapter 6

Exploring the Use of Blockchain Technology in IoT Applications

Sergey Khvan, Refik Caglar Kizilirmak and Mehdi Shafiee

Abstract

The integration of blockchain and IoT presents tremendous potential for unlocking new opportunities and capabilities. With additive decentralized features, businesses and individuals can benefit from increased security, transparency, and efficiency in various applications. This chapter first presents the technical aspects of this integration, including the role of smart contracts in decentralized IoT systems and how blockchain enhances the security, stability, and transparency of IoT networks. Then, a step-by-step tutorial for developing smart contracts and ledger on Ethereum blockchain is presented, particularly from the perspective of IoT nodes. The considered scenario is for an IoT device that writes/retrieves data from the blockchain; however, the presented methodology can easily be extended for different use cases.

Keywords: Internet of Things (IoT), blockchain, smart contract, Ethereum, decentralized systems

1. Introduction

The Internet of Things (IoT) systems have become increasingly popular in several applications ranging from smart homes, automation, and healthcare to smart transportation [1]. The IoT infrastructure mainly interconnects countless devices, sensors, and systems over the existing Internet Protocol (IP) to collect, manipulate, and visualize the data for intelligent decision-making. It is a proven technology that enhances the efficiency and productivity of many processes in several industries [1]. The growing interest in academia and industry will lead to new innovations in the field, which will have a more visible impact on our daily lives.

To fully exploit the potential of IoT systems and accommodate a massive number of devices in the network, resource-efficient (e.g., energy consumption, spectrum usage, computational resources) multiplexing methods play a key role [2]. IoT multiplexing methods combine multiple data streams from several devices into a single channel. The effective use of multiplexing method reduces the use of network resources resulting in reliable and sustainable network performance. Mainly, when the limited memory, processing power, and battery life of an IoT device are considered, the importance of these multiplexing methods is more evident. Quality of service (QoS) is another crucial aspect of IoT networks, as different applications or different devices in the same network may require different QoS levels [2]. The multiplexing methods may also help to reach desired QoS levels by optimally allocating the resources among the devices. IoT systems may also suffer from interference in case multiple devices share the same spectrum [3]. Multiplexing methods should also consider interference management while sustaining efficient spectrum usage. Moreover, the security of IoT data is of concern in many applications. Multiplexing methods should consider security threats and ensure the isolation of data streams from different IoT devices to prevent unauthorized access or interference. Furthermore, the scalability of the multiplexing methods is important in IoT networks since the number of IoT devices and associated data can grow rapidly. When accommodating a massive number of IoT devices, multiplexing methods should be able to adjust and optimize resource allocation while still maintaining the QoS requirements of the devices. Lastly, the real-time nature of IoT networks necessitates more computationally efficient multiplexing methods, for example, with less control signaling, so that the devices can join or leave the network and are assigned their channels in a lightweight manner. Considering all these challenges, the design and development of IoT multiplexing methods is an active research field targeting efficient, reliable, and secure communication among connected devices.

The multiplexing methods mainly refer to physical layer processing, such as time division multiplexing (TDM) and frequency division multiplexing (FDM). TDM primarily shares the spectrum in time among the devices, whereas FDM shares the spectrum by dividing it into multiple slots. Multiplexing can sometimes occur using non-orthogonal methods where devices simultaneously operate in the entire spectrum using signal processing methods such as spread spectrum or interference cancelation. There are several works in the literature that optimizes the IoT network performance using these methods in the physical layer [4–6]. In practice, all these physical layer multiplexing methods occur between the devices and the first-hop router and today implementations are based on well-known link-layer standards such as LoRaWAN [7], 802.11 (Wi-Fi) [8], and 802.15.4 (ZigBee) [9]. Some versions of LoRaWAN use spread spectrum, 802.11 uses orthogonal frequency division multiplexing (OFDM), and 802.15.4 employs TDMA or carrier sense multiple access (CSMA). Most of the off-the-shelf IoT devices support either of these standards, and developers are not allowed to modify the physical layer specifications, including the multiplexing method implemented.

The multiplexing in IoT can also refer to the methods implemented in upper layers, such as efficient routing for low-power wireless packet-switched networks such as 6LoWPAN [10]. 6LowPAN protocol runs in the network layer, specifically in IPv6, and facilitates the integration of the IP-based network layer to the link layer (such as Wi-Fi, ZigBee) by allowing mesh networking among IoT devices. Furthermore, routing protocol for low power and lossy networks (RPL) is another network layer protocol proposed for IoT devices for efficient routing of the packets arriving from different IoT devices [11].

In the application layer, there are other protocols that consider the power constraint of the IoT devices, such as MQ telemetry transport (MQTT) and constrained application protocol (CoAP). MQTT is a lightweight application layer protocol based on publish-subscribe messaging pattern, which requires a central intermediary node called broker to exchange data between the devices and servers [12]. CoAP, on the other hand, which is again a lightweight protocol, allows devices to communicate with each other through mesh topology using client-server model [13]. Both are widely used in IoT domain.

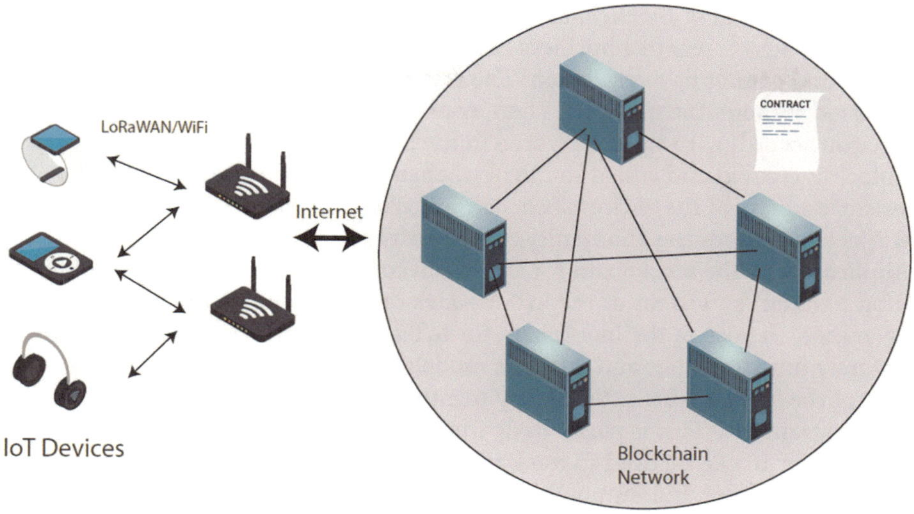

Figure 1.
Illustration of a blockchain-based IoT system.

Recently, the decentralization of IoT systems using blockchain has also emerged as an alternative solution that addresses the aforementioned scalability, reliability, and security issues. First of all, using smart contracts that are programmable agreements executed on blockchain can manage the access rights of IoT devices that inherently give control over the control of QoS requirement of different devices [14]. The same approach can also be used to allocate resources efficiently while each device is multiplexed in the same channel. Another solution that blockchain brings is its enhanced security and privacy features. In blockchain, each transaction is transparent, meaning that multiple devices can access it. Data stored on the blockchain is tampered-proof that ensures data integrity and eliminates the risk of unauthorized modifications.

Furthermore, blockchain can store and process data securely, either locally or in a distributed manner. IoT devices can participate as "full nodes" in the blockchain's consensus mechanisms. This approach may reduce the latency in the network. However, full nodes need to store entire blockchain data, which is not desired for IoT devices with limited memory storage. Therefore, a more preferred approach is that IoT devices implementing "wallet" interact with the blockchain through transactions of smart contracts to write and retrieve data from the blockchain. **Figure 1** shows the scenario considered in this chapter. In Section 2, we give more insights of blockchain-based systems. In Section 3, we discuss the advantages of the integration of blockchain and IoT. In Section 4, we show the building and deployment of a smart contract for a simple scenario and IoT implementation with blockchain. Finally, we conclude in Section 6.

2. Blockchain

Blockchain technology is a versatile and secure ledger system that can be used in various industries. The first idea of blockchain technology was introduced in 2008 by

Satoshi Nakamoto [15]. Blockchain is a shared, immutable ledger that records transactions and tracks assets in a business network. Blocks are linked together using hash addresses and cannot be overwritten. The transaction process starts with a request broadcasted through the network. Then, consensus algorithm is used to verify the transaction according to the data stored in the blockchain. After the verification, a new block is created and added to the blockchain. To provide better reliability, full nodes store a copy of the entire blockchain. Blockchain brings trust to peer-to-peer networks and ensures the anonymity and security of the users.

Application of the blockchain for the IoT becomes more popular, as it brings the solution to main drawbacks of the IoT. Besides the enhanced security, privacy, and transparency, the use of the blockchain for IoT applications allows the implementation of new functionalities and business models [16].

One of the key benefits is the ability to ensure transaction authenticity and record ownership transfers. This is particularly important in supply chain management, where blockchain can be used to track the sources of insecurity in IoT devices and provide a transparent and immutable record of product information, such as origin, processing method, and transportation route [17].

In **Figure 2**, a simple blockchain schema is given, where the genesis block is the first block of the blockchain. In the IoT example that we present in Section 4, we will deploy the smart contract on this block. Each block of the blockchain stores the hash code of the next block. In the blockchain, no other block can be inserted in between the blocks; therefore, the history of transactions could be secured.

2.1 Consensus

Consensus is a fundamental aspect of blockchain technology that ensures agreement among participants in the network regarding the validity of transactions and the state of the blockchain [18]. A consensus protocol is used to assign the contribution of nodes(miners) that will be used to verify each transaction. Consensus protocol makes transactions more efficient, secure, binds them to time, and allows the creation of new functionality. It is achieved through various consensus mechanisms, such as Proof of Work (PoW), Proof of Stake (PoS), Proof of Authority (PoA), and Proof of Luck (PoL) [19]. After achieving consensus, new blocks are added to the blockchain.

The most common algorithms are Proof of Work (PoW) and Proof of Stake (PoS). Proof of Work (PoW) uses miners to confirm transactions. Miners are "unreliable" users/actors who compete in solving a mathematical puzzle or a challenge to have the

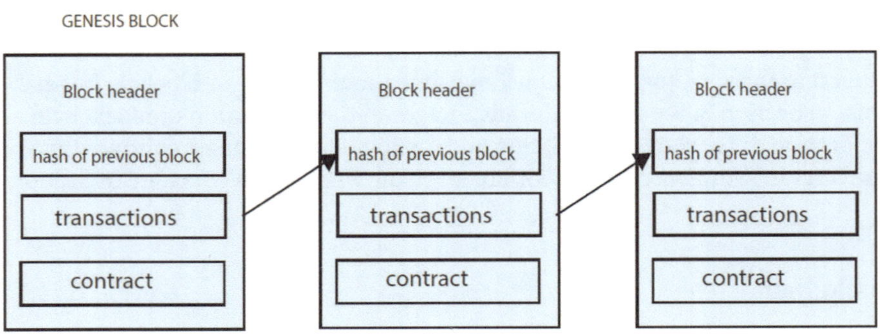

Figure 2.
Illustration of a blockchain.

new block accepted by the blockchain. This process is called mining and is designed as a way to be easily solvable by the blockchain, but requires significant computational power from the user. Limitations in scalability and vulnerability to attack are the main drawbacks of PoW [20]. Those limitations and possible environmental impacts due to low energy efficiency [21] are the main reason for the growing popularity of other algorithms.

Proof of Stake (PoS), on the other hand, selects validators based on the amount of cryptocurrency on the account and willingness to "stake" as collateral [22]. To validate the transaction more than half of the selected users must accept the information, which is passed as a request. In comparison with PoW, PoS reduces energy consumption due to the absence of mining [21]. Even though PoS became more popular due to better energy efficiency, it also has its challenges. The main ones are "nothing at stake" problem and potential centralization tendencies [20]. Therefore, the choice of the right consensus algorithm should be carefully considered according to the requirements for the implementation.

2.2 Smart contracts

Smart contracts is a code, which is stored in the blockchain. Their functionality can be executed by the nodes of the blockchain, when certain conditions are met. It eliminates the need for intermediaries and increases efficiency and transparency in various applications [23]. Smart contracts are a key feature of blockchain technology and enable the automation of complex processes and the creation of decentralized applications (DApps) [24].

2.3 Challenges

As any other technology blockchain faces several challenges. Those are scalability, throughput, latency, privacy, security, interoperability, and regulatory and legislative issues [18, 24, 25]. Scalability is a major concern as blockchain networks need to handle a large number of transactions while maintaining decentralization and security [25]. Moreover, it may require a lot of storage in the nodes of the blockchain, as they store full copies of the entire chain. Another crucial part is privacy and security, as blockchain transactions are transparent and immutable, raising concerns about data protection and confidentiality [25]. Loss of the data may lead to new issues related to legal rights. Interoperability is another challenge, as different blockchain platforms may have different consensus mechanisms, governance models, and technical specifications, making it difficult to integrate and exchange data between them [26].

3. Integration of blockchain and IoT

Most IoT systems today operate on centralized server systems. These server systems have the task of storing, maintaining, and retrieving IoT data. They employ powerful data analytics tools capable of handling large volumes of data, enabling organizations to analyze, apply machine learning techniques, and visualize the data. These centralized systems also rely on various communication, data management, and security protocols to safeguard and sustain their operations. However, despite the prevalent use of centralized systems in the IoT domain, they face challenges related to scalability, latency, and the potential for a single point of failure, which undermines the feasibility of IoT systems [14].

The use of blockchain technology offers several advantages to overcome the aforementioned challenges. Some of these advantages include:

- Decentralization: In a decentralized network, multiple nodes participate in verifying and validating transactions. This completely removes the need for a single central server and reduces the risks associated with a single point of failure. For example, well-known denial of service (DoS) attacks are common security threats in centralized systems.

- Immutability and transparency: The data stored on a blockchain is permenant and cannot be altered. This feature is particularly useful in applications where multiple entities need to trust the data on the blockchain. In contrast, centralized systems are controlled by a single authority, which lacks transparency and raises concerns in applications where data ownership and privacy are important.

- Enhanced security: Public key cryptography is widely used in many blockchain systems. It enhances data security through digital signatures that ensure the integrity of data. Furthermore, the validity of the transaction is verified by multiple participants *via* consensus mechanisms. This inherent characteristic significantly strengthens the system's resilience against unauthorized data tampering.

- Smart contracts: Smart contracts form the foundation of data exchange in a blockchain-based IoT systems. They are self-executing agreements with predefined rules deployed on the blockchain. They enable interactions between IoT devices and allow secure and autonomous transactions by eliminating the need for intermediate devices. Smart contracts can facilitate trust and streamline processes within IoT networks.

- Scalability: In the context of blockchain, scalability refers to the ability to handle a high number of transactions per second. Traditional blockchains may face scalability challenges as network traffic grows. Several methods have been proposed to overcome these challenges, such as off-chain solutions, also known as layer-2 solutions. These solutions allow transactions to be processed outside the main blockchain, creating additional space and reducing the change of congestion. In the domain of IoT, this becomes particularly useful as the number of IoT devices and associated data grow. Moreover, these layer-2 solutions bring additional security and privacy benefits of their own.

4. Explaining blockchain technology and working with Alchemy

This section presents a step-by-step tutorial for smart contract deployment on the Ethereum blockchain and writing/retrieving data through it, for IoT applications. We use Alchemy blockchain development platform, which is a popular tool for software engineers to develop their DApps [27]. It provides a set of APIs, tools, and other solutions to facilitate the development of blockchain applications. Alchemy allows building and effectively deploying smart contacts on several public blockchain networks, including popular Ethereum [28] and Solana blockchains.

The popularity of Alchemy has increased recently with the growing momentum in decentralized applications with its friendly graphical user interface (GUI) and specific tools for DApps. The process of DApp development starts with building a smart contract for a specific IoT scenario that runs on a selected blockchain. Then, the contract is deployed and tested on a testnet in order to verify its functionalities of storing and reading data from the blockchain. In this section, we consider Goerli Ethereum testnet which is a separate blockchain that mimics the original Ethereum blockchain allowing developers to test their DApps without interacting with the main Ethereum network. Goerli testnet tools are also available in Alchemy platform. Please note that we are not discussing the implementation of a full Ethereum validating node; rather, we are focusing on smart contract development. Any workstation connected to the Internet would suffice for creating and uploading smart contracts to the blockchain. We also demonstrate how this smart contract is utilized within a DApp created using Alchemy, and we showcase how IoT devices interact with this DApp. Here are other prerequisites for the development of DApp at the workstation.

Prerequisites:

- Alchemy account: A service providing APIs and tools for blockchain development and interaction.

- MetaMask Wallet: Browser extension wallet for Ethereum transactions with a small amount of Ether (ETH) for fees. 0.001 ETH is required in mainnet to obtain the testing cryptocurrency (Goerli ETH).

- VSCode: Microsoft's code editor offering extensions for various languages, including Python and Solidity that we consider in this tutorial.

- Python 3.9+: Programming language required for Ethereum and blockchain development.

- Solidity: Ethereum's programming language for creating smart contracts.

- Web3: Python library enabling interaction with Ethereum nodes and smart contracts.

- Solcx: Python library for compiling Solidity smart contracts for Ethereum.

Installation of web3 and solcx using terminal.

To install "web3" and "solcx" libraries, the following commands should be entered in the command prompt.

The first command in **Figure 3** will download and install the necessary files for the "solcx" library, which is used for Solidity contract compilation. The second command is for "web3" library installation, which is essential for interacting with Ethereum blockchain networks using Python. After running these commands, the installation process for both libraries should begin. Once the installation is completed, they can be used in Python projects on the workstation to interact with Ethereum smart contracts and implement blockchain functionality.

```
$pip install py-solc-x
$pip install web3
```

Figure 3.
Installing py-solc-x and web3 libraries.

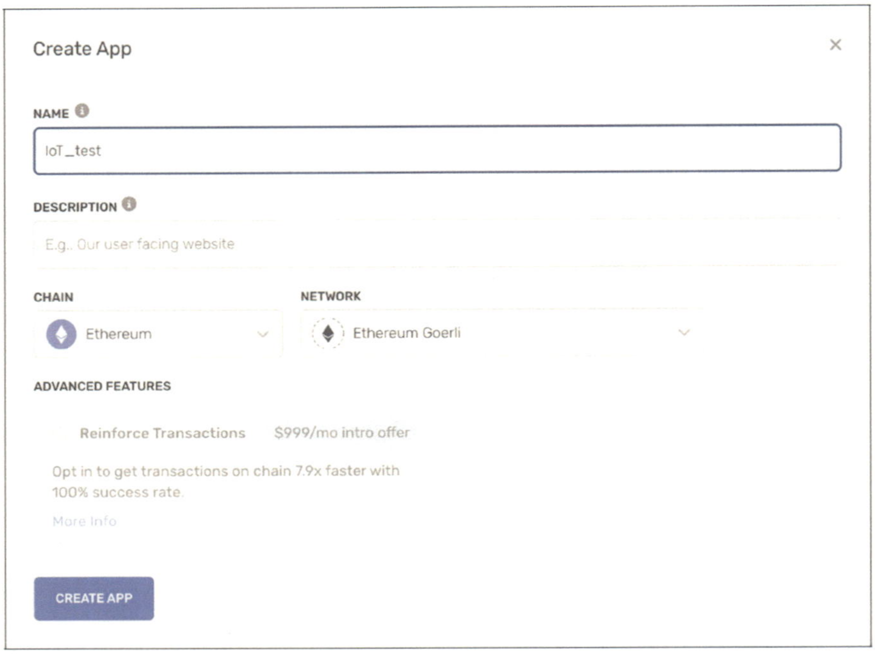

Figure 4.
Creating a new DApp, named IoT_test, using Alchemy.

After preparing the development environment, in the following sections, we describe each phase of building a blockchain-based IoT system. We start with creating a DApp with Alchemy in Section 4.1, and then proceed to create a smart contract in Section 4.2, followed by deploying the smart contract to the blockchain in Section 4.3. Lastly, reading and writing data from the blockchain are described in Section 4.4. While our discussion can be applied to various scenarios, we are specifically demonstrating a scenario in which an IoT device writes its sensor reading to the blockchain and is also able to read other data from the blockchain.

4.1 Creating a DApp with Alchemy

DApps can be created using Alchemy development platform. For that purpose, users should register and log into https://www.alchemy.com/. The dashboard is given in **Figure 4** where users can create a new DApp after selecting Ethereum Goerli. After clicking "Create App," a DApp named IoT_test will be generated on the Ethereum Goerli blockchain, and users will encounter the interface shown in **Figure 5**. The API key of the DApp can be obtained by selecting "View Key." This key will be utilized later when deploying our smart contract to the blockchain. It plays a crucial role in enabling the DApp to establish communication and interaction with the deployed

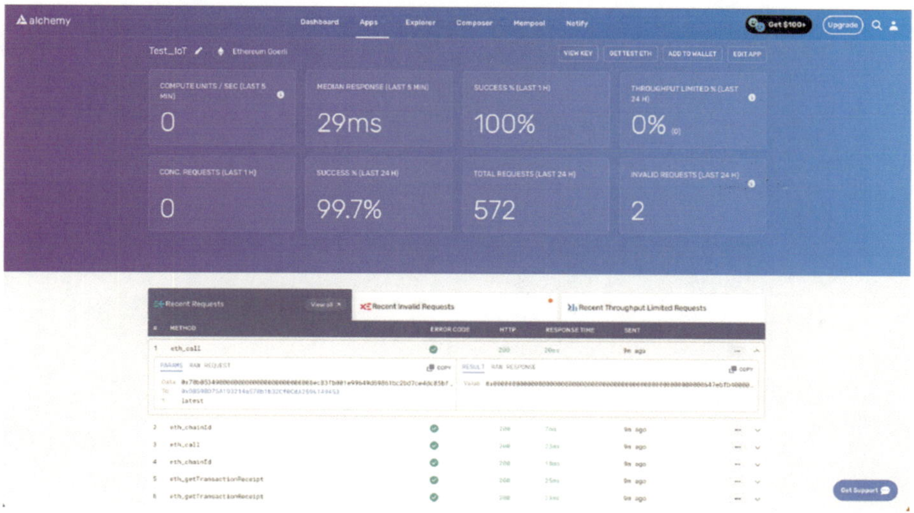

Figure 5.
Alchemy dashboard of created app.

smart contract. The API key is an authentication mechanism that allows the DApp to access and execute functions within the smart contract securely.

Testing the DApp without deploying any smart contract involves installing the Metamask wallet, obtaining test ETH from https://goerlifaucet.com/, and connecting to the testnet. This allows exploration and interaction with the DApp on the testnet to ensure proper functionality before deploying smart contracts. Note that there are no legal Ethereum rules that mandate testing. For additional guidance on testing the DApp, please refer to Ref. [29]).

4.2 Building the contract

Developers utilize the Solidity programming language to create smart contracts for Ethereum blockchain. Alchemy provides tools for streamlined deployment and interaction of these contracts within their DApps on the blockchain. For this example, we present a smart contract for a simple IoT scenario through which IoT device will collect data from its sensor and store it in the blockchain. The Solidity code can be found in **Figure 6**. This smart contract, named IoT_SmartContract, is created using Solidity programming language; hence, smart contracts have .sol extension. Through this smart contract, the IoT device stores the value of sensor reading and timestamp representing the time when the data was collected in value and timestamp variables, respectively. There are three functions defined in the smart contract, namely addReading (adds a value from the sensor with timestamp as an array [timestamp, value]), getReadingCount returns the number of the blocks in the blockchain, and getReading requires the index of the block to retrieve data from.

4.3 Deploying the contract

After saving the IoT_SmartContract.sol file, it needs to be deployed on the Ethereum blockchain. The code in **Figure 7** deploys the smart contract created above on the blockchain; in our case it is Ethereum Goerli. For the DApp, we created earlier using Alchemy to interact with this uploaded smart contract ALCHEMY_API_KEY

```
# Smart Contract
pragma solidity ^0.8.0;

contract IoT_SmartContract {
                    struct SensorReading {
                    uint256 timestamp;
                    uint256 value;
                    }

mapping(address => SensorReading[]) public readings;

function addReading(uint256 _value) public {
SensorReading memory reading = SensorReading(block.timestamp, _value);
readings[msg.sender].push(reading);
}

function getReadingCount(address _owner) public view returns (uint256) {
return readings[_owner].length;
}

function getReading(address _owner, uint256 _index) public view returns
     (uint256, uint256) {
require(_index < readings[_owner].length, "Invalid index");
SensorReading storage reading = readings[_owner][_index];
return (reading.timestamp, reading.value);
}
}

}
```

Figure 6.
Sample IoT smart contract (IoT_SmartContract.Sol) created using solidity.

and ALCHEMY_URL should be set. The ALCHEMY_API_KEY is the API key obtained earlier from the "View Key" option in the Alchemy dashboard of the created app, shown in **Figure 5**. ALCHEMY_URL should be set as "https://eth-goerli.g.alchemy.com/v2/ALCHEMY_API_KEY." This URL is also available at the Alchemy dashboard of the DApp. Furthermore, in the code, IoT_SmartContract.sol file location should also be assigned to contract_file_path. After running the code, the smart contract will be deployed on the blockchain and it will print the address of the block at which it was deployed. When a smart contract is deployed on a blockchain, it is assigned a unique address on that blockchain. For example, we present the block address in which our smart contract is written in **Figure 8**. This address should be kept for later use as one of the required inputs on the IoT device and assigned to contract_address when writing/retrieving data, as described in the next section.

4.4 Interacting with IoT devices and the blockchain for data exchange

The following describes the process for writing and retrieving data from the blockchain. The code is provided in **Figure 9**. While any device with the DApp's API key, an ETH wallet, and the DApp's smart contract address can read and write data on the blockchain, our scenario specifically focuses on IoT devices writing sensor readings and subsequently retrieving data of other sensors.

Note that the code in **Figure 9** is given for a computer development environment. When IoT microcontrollers are used to read and write data, minor modifications to suit the specific microcontroller are required. Nonetheless, the procedure remains the same across different microcontrollers and the fundamental principles of interacting with the blockchain are the same.

```python
# Deploying the smart contract on blockchain
from web3 import Web3
import solcx
from eth_account import Account
from eth_account.signers.local import LocalAccount

# Set up Alchemy provider
ALCHEMY_API_KEY = "<your alchemy app API key>" # put your API key from the alchemy app
ALCHEMY_URL = f"https://eth-goerli.g.alchemy.com/v2/{ALCHEMY_API_KEY}"

# Solidity contract source code in a separate .sol file
contract_file_path = "<path to your file (contract/contract.sol)>" # put relative or absolute path to created .sol file

# Uncomment the following lines to read the contract source code from the file
# with open(contract_file_path, "r") as f:
# contract_source_code = f.read()

def compile_source_file(file_path):
solcx.install_solc(version='0.8.9')
solcx.set_solc_version('0.8.9')
with open(file_path, 'r') as f:
source = f.read()
print(source)
return solcx.compile_source(source)

# Compile the contract
compiled_contract = compile_source_file(contract_file_path)
contract_interface = compiled_contract["<stdin>:IoT_SmartContract"]

# Set up web3 instance
w3 = Web3(Web3.HTTPProvider(ALCHEMY_URL))

# Set up account and private key
private_key = "<your private key from the metamask wallet>" #in metamask extension go to account details and export private key
account: LocalAccount = Account.from_key(private_key)

# Deploy the contract
contract = w3.eth.contract(abi=contract_interface["abi"], bytecode=contract_interface["bin"])
deploy_txn = contract.constructor().build_transaction({
"from": account.address,
"nonce": w3.eth.get_transaction_count(account.address),
"gas": 2000000, # you can change the gas price here
})

signed_txn = w3.eth.account.sign_transaction(deploy_txn, private_key=private_key)
tx_hash = w3.eth.send_raw_transaction(signed_txn.rawTransaction)

# Wait for the transaction to be mined
tx_receipt = w3.eth.wait_for_transaction_receipt(tx_hash)

# Get the contract address from the transaction receipt
contract_address = tx_receipt["contractAddress"]

print(f"Contract deployed at the address: {contract_address}") # You will need this address later
```

Figure 7.
Deploying the smart contract on blockchain, created using Python.

In the code, the sensor reading from an IoT device, represented by the value stored in the variable reading_value, is written to the blockchain along with a timestamp. For this example, we assigned one integer value of "45" to reading_value as a sample

```
Contract deployed at the address:
0xD8598D75A193214a578b1b32Cf0CdA2596149453
```

Figure 8.
Output prompt from the terminal after contract deployment.

sensor reading. However, it can be changed according to the user's need, such as real-time sensor reading. After executing the code, this reading value will be written to the blockchain.

In the same run, we also provide retrieving data from the blockchain. Please note that the reading and retrieving portions of the code can be separated as needed; however, up to line-42 should remain common. The code will display the count of stored sensor reading data on the blockchain. Note that the index of the first block is 0. In order to retrieve the data stored, the user needs to provide the index of the block. **Figure 10** shows the code output. For example, it displays that there are currently four data entries in the blockchain. After entering the block index of the data to be retrieved, the code returns the timestamp and data. In this example, block index is entered as 1 and the associated data is [1,686,028,212,45]. The format of the time is in Unix timestamp format.

In using public blockchains, there is a cost for each transaction to write data on blockchain. When a transaction is submitted, a certain amount of cryptocurrency, known as a transaction fee, should be paid to compensate the network nodes for the resources consumed in validating the transaction. In the context of Ethereum, the native token of the blockchain is ETH and the amount to be paid should be stored in the wallet of the IoT devices that are submitting the transactions. In **Figure 10**, the node_address should be set to the Ethereum wallet address of the IoT device and private_key should store the private key associated with the wallet. After each transaction, the corresponding transaction fee will be deducted from this address. Transaction fees in Ethereum, often referred to as gas fees, are measured in units of Gwei. Users may opt to pay a higher fee for an increased transaction speed. In **Figure 10**, the gas: value can be changed based on network conditions and user preferences. Note that reading the data from the blockchain does not require a transaction fee.

The transactions in the DApp can be viewed in the Alchemy dashboard (see **Figure 5**). Here, each transaction or request to the API could be tracked. Also, the addresses of the previous requests could be found. Error codes of the failed transactions are also shown in the result window.

After completing the testing phase on the testnet, the transition to the Ethereum mainnet necessitates the creation of a new DApp. Users need to establish a separate DApp within the Alchemy platform, selecting the Ethereum mainnet environment. The Goerli-based application remains essential for code testing purposes. The same codes we provided above can be used in mainnet, except for the Alchemy_API_Key and Alchemy_URL, which should be configured for the DApp created on mainnet.

5. Conclusions

In this chapter, we addressed the main challenges of IoT systems and discussed how blockchain-based IoT systems can address these challenges. Specifically, we asserted that the reliability, security, transparency, immutability, and scalability aspects of IoT networks can be enhanced with blockchain systems. We then provided

```
# Writing data to the blockchain
from web3 import Web3
from web3.middleware import geth_poa_middleware
from eth_account import Account
import solcx

# Set up Alchemy provider
ALCHEMY_API_KEY = "your_key" # Same key as before
ALCHEMY_URL = f"https://eth-goerli.g.alchemy.com/v2/{ALCHEMY_API_KEY}"

contract_address = "<contract address from the deployment>" # Put the saved address from the previous file

node_address = "<address of the wallet>" # put address of the account in the metamask
private_key = "<privater key of the wallet>" # private key from that account
account = Account.from_key(private_key)

# Set up web3 instance
w3 = Web3(Web3.HTTPProvider(ALCHEMY_URL))
w3.middleware_onion.inject(geth_poa_middleware, layer=0)

# Solidity contract source code in a separate .sol file
contract_file_path = "contracts/IoT_SmartContract.sol" # put your own path here

# Read the contract source code from the file
# with open(contract_file_path, "r") as f:
# contract_source_code = f.read()

def compile_source_file(file_path):
solcx.install_solc(version='0.8.9')
solcx.set_solc_version('0.8.9')
with open(file_path, 'r') as f:
source = f.read()
print(source)
return solcx.compile_source(source)

# Compile the contract
compiled_contract = compile_source_file(contract_file_path)
contract_interface = compiled_contract["<stdin>:IoT_SmartContract"]

contract = w3.eth.contract(address=contract_address, abi=contract_interface["abi"])

# Simulate IoT node readings
reading_value = 45 # this variable will be stored as an example


# Add a reading to the smart contract
add_reading_txn = contract.functions.addReading(reading_value).build_transaction({
"from": node_address,
"nonce": w3.eth.get_transaction_count(node_address),
"gas": 2000000, # price of each transaction to store the data
"gasPrice": w3.to_wei(10, "gwei")
})

signed_txn = w3.eth.account.sign_transaction(add_reading_txn, private_key=private_key)
tx_hash = w3.eth.send_raw_transaction(signed_txn.rawTransaction)


# Wait for the transaction to be mined
tx_receipt = w3.eth.wait_for_transaction_receipt(tx_hash)
print(f"Reading added.")

# Get the reading count for the node
reading_count = contract.functions.getReadingCount(node_address).call()
print(f"Reading count: {reading_count}") # returns the number of blocks in the blockhain

block_number = int(input("Please enter the index of the block to retrieve data from: "))# index of the required block to be read
if block_number != '':
values_block = contract.functions.getReading(node_address, block_number).call()
print(values_block)# is a list of 2 values 1 is a timestamp and second is stored reading at this time
print(f"Reading from the sensor:{values_block[1]}, at {values_block[0]}")
```

Figure 9.
Writing and retrieving data from the blockchain, created using Python.

```
Reading count: 3
Please enter the index of the block to retrieve data from: 1
[1686028212, 45]
Reading from the sensor: 45, at 1686028212
```

Figure 10.
Output prompt from the terminal to retrieve data.

a step-by-step tutorial with a detailed list of used tools on how to build and implement an IoT system on a blockchain. We used the most widely used platforms and public blockchain. We considered a simple scenario of reading sensor data at an IoT device and writing data on a blockchain. We provided source codes for building smart contract, deploying it on a blockchain and writing/retrieving data from the blockchain. Our scenario includes the case where the devices interact with the blockchain network only. The work can be further expanded by allowing interactions between the devices, as well as incorporating hybrid solutions with a centralized server.

Acknowledgements

This work was supported by the Faculty Development Competitive Research Grant Programs of Nazarbayev University (grant no. 20122022FD4125 and grant no. 20122022FD4112).

Conflict of interest

The authors declare no conflict of interest.

Abbreviations

DApp	decentralized application
IoT	Internet of Things
GUI	graphical user interface
QoS	quality of service
TDM	time division multiplexing
FDM	frequency division multiplexing
CSMA	carrier sense multiple access
MQTT	MQ telemetry transport
CoAP	constrained application protocol
ETH	ether
RPL	routing protocol for low power and lossy networks
OFDM	orthogonal frequency division multiplexing
API	application programming interface
PoS	proof of stake
PoW	proof of work
PoL	proof of luck
PoA	proof of authority

DOI: http://dx.doi.org/10.5772/intechopen.1003635

Author details

Sergey Khvan†, Refik Caglar Kizilirmak*† and Mehdi Shafiee
Department of Electrical and Computer Engineering, Nazarbayev University, Kazakhstan

*Address all correspondence to: refik.kizilirmak@nu.edu.kz

† These authors contributed equally.

References

[1] Hassan WH. Current research on Internet of Things (IoT) security: A survey. Computer Networks. 2019;**148**: 283-294

[2] Oliveira L, Rodrigues JJPC, Kozlov SA, Rabêlo RAL, de Albuquerque VHC. MAC layer protocols for Internet of Things: A survey. Future Internet. 2019; **11**(1):16

[3] Sarma SS, Hazra R, Mukherjee A. Symbiosis between D2D communication and industrial IoT for industry 5.0 in 5G mm-wave cellular network: An interference management approach. IEEE Transactions on Industrial Informatics. 2021;**18**(8):5527-5536

[4] An S, Wang H, Sun Y, Lu Z, Yu Q. Time domain multiplexed LoRa modulation waveform design for IoT communication. IEEE Communications Letters. 2022;**26**(4):838-842

[5] Jia M, Yin Z, Guo Q, Liu G, Gu X. Downlink design for spectrum efficient IoT network. IEEE Internet of Things Journal. 2017;**5**(5):3397-3404

[6] Wu Q, Chen W, Ng DW, Schober R. Spectral and energy-efficient wireless powered IoT networks: NOMA or TDMA? IEEE Transactions on Vehicular Technology. 2018;**67**(7):6663-6667

[7] Haxhibeqiri J, De Poorter E, Moerman I, Hoebeke J. A survey of LoRaWAN for IoT: From technology to application. Sensors. 2018; **18**(11):3995

[8] Banerji S, Chowdhury RS. On IEEE 802.11: Wireless LAN technology. 2013. arXiv preprint arXiv:1307.2661

[9] Ndih ED, Cherkaoui S. On enhancing technology coexistence in the IoT era: ZigBee and 802.11 case. IEEE Access. 2016;**4**:1835-1844

[10] Yang Z, Chang CH. 6LoWPAN overview and implementations. In: Proceedings of the 2019 International Conference on Embedded Wireless Systems and Networks (EWSN); China: ACM; 2019. pp. 357-361

[11] Iova O, Picco P, Istomin T, Kiraly C. RPL: The routing standard for the Internet of Things... Or is it? IEEE Communications Magazine. 2016; **54**(12):16-22

[12] Yassein MB, Shatnawi MQ, Aljwarneh S, Al-Hatmi R. Internet of Things: Survey and open issues of MQTT protocol. In: 2017 International Conference on Engineering & MIS (ICEMIS); Tunusia: IEEE; 2017. pp. 1-6

[13] Tariq MA, Khan M, Raza Khan MT, Kim D. Enhancements and challenges in CoAP—A survey. Sensors. 2020;**20**(21): 6391

[14] Zhang Y, Kasahara S, Shen Y, Jiang X, Wan J. Smart contract-based access control for the Internet of Things. IEEE Internet of Things Journal. 2018;**6**(2): 1594-1605

[15] Nakamoto S. Bitcoin: A peer-to-peer electronic cash system. Decentralized Business Review. 2008

[16] Dai HN, Zheng Z, Zhang Y. Blockchain for Internet of Things: A survey. IEEE Internet of Things Journal. 2019;**6**(5):8076-8094

[17] Rejeb A, Keogh JG, Treiblmaier H. Leveraging the Internet of Things and blockchain technology in supply chain management. Future Internet. 2019; **11**(7):161

[18] Islam S, Islam MJ, Hossain M, Noor S, Kwak KS, Islam SR. A survey on consensus algorithms in blockchain-based applications: Architecture, taxonomy, and operational issues. IEEE Access. 2023

[19] Alrowaily MA, Alghamdi M, Alkhazi I, Hassanat AB, Arbab MM, Liu CZ. Modeling and analysis of proof-based strategies for distributed consensus in blockchain-based peer-to-peer networks. Sustainability. 2023;**15**(2):1478

[20] Rebello GA, Camilo GF, Guimaraes LC, de Souza LA, Thomaz GA, Duarte OC. A security and performance analysis of proof-based consensus protocols. Annals of Telecommunications. 2021;**77**: 517-537

[21] Shi X, Xiao H, Liu W, Lackner KS, Buterin V, Stocker TF. Confronting the carbon-footprint challenge of blockchain. Environmental Science Technology. 2023;**57**(3):1403-1410

[22] Bala K, Kaur PD. A novel game theory based reliable proof-of-stake consensus mechanism for blockchain. Transactions on Emerging Telecommunications Technologies. 2022;**33**(9):e4525

[23] Zehir C, Zehir M. Emerging blockchain solutions in the mobility ecosystem: Associated risks and areas for applications. Bussecon Review of Social Sciences (2687–2285). 2022;**4**(2):1-14

[24] Trivedi S, Mehta K, Sharma R. Systematic literature review on application of blockchain technology in E-finance and financial services. Journal of Technology Management Innovation. 2021;**16**(3):89-102

[25] Yli-Huumo J, Ko D, Choi S, Park S, Smolander K. Where is current research on blockchain technology?—A systematic review. PLoS One. 2016;**11** (10):e0163477

[26] Abdullah S, Arshad J, Alsadi M. Chain-net: An internet-inspired framework for interoperable blockchains. Distributed Ledger Technologies: Research and Practice. 2022. DOI: 10.1145/3554761

[27] Alchemy - the web3 development platform. Available from: https://www.alchemy.com/ [Accessed: June 29, 2023]

[28] Ethereum Foundation. Available from: https://ethereum.org/en/ [Accessed: June 29, 2023]

[29] A guide to building, testing, and deploying your first DApp with Truffle, Ethers.js, Ganache, and React. Available from: https://dev.to/heydamali/a-guide-to-building-testing-and-deploying-your-\first-dapp-with-truffle-ethersjs-ganache-and-react-1mh0 [Accessed: September 2, 2023]

Chapter 7

Perspective Chapter: Leveraging Self-Sovereign Identity to Introduce ReCert – A Foundational Framework for Decentralized BCTE Solutions

Saqib Rasool and Rune Hylsberg Jacobsen

Abstract

Blockchain-enabled Transactive Energy (BCTE) heralds a revolutionary departure from traditional paradigms to achieve decentralization and its benefits in the energy sector. Despite the foundational insights provided by the IEEE's seminal position paper in 2021, the practical realization of BCTE still needs to be achieved, necessitating substantial research and development endeavors toward the real-world realization of BCTE. Our study responds to this imperative by presenting a foundational framework of ReCert that aims to unlock the full potential of BCTE through a prosumer-centric approach and sets a cornerstone to advance toward a fully functional BCTE solution.

ReCert[1] introduces a Re-Certification mechanism that operates over Self-sovereign Identity (SSI), which also serves as a gluing force between the DLT and blockchain components of the ReCert framework to tackle the challenges of the blockchain trilemma. This study shows the feasibility of the ReCert framework in supporting the BCTE modules of Granular Certificates (GC), Decentralized Identity (DI), and aggregation that operate through the concepts of SSI. The evolutionary framework of ReCert follows the layered approach to establish the groundwork for transforming into a fully decentralized BCTE solution.

Keywords: blockchain-enabled transactive energy, BCTE, DIDs, self-sovereign identity, blockchain trilemma, decentralized energy systems, prosumer-driven, granular certificates, concordium, IOTA tangle, aggregation, ReCert

1. Introduction

The energy sector's transformation toward a more sustainable future drives innovation in renewable energy production and its efficient integration within the power grid. BCTE

[1] http://ReCert.org

has emerged as a promising vision to address the associated challenges through decentralization. It leverages blockchain technology to create a secure, transparent, and automated system for managing energy transactions between various participants in the grid, including prosumers who act both as producers and consumers of energy [1]. This decentralized approach could revolutionize the energy sector by enabling peer-to-peer energy trading, improving grid flexibility, and incentivizing renewable energy adoption [2].

The position paper released by the IEEE in 2021 [3] presents a persuasive vision of BCTE that still needs adoption in the production environment, necessitating a detailed implementation strategy. BCTE is a complex system with many modules, including identity management, energy data acquisition, aggregation and indexing, a decentralized marketplace, and many more. Developing a robust BCTE solution necessitates a step-by-step approach, starting with core features and gradually integrating additional functionalities. In this study, we envision this strategy through the presentation of a foundational framework of ReCert [4] that can evolve to transform into a fully functional BCTE.

The ReCert framework introduces the Self-sovereign Identity (SSI)-driven ReCert certificates. We have focused explicitly on three BCTE modules, viz. 1) Decentralized Identity (DI), 2) Indexing through Aggregation (IA), and 3) Granular Certificates (GC). All of these modules of ReCert leverage the concepts of SSI. The first module of DI uses the Decentralized Identifiers (DIDs) of SSI to manage the identity of all the participants of ReCert. The second module of IA aggregates ReCert certificates by using a Merkle tree data structure to index the certificates of a single prosumer meter in a single Merkle tree [4], using the concept of edge computing [5]. The third module of GC utilizes the Verifiable Credentials (VC) and Verifiable Presentations (VPs) of SSI along with the innovative concept of GC from the project of Energy Track and Trace (ETT) [6] to issue, manage, and verify the Renewable Energy Certificates (RECs).

Using blockchain to issue RECs [7] is a popular way to verify the source and origin of renewable energy, providing consumers with assurance that they are getting the clean energy they have paid for. REC is a type of EAC (Energy Attribute Certificate) that helps in avoiding greenwashing [8], where companies not using renewable energy sources falsely claim the rewards of using them for energy production. GCs of ETT and ReCert, which handle the certificates at the granular level, also fall under the category of EACs. Hence, GCs can replace the REC or other types of EACs. However, GCs, a single REC certificate operating at the watt per hour, must be replaced with a higher number of GCs operating at the minute level for less energy. Hence, a GC-supporting system is required to support the high throughput to handle the high volume of transactions generated for shorter time intervals in minutes by thousands of consumer meters connected to a registry in a specific vicinity. The ETT project handles this requirement through pre-trusted registries acting as centralized Distribution System Operators (DSO) [9], which is against the BCTE's decentralization promise and thus requires a more decentralized solution like ReCert [1, 4].

ReCert utilizes the prosumer meters to offer a decentralized alternative to the centralized registries of ETT and establish a foundation for a decentralized BCTE solution. However, accommodating the massive number of GCs is challenging. Hence, ReCert has introduced the concept of Re-Certification to aggregate many certificates at the prosumer meters' level that are Re-Certified by the IOTA-driven registries. Although we have already presented ReCert as an aggregation framework [4], this study focuses on its potential as a foundational framework that can evolve into a fully functional decentralized BCTE solution. ReCert is derived from our already proposed hybrid framework [1] to tackle the blockchain trilemma, which states that we can fully optimize only two of the three properties of blockchain solutions: scalability, security, and decentralization [10]. As shown in **Figure 1**, our proposed hybrid approach in ReCert addresses the blockchain trilemma by integrating the DAG of the IOTA Tangle with a public blockchain.

SSI plays a vital role in ReCert, where prosumer meters issue GCs through SSI VCs over the DLT of IOTA at the DSO level. Hence, the feeless transaction model of IOTA offers the economic feasibility to support the high volume of GCs at each DSO level, resulting in the aggregation of numerous GCs in Merkle trees. Each Merkle tree is then anchored to the public blockchain through a single transaction of a public blockchain to avail the security and reliability of the public blockchains. Hence, a single gas fee is enough to preserve the integrity and offers the immutability of all the GCs anchored in a single Merkle tree. It is essential to mention that ReCert is just a conceptual framework without a concrete implementation. Hence, this perspective study highlights the need and significance of ReCert as a foundational framework for a decentralized BCTE.

Figure 1 presents the three-layered architecture of our proposed solution, which supports all three properties of the blockchain trilemma. The lower layer of the public blockchain receives negligible transactions to reduce the operational cost by reducing the number of transactions that require the transaction fee for execution. The DLT-driven middle layer handles most of the transactions from the prosumer meters through the feeless transaction model of the IOTA Tangle to improve the economic feasibility of the proposed system. This integration aims to marry IOTA's scalability and feeless transaction model with the security and decentralization of public blockchains. **Figure 2** shows the extended version of **Figure 1** and presents the evolutionary nature of ReCert that makes it extendable to transform into a decentralized BCTE solution.

We break down the contents of this book chapter into the following sections:

- *Section 2* presents the significance of BCTE and highlights the requirements for a foundational framework that can grow into a complete BCTE solution.
- *Section 3* explains the SSI and its pivotal role in the realization of ReCert.
- *Section 4* delves into the concept of blockchain technology and introduces the challenges of solving the blockchain trilemma. This section also justifies the addition of an extra DLT layer to manage the high volume of transactions associated with granular ReCert certificates.
- *Section 5* presents our proposed solution, encompassing GCs, DLT, blockchain, and VCs/VPs of SSI, all working in collaboration to support the claimed features of our proposed solution of the ReCert framework.

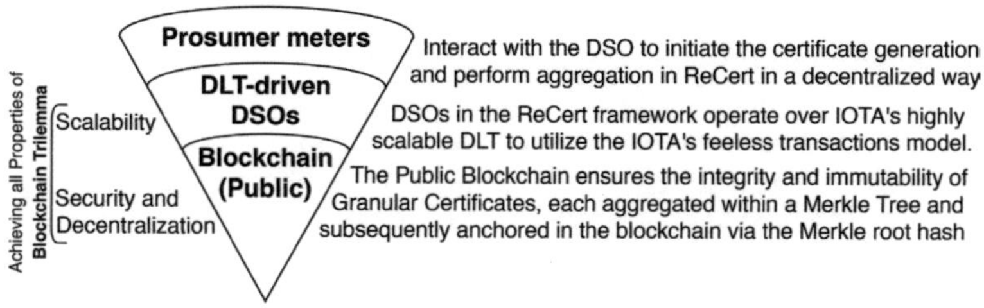

Figure 1.
Layered architecture of ReCert to solve the blockchain trilemma to handle the granular ReCert certificates.

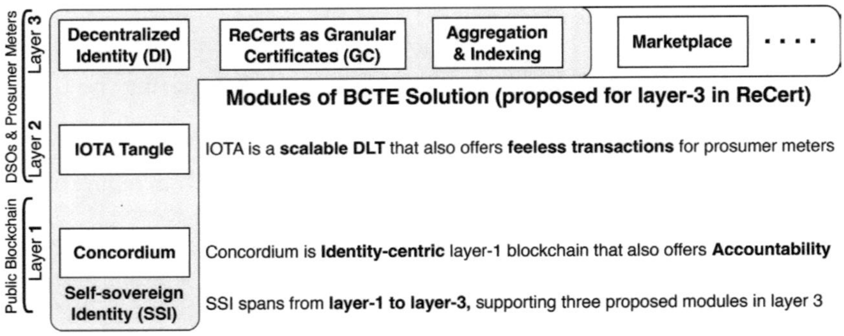

Figure 2.
ReCerts adopts a layered approach, wherein Layer 3 actively supports the integration of additional BCTE modules, further building upon the foundational functionalities of Layers 1 and 2.

- *Section 6* justifies the technologies adopted in our proposed solution of ReCert. It also shows the feasibility of our proposed solution as the foundational framework that can transform it into a fully decentralized BCTE solution.
- *Section 7* compares our work with relevant research studies and highlights our scholarly contributions compared to existing research efforts.
- *The last section* concludes this chapter and presents future research directions.

2. Need and significance of blockchain-enabled transactive energy

In this section, we highlight the significance of BCTE and outline the prerequisites for a foundational framework capable of evolving into a fully operational, decentralized BCTE solution. Our analysis delves into two specific scenarios to illustrate the varying degrees of effort needed to implement BCTE in developed and developing countries. For developed countries, we examine the ETT project operating across four European nations [6]: Denmark, Germany, Belgium, and Estonia. Regarding developing countries, we considered the case study of Pakistan to highlight the limitations of adopting BCTE and the different benefits we can achieve through this adoption in developing countries.

2.1 Use case of developed countries of Europe

The ETT project is a joint initiative of four TSOs: 50 Hertz from Germany, Elering from Estonia, Elia from Belgium, and Energinet from Denmark. Its main goal is to create a system for monitoring and tracing sustainable energy from its origin to its use. ETT has also introduced the concept of GCs to operate these at a fine-grained level to more accurately match the production and consumption of energy from renewable resources. The findings from the experimental study by ETT demonstrate the effectiveness of GCs in achieving the goal of more accurately measuring the generation of renewable energy [11].

ETT allows the registries (DSOs) to collect data on production and consumption certificates and aggregate these into Merkle trees while operating under centralized control. This centralization is the most significant limitation of ETT, as the centralized registries have complete control over the collection and aggregation of production and consumption data, which hinders its potential to serve as a foundational framework for a fully operational BCTE system [6]. To address this limitation, we propose to utilize the DLT of IOTA at the DSO level to enhance transparency in their operations while constructing Merkle trees [1]. ReCert goes one step further by utilizing edge computing [5] to perform this aggregation at the prosumer level. Researchers have already discussed the benefits of shifting this aggregation from DSO to the prosumers [4]. Hence, adapting ReCert concepts of aggregating certificates at the prosumer level improves decentralization and helps achieve a decentralized BCTE solution.

2.2 Use case of the developing country of Pakistan

After demonstrating the effectiveness of our proposed solution in achieving BCTE in developed countries, we now focus on its potential impact in developing countries, with a particular focus on Pakistan. Given the adoption challenges faced by such regions [12], we propose a phased integration of BCTE at a limited scale to deliver benefits tailored to the specific needs of developing countries. In this context, we have highlighted blockchain integration at the distribution transformer level of a DSO along with the associated benefits.

In Pakistan, the power grid consists of the National Grid Company (NGC) of NTDC, which operates a 220 kV and 500 kV transmission network connecting power generation plants throughout the country to various regional Distribution Companies (DISCOs) and K-Electric, a private company responsible for generation, transmission, and distribution. DISCOs manage a 132 kV sub-transmission network and a distribution network that operates at 11 kV and down to 400/230 V voltage levels. Consumers receive the energy/power from 132 kV substations via 11 kV feeders, which pass through one or more distribution transformers to step down the voltage for local use. In recent years, Pakistan has introduced net metering for prosumers; however, the current meters lack the real-time communication capabilities necessary for blockchain-based, prosumer-driven solutions [1, 4]. Hence, we can initiate blockchain integration at the distribution transformer level to address this limitation, reducing Pakistan's high distribution losses, currently at 17.4% [12], and offering a practical solution for developing countries with limited smart metering infrastructure. The government of Pakistan has already shown commitment to installing smart devices at distribution transformers for real-time data transmission, paving the way for transformer-driven BCTE solutions in developing countries like Pakistan.

2.3 Requirements for the foundational framework of BCTE

We have presented the need for two different levels of BCTE solutions. We proposed using a prosumer-driven BCTE framework in developed countries with smart meters installed at the household level and the transformer-driven BCTE solution for developing countries that lack smart meters at the consumer level. For clarity, we have confined this study to ReCert's prosumer-driven solution, and, as a future work, we can work on a different set of features to present another version of ReCert for the transformer-driven BCTE framework. Following are the five essential requirements that we have highlighted for a potential foundational framework that can set the cornerstone for a decentralized BCTE solution. Each of the following five points highlights one requirement, and each requirement points to the exact section or sub-section of this study where we address that requirement in our ReCert solution.

1. The foundational framework of BCTE must operate over the DI to adhere to the decentralization promise of BCTE. We propose achieving this requirement through SSI, which the upcoming Section 4 covers in detail.

2. The foundational framework of BCTE must manage the certificates at a fine-grained level along with the support of slicing and merging of certificates for matching the production and consumption level of individual prosumer meters, and for that, we have proposed the use of VCs/VPs of SSI to issue and verify certificates, respectively. Section 4 and sub-section 6.3 will provide more details of our proposed handling of this requirement.

3. The government agencies must have access to intervene by relating the real identities of stakeholders against their DIDs stored on the ledger to achieve better accountability in the BCTE. We proposed offering this feature through Concordium, as detailed in sub-section 6.1.

4. The registry must operate with the less operational cost of decentralization as it has to handle high throughput due to a massive number of requests from many prosumer meters. We propose using IOTA at the registry level to utilize its feeless transaction model, with further details presented in sub-Section 6.2.

5. The proposed framework must be flexible enough to evolve to a fully operational BCTE solution, and sub-Section 6.4 presents this extendable and evolutionary nature of our proposed solution to allow the transformation into a fully functional BCTE solution in the future.

3. Role of self-sovereign identity toward the realization of ReCert

SSI has emerged as the primary solution for decentralized identity implementation. Its functionality extends beyond identity management, offering features such as certificate management through VCs/VPs of SSI [13]. Additionally, SSI allows for the combination of multiple VCs to create a VP and partially includes a VC in different VPs [14]. Therefore, we advocate implementing BCTE over SSI. We have included the content of this section from our already published paper on the SSI-based proposed architecture [1] that provided the basis for understanding the role of SSI in offering the ReCert solution. Section 7 of the state-of-the-art compares our current study on ReCert with our two previously published papers [1, 4] on the same solution.

3.1 Root of trust (RoT) in public key infrastructure (PKI)

PKI is a foundational pillar in contemporary digital security, offering a structured mechanism for secure digital data exchange and communication. Central to PKI is employing a system encompassing digital certificates and keys administered by entities recognized as Certificate Authorities (CAs). This framework engenders a *Chain of Trust*, wherein each participating entity receives certification from a higher authority, culminating in a *Root CA*. The reliance within a PKI architecture is thus inherently placed on the operational integrity and security of these CAs. Nonetheless, this model intrinsically centralizes trust within a limited number of organizations, identified as *Root CAs*, thereby rendering the entire system susceptible to a singular point of failure. The compromise of a *Root CA* consequently jeopardizes the whole chain of trust of subordinate CAs. In juxtaposition to the imperative of decentralization in BCTE, the implicit trust characteristic of PKI signifies a dependency on centralized, authoritative bodies to validate and safeguard communications. Users and systems trust certificates disseminated by these CAs under the presumption of stringent verification processes. However, this trust model is increasingly being questioned in light of the complexity and magnitude of contemporary digital interactions, accentuating the necessity for more dispersed and robust trust frameworks, as discussed in the subsequent sub-section. Aligned with the traditional paradigms of PKI, the initiative of ETT [6] and the extant scholarly discourse surrounding it [9] rely on the principle of centralization through pre-trusted registries at DSOs.

The centralization in ETT aims to streamline the issuance and management of energy certificates by eliminating the transaction fees associated with a blockchain-based certification system. Entrusting these registries presupposes their operational integrity and security, simplifying the infrastructure and introducing potential vulnerabilities and avenues for security breaches. Although advantageous in terms of operational efficiency and management, this centralized trust model engenders apprehensions regarding the reliability and overall trustworthiness of the system. Within the sphere of energy certification, any compromise of these registries could have profound implications on the integrity of certification. It underscores the intrinsic limitation of implicit trust in the foundational framework [9], a compelling exploration into more decentralized and distributed trust models like the one proposed herein for prosumer-driven certification predicated on SSI.

3.2 SSI and its effectiveness in decentralized identity

The concept of SSI, as delineated in Preukschat and Reed [15], represents a fundamental shift in the paradigm governing the management of digital identities and trust mechanisms. SSI vests individuals with the autonomy to maintain and control their digital identities without relying on centralized authorities. This paradigm challenges the conventional centralized trust frameworks by facilitating individuals with the capability to generate and manage their credentials. These credentials can be verified autonomously, aligning with the principles of the zero-trust model. An elaborate illustration of the interactions among three critical entities within the SSI ecosystem—namely, the certificate issuer, the user, and the verifier—is provided in **Figure 3**.

Within the depicted workflow in **Figure 3**, the blockchain infrastructure accommodates two primary registries: The Verifiable Data Registry (VDR) [16] functions as a repository for all disseminated certificates, whereas the Revocation Registry (RR) [17] enables issuers to invalidate any certificate previously issued. In this context, the prosumer meter device represents the user, capable of orchestrating the Root of Trust through algorithmic and autonomic trust mechanisms, further expounded in subsequent sections. The workflow delineated in **Figure 3** unfolds as follows:

1. *Key generation and DID registration*: The initial step involves the issuer and the user independently generating their public-private key pairs. Subsequently, they

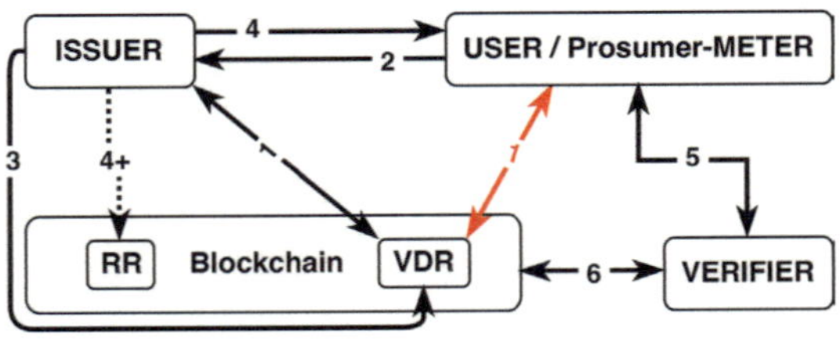

Figure 3.
Facilitation of SSI in self-certification of prosumer meters in our proposed solution of ReCert.

register their Decentralized Identifiers (DIDs) within the VDR, establishing a unique association between each DID and its corresponding public key.

2. *DID share for certificate issuance*: The user shares their DID with the issuer, a critical step that allows the issuer to tailor the certificate specifically to the user's DID, thereby ensuring a secure and personalized certificate issuance process.

3. *Creation of the Verifiable Credential (VC)*: The VC comprises the user's DID, verifiable claims, and the issuer's digital signature, among other pertinent information, encapsulating the user's credentials as authenticated by the issuer.

4. *Transmission of VC and revocation potential*: Following the VC's transmission to the user, the issuer retains the right to revoke the issued certificate at any given time, a capability represented by the dotted line in **Figure 3**.

5. *User-controlled privacy via VP*: The user is allowed to employ methodologies such as selective disclosure [18] or zero-knowledge proofs [19] to convert the VC into a VP. This transformation permits the user to dictate the privacy level of their data, enabling the disclosure of selective information to the verifier rather than the entirety of the VC's content.

6. *Verification by consulting RR and VDR*: In the final step, the verifier assesses the certificate's authenticity and validity by referencing both the RR and the VDR on the blockchain, ensuring the certificate's legitimacy and active status.

Figure 3 adeptly encapsulates the intricate yet coherent sequence of operations in the certificate issuance and verification process within the SSI framework, underpinned by blockchain technology. This methodology heralds a significant progression in digital identity management, offering heightened security, privacy, and user autonomy.

3.3 SSI and algorithmic trust (transactional roots of trust)

In the context of SSI, algorithmic trust, also known as the *Transactional Roots of Trust*, relies on cryptographic technologies to establish trust independently of institutional reputation. The security and integrity of algorithms create and verify this trust in digital credentials. For example, digital signatures, a critical component of SSI, provide a secure and tamper-evident way to establish the authenticity of digital information. In this model, trust is derived from the mathematical certainty of cryptographic operations, ensuring that credentials are genuine and untampered. This reliance on algorithmic trust represents a significant departure from traditional trust models, such as the *Administrative Roots of Trust* in PKI, where humans define the Root CA. Different machines collaboratively establish trust in the case of *Algorithmic Trust*. It offers a more secure and transparent approach to identity verification, free from the biases and vulnerabilities inherent in centralized systems. In an SSI framework, the authenticity of an individual's credentials is always verifiable through cryptographic means, providing a solid foundation for secure and trustworthy digital interactions even without relying on the issuers of the identities.

3.4 SSI and autonomic trust (self-certifying roots of trust)

Autonomic Trust delineated as the *Self-certifying Roots of Trust* within the domain of SSI, emerges as a crucial byproduct of the decentralized and autonomously managed nature of identities inherent to these systems. This paradigm grants each participant within the network the autonomy to manage their identity, credentials, and trust relationships independently. Such an approach engenders a dynamic and responsive trust model predicated upon direct, peer-to-peer interactions and the verifiable authenticity of credentials, thereby fostering an environment where entities can engage in transactions with enhanced confidence and security. It is primarily because each participant's identity and credentials can be independently verified, obviating the need for centralized authority. SSI demonstrates significant utility in dynamic and decentralized environments like prosumer energy networks. The capability of each participant to autonomously manage and present their credentials underpins a more fluid and responsive trust model. This model facilitates a system wherein trust is not perceived as static but evolves with each interaction, providing a robust and flexible framework for secure and efficient energy certification and transaction processes. It enables explicitly prosumer meters to generate the certificates as VCs to be forwarded to the corresponding registry and generate VPs to facilitate the verification of certificates, enhancing the overall trustworthiness and efficiency of the system.

3.5 SSI support in DLT of IOTA and blockchain of Concordium

Concordium is a public blockchain that focuses on maintaining identity information and offers support for SSI at the ledger level. However, there may be more cost-effective options for directly storing green energy certificates [9]. To address this, we have proposed an intermediary layer of DLT using IOTA Tangle [10]. The latest version of IOTA enables SSI implementation over the IOTA Tangle through its support for smart contracts [20]. Sub-sections 6.1 and 6.2 discuss the significance of selecting consortium and IOTA in our proposed ReCert solution, respectively.

4. Inherent limitations of blockchain due to its scalability trilemma

Figure 4 shows the shift from distributed databases to blockchain, ultimately leading to the development of DLT. This transition also highlights the similarity between the limitations posed by the CAP theorem in distributed databases and the scalability challenge of the blockchain trilemma [10]. Additionally, **Figure 4**

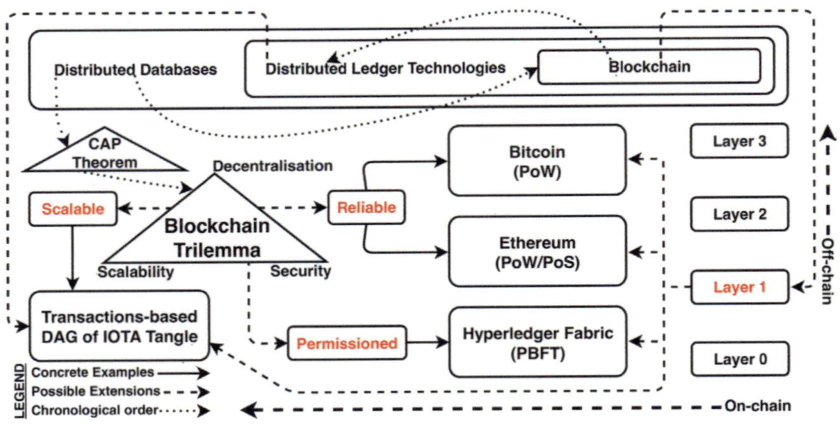

Figure 4.
Blockchain scalability trilemma that inspired us to introduce the DLT in our proposed solution.

presents two potential directions of on-chain and off-chain to address the blockchain trilemma. On-chain solutions employ ledger-driven approaches with various consensus algorithms to enhance scalability compared to traditional public blockchain platforms. Conversely, off-chain solutions are built upon existing layer-1 solutions to tackle the scalability issue presented by the blockchain trilemma. This section covers **Figure 4** in detail and lays a foundation for our hybrid solution, which we will cover in the upcoming section.

4.1 From distributed databases to distributed ledger technologies

A database constitutes an essential application that abstracts the operations related to data handling within a system. Due to exponential growth in data production capabilities, databases increasingly need to scale data and computational resources. We can address this difficulty through two distinct methodologies: vertical and horizontal scaling [21]. Vertical scaling pertains to enhancing the capabilities of the system hosting the database application. Nevertheless, this approach encounters limitations at a more substantial scale, necessitating the adoption of horizontal scaling to accommodate the escalating demands of data management. Horizontal scaling leverages multiple computing nodes to disperse the computational burden across several machines. Implementing horizontal scaling is relatively more straightforward for stateless applications, which solely necessitate the distribution of computational loads among various nodes. Conversely, this strategy presents significant challenges for stateful applications requiring a balance in computational and storage loads. Efforts in vertical scaling may also encompass code optimizations, particularly in the context of microservices or the transition to event-driven architecture, necessitating code modifications to achieve database-level horizontal scalability.

Horizontal scalability in Distributed Database Management Systems (DDMS) presents solutions that demand minimal or no alterations to the existing code as the database engine handles the distribution of load across multiple nodes of a distributed database. DDMS paved the way for blockchain technology, which we achieved by applying multiple constraints over the DDMS through a consensus mechanism. A conventional database facilitates four CRUD (Create, Read, Update, and Delete) operations, whereas a blockchain only supports the create and read functionalities.

Blockchain also enables the simulation of update operations by appending new values to the ledger where previous entries remain intact, preventing the replacement of existing values in the blockchain ledger.

Conceptually, a blockchain mirrors the data structure of a linked list, wherein data blocks are interconnected in a sequential chain and safeguarded via cryptographic hashes [22]. However, the advent of more complex data structures has led to the proposal of systems that emulate blockchain functionalities without using the linked list-like structure of the blockchain, and all these solutions are collectively known as Distributed Ledger Technologies (DLTs). For instance, IOTA employs the Directed Acyclic Graph (DAG) data structure instead of a linked list to offer functionalities analogous to those of blockchain systems. Since the DLTs evolved from the blockchain, we can refer to all blockchains as DLTs, but only some DLTs are blockchains because a DLT can only qualify to be termed the blockchain if it has the ledger based on the data structure of the link list.

4.2 From CAP theorem to blockchain trilemma

The conceptual framework illustrated in **Figure 4** delineates the CAP theorem [10], articulating three pivotal properties: Consistency, Availability, and Partition Tolerance. Although we can manifest these three attributes concurrently within centralized systems, distributed architectures face inherent limitations that preclude the simultaneous realization of all three. In distributed systems, a trichotomy emerges, allowing for the robust attainment of merely two CAP properties, thus necessitating a compromise on the third. This trichotomy, manifested as CA, CP, or AP pairs, significantly influences the operational dynamics of distributed applications. Consequently, the specific requisites of an application predominantly guide the strategic decision-making process regarding this compromise.

In blockchain, combining multiple transactions into a block before appending the block to the ledger is necessary. This process often requires additional time in the form of block confirmation time. The consensus algorithm oversees the creation of new blocks. It operates under the assumption that different participants may have differing opinions but can still agree on appending the same block to their ledgers. As a result, blockchain operates with the belief that participants must eventually have consistent views by not compromising on the consistency property of the CAP theorem. Therefore, we focus on the availability and partition tolerance of the CAP theorem in blockchain.

However, as pointed out by Vitalik Buterin, the co-founder of Ethereum, blockchain systems face a trilemma similar to the CAP theorem, where we can only fully optimize two properties out of security, scalability, and decentralization. Therefore, when designing blockchain-based solutions, we must consider the challenge of the blockchain trilemma, given in **Figure 4**. Following are the three broader categories for designing blockchain solutions while considering the limitations of the blockchain trilemma. Each of these categories compromises one of the three properties of the blockchain trilemma.

1. *Reliable blockchain solutions*: The pioneering blockchain consensus algorithm, PoW (Proof of Work), presents first-generation solutions by adhering to the *order-execute* paradigm. This model prioritizes transaction sequencing before their execution. PoW is the most secure blockchain consensus algorithm as it compromises on scalability to achieve security and decentralization. As shown in **Figure 4**,

bitcoin uses this consensus algorithm of PoW. Ethereum was initially based on the same consensus algorithm but later moved to the PoS (Proof of Stake) consensus algorithm to achieve a reliable system after compromising scalability [23].

2. *Permissioned blockchain solutions*: Hyperledger Fabric's permissioned blockchain employs the consensus algorithm of PBFT (Practical Byzantine Fault Tolerance) to compromise on decentralization and offer more scalable and privacy-enhanced centralized blockchain solutions. The Hyperledger Fabric framework initially introduced this approach, characterized by an *execute-order-validate* sequence where transactions are first executed and then forwarded to an orderer node for ordering the transactions in a block. It is against the conventional *order-execute-validate* paradigm of the popular blockchain solutions of Bitcoin and Ethereum.

3. *Scalable blockchain solutions*: The consensus mechanism underlying IOTA departs from conventional models by adopting a transactions-based DAG (Directed Acyclic Graph) to facilitate scalability and decentralization while conceding the security property of the blockchain trilemma. Designed to process numerous parallel IoT transactions, it departs from the conventional link list-like structure of the blockchain and introduces a tree-like structure that makes it a DLT and not a blockchain. Academic researchers and industry practitioners are continuously trying to address the challenges of the blockchain trilemma to optimize all three properties. The upcoming sub-sections elaborate on these solutions to address the blockchain trilemma limitation by categorizing them broadly into on-chain and off-chain solutions.

4.3 Layer-1 on-chain solutions to address the blockchain trilemma

Efforts to address the blockchain trilemma have led to creating different consensus mechanisms, each aimed at supporting a self-governing data ledger. These on-chain approaches that seek to overcome the trilemma's inherent challenges while maintaining an independent ledger are also known as layer- 1 blockchains. Projects such as Kaspa [24], operating as a layer-1 blockchain solution, assert that it can resolve the blockchain trilemma by removing the requirement for block finalization time [25] to achieve scalability while maintaining the existing properties of security and decentralization. **Figure 5** in sub-Section 6.1 provides more details on the block creation and the transaction confirmation time.

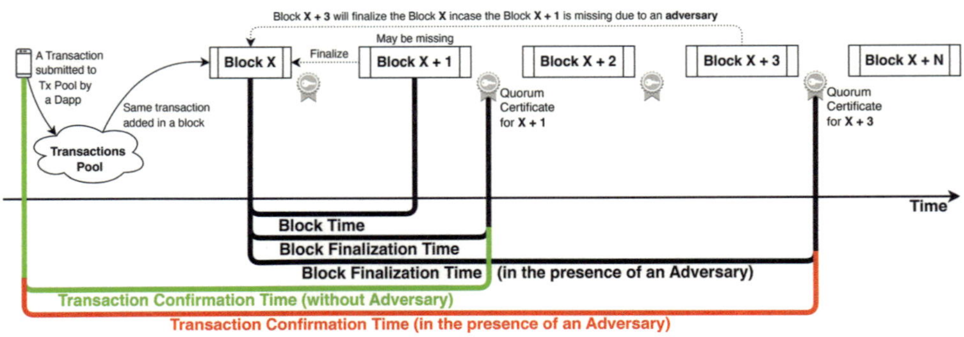

Figure 5.
Impact of an adversary on the transaction confirmation time.

4.4 Layer-2/Layer-3 off-chain solutions to address the blockchain trilemma

In addition to on-chain solutions, the blockchain ecosystem has seen the development of off-chain strategies that eliminate the necessity for a separate blockchain ledger. These solutions, known as layer-2 and layer-3 blockchains, leverage existing layer-1 solutions without maintaining their independent ledgers. Layer-2 solutions focus on enhancing the scalability of public blockchains that have already prioritized decentralization and security. In contrast, layer-3 solutions are customized for specific applications and use cases, expanding upon the capabilities of layer-2 frameworks.

4.5 Our proposed hybrid approach following both on-chain and off-chain

Our proposed solution of ReCert combines on-chain and off-chain strategies to tackle the blockchain trilemma. We can introduce scalability into the equation by integrating Concordium's public blockchain's decentralized and secure framework with the IOTA tangle's scalable solution. These projects operate as layer-1 blockchains, maintaining independent ledgers as the on-chain solution. However, we have combined them in a layered approach similar to off-chain solutions, allowing IOTA to operate over the underlying layer of Concordium to leverage the security and decentralization of the public blockchain solution. Additionally, we have introduced two proposed modules of the BCTE foundational framework as layer-3 blockchain solutions, as depicted in **Figure 2**. Despite their distinct functionalities, SSI is the connecting bond among all three layers. We give more details of our proposed solution in sections 5 and 6.

5. Proposal of ReCert framework and ReCert certificates

This section presents an overview of the ReCert framework, which combines Concordium's public blockchain for reliability, security, and decentralization with the scalability and feeless transactions offered by the DLT of IOTA. The VCs and VPs of SSI play an integral role in bridging these two layer-1 blockchain platforms. Besides being a layer-1 solution, IOTA acts as a layer-2 solution using the underlying Concordium blockchain as its layer-1 counterpart. This section also explains the interaction patterns of four key entities, each playing a critical role in ensuring the integrity and verification of ReCert certification. We have also presented the life cycle of a ReCert certificate and the crucial role of SSI and Merkle tree in realizing the stated goals of the ReCert framework.

5.1 Key entities in the ReCert framework

The following four entities collaborate to operate the proposed framework of ReCert successfully.

5.1.1 Advanced prosumer meters

These devices represent the forefront of smart home technology, equipped with the capability to produce green energy via solar panels. We focus on the cutting-edge prosumer meters developed by Develco Products [26], transcending traditional electricity consumption metrics. These meters can differentiate the source of electricity,

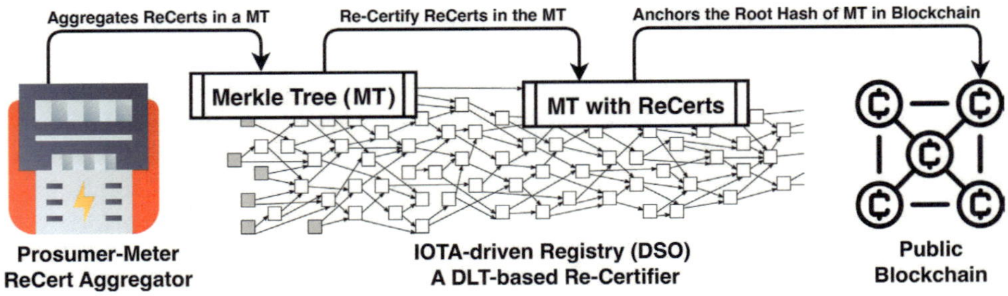

Figure 6.
The proposed solution of ReCert framework based on the DLT of IOTA and the public blockchain of Concordium.

discerning between grid-supplied and solar-generated energy at prosumer locations. Such distinction is paramount for the automated issuance of green energy certificates, as delineated in **Figure 6**. By transmuting these certificates into digital currency, we aim to substantially mitigate incidents of greenwashing, thereby providing a more genuine reflection of green energy contributions.

5.1.2 Energy distribution registries/DSOs

These entities oversee electricity distribution within their jurisdictions and serve as DSOs. A predominant challenge involves distinguishing electricity's origin once it mixes into the distribution network. A proposed remedy involves labeling energy at its inception; however, traditional methodologies heavily rely on the registries' integrity for green energy labeling, contradicting BCTE's promise. Consequently, ReCert advocates adopting DLT-driven registries to cultivate transparency and reinforce trust within the energy distribution framework.

5.1.3 Public blockchain ledger

We envisage this ledger as the single source of truth within our framework. Establishing a direct linkage between energy production sources and the public blockchain incurs operational overhead. To tackle this challenge, we introduce an intermediary DLT layer, based explicitly on the feeless transactional model of IOTA Tangle, to bridge many green energy sources with the public blockchain. This methodology is particularly advantageous for prosumers, given their numerical superiority over larger green energy producers like solar farms or wind turbines.

5.1.4 Auditors/verifiers

These entities are instrumental in incentivizing green energy production, aiming to eradicate greenwashing practices—the deceptive claim of green energy utilization for obtaining incentives. Our architecture leverages blockchain technology as the single source of truth, effectively nullifying the participation of entities engaged in greenwashing. The blockchain exclusively acknowledges data from the registries, originating at the prosumer meters, thereby decentralizing trust from central registries to the end-users.

Figure 7.
Lifecycle of a ReCert certificate.

5.2 Lifecycle of a ReCert certificate

We have proposed the ReCert framework for the ReCert certificates, and **Figure 7** shows the crucial stages of the lifecycle of a ReCert certificate. Each ReCert holder (prosumer meter) gets the ReCert certificate as a VC of SSI. It can transfer the ownership of a ReCert certificate by issuing a VC to the other prosumer meters or can claim the benefits of a ReCert certificate by presenting it as a VP of SSI that ends up the retirement of an already issued ReCert certificate. We have already explained this whole lifecycle of a ReCert certificate in our published paper [4].

5.3 ReCert certificates and SSI

The ReCert framework proposes implementing SSI at the prosumer meters to issue ReCert certificates and record energy distribution in an IOTA-driven registry (DSO). The prosumer meters can collect the stored certificates in bulk to aggregate in a Merkle tree and forward them to the registry that anchors the Merkle tree within the Concordium blockchain after the Re-Certification [4]. The energy attributes are first converted into verifiable claims and forwarded to the registries that store those claims in the form of VCs of SSI. Prosumer meters can collect the stored VCs from the registries to convert them into VPs of SSI and aggregate those in the Merkle trees before forwarding those Merkle trees for Re-Certification to the corresponding registry. In this way, the concepts of VCs and VPs of SSI play an integral role in issuing and verifying ReCert certificates stored in the Merkle tree's data structure, explained in the upcoming sub-section.

5.4 Merkle tree-based aggregation of ReCert certificates

The Merkle tree data structure is a crucial component of the ReCert framework, which has already been explained in our foundational paper [1]. Merkle tree utilizes a hierarchical node system, where each leaf node represents the hash of a ReCert certificate, and each non-leaf node is a hash of its child nodes. This structure enables efficient and secure certificate verification and maintains the entire dataset's integrity through its root hash. The root hash serves as a sensitive indicator for detecting changes in data, making the Merkle tree an ideal choice for our ReCert framework, where rapid verification and unwavering data integrity are required.

6. ReCert as a foundational framework for fully functional BCTE

In the last section, we explained how the main components of the proposed ReCert framework work. In contrast, this section describes the significance of the selection of technologies proposed for implementing the framework and certificates of ReCert. At the framework level, we justified the choice of Concordium and IOTA for implementing the ReCert framework. For the certificates, we explained the significance of selecting the SSI for the ReCert certificates. This section also highlights the potential for our proposed solution to develop and grow into a fully functional BCTE.

6.1 Importance of Concordium blockchain as a single source of truth

Concordium is the first blockchain to inherently support decentralized identity at the ledger level. It also offers accountability through a feature that reveals the original identity of users upon government intervention. As a result, Concordium's public blockchain can serve as a crucial single source of truth for implementing a fully operational country-wide BCTE solution. **Figure 5** shows the transaction confirmation time in the latest upgrade to the Concordium consensus algorithm. When there is no adversary, the transaction confirmation time is typically very fast, as it only needs the generation of one new block to verify the previous block, allowing us to run a fully operational BCTE on the Concordium blockchain effectively. In the case of an adversary, it needs the issuance of two consecutive legitimate blocks to verify the previous blocks that were not able to be verified due to the missing blocks due to the presence of an adversary.

In **Figure 5**, if there is no adversary, the consensus algorithm of Concordium will be able to finalize the transaction placed in block X after issuing the Quorum certificate against block X + 1. This issuance of a Quorum certificate verifies the legitimate generation of block X + 1. However, if an adversary produces block X + 1, the algorithm will not issue the Quorum certificate against that block, flagging block X + 1 as a missing block. In that case, the same transaction of block X gets finalized after the issuance of the Quorum certificate for block X + 3, as the issuance of two consecutive blocks (X + 2 and X + 3) finalizes all the non-finalized transactions placed in the already issued blocks in the Concordium ledger.

6.2 Role of IOTA in handling a large number of prosumer meter transactions

We propose a prosumer-centric solution that operates over numerous prosumer meters, generating a high volume of transactions of granular ReCert certificates. The feeless model of IOTA is ideal for managing this large number of transactions without incurring additional operational costs in transaction fees. However, the DLT of IOTA relies on the identity management features of the Concordium blockchain. Therefore, we utilize the IOTA ledger as a short-term backup for constructing the Merkle tree. Once we have successfully anchored a Merkle tree in Concordium's public blockchain, we can remove the older nodes of the duplicate certificates from the IOTA Tangle to reduce the operational costs at the registry level.

6.3 Importance of SSI to support granular ReCert certificates

Our recommended solution operates at the fine-grained level to align with the operational capabilities of the household prosumer meters. Selecting technology that supports the slicing and merging of certificates is crucial. Since the SSI allows splitting a single VC into multiple VPs and merging multiple VCs into a single VP, it can support our stated aim of operating the granular ReCert certificates at the fine-grained level. Issuers have utilized NFTs and SFTs to issue and manage the GC, but neither supports the slicing feature. Therefore, we propose using SSI-based certificates to manage the granular certificates of ReCert in the ReCert framework.

6.4 Potential to evolve ReCert into a fully operational BCTE solution

Figure 2 illustrates the architecture of the ReCert framework, which has a hierarchical structure across three layers. Public blockchain technology underpins the foundational layer, serving as the single source of truth for BCTE. The intermediary layer (Layer Two) uses the DLT, specifically tailored to scale for the enormous number of transactions originating from the BCTE. Although the current version of ReCert utilizes the DLT of IOTA, an optimized BCTE-specific solution might replace IOTA, depending on its economic viability, operational cost-effectiveness, and inherent scalability, to meet the extensive transactional needs of BCTE.

Layer 3 in **Figure 2** necessitates comprehensive developmental efforts, given its critical role in augmenting the BCTE infrastructure with additional modules essential for expanding the feature set of BCTE. Consequently, the foundational layer mandates minimal alterations, whereas the third layer is subject to extensive modifications to facilitate the integration of more BCTE modules. Although the secondary layer addresses the difficulties of extant BCTE modules within the third layer, evolving requirements prompted by incorporating new modules may require introducing a more optimized solution at layer two.

7. State of the art

This study covers the third iteration of our proposed ReCert solution. In the first version [1], we introduced the concept of an IOTA-driven registry to replace the existing centralized registries. However, the feature of aggregating the green energy certificates remained confined to the IOTA-driven registry, which we shifted to the prosumer meters in the second version [4] of ReCert. This study presents the third iteration of our proposed solution that covers the potential of the ReCert framework to act as a foundational framework, with the potential to evolve into a fully operational, decentralized BCTE framework.

In green energy certificate issuance, the existing methodology currently involves using Non-Fungible Tokens (NFTs) and Semi-NFTs [1]. These tokens are typically associated with fixed assets. However, recent advancements in SSI technology have demonstrated its superiority in handling flexible assets, as opposed to the rigidity of NFTs [27]. Our research focuses on issuing sliceable granular ReCerts [9], which inherently requires a flexible approach, resulting in preferring the SSI over NFTs and SFTs. This decision also aligns with our goal of facilitating a more adaptable and decentralized way of managing ReCerts.

Our research builds upon the concepts introduced in a recent publication [9], which set the foundation for issuing sliceable green energy certificates with improved privacy measures. However, this approach relies solely on pre-trusted registries to issue the certificates, which may not be the most reliable method. The *Verra Scandal* report [28] exposed that a significant organization certified over 90% of rainforest carbon offsets as worthless. As a result, we have proposed a fully decentralized alternative that utilizes a DLT at the registry level and involves prosumer meters in the certificate generation process to enhance reliability through decentralization. Our approach also draws inspiration from two additional studies [7, 29].

Studies	Prosumer-driven	Smart meter	SSI	NFTs	Hybrid	Merkle tree	Nature of registry
ReCert	✓	✓	✓	—	✓	✓[a]	IOTA-based Decentralized
[9]	—	—	—	—	—	✓	Pre-trusted (no blockchain)
[7]	—	✓	—	✓	—	✓	Multichain-based Consortium
[29]	✓	—	✓	—	—	✓	Blockchain-based Decentralized

[a]*Our proposed hybrid approach utilizes both blockchain and DLT at layer-1 and layer-2 respectively.*

Table 1.
Comparative analysis of our proposed solution with the relevant research studies.

These papers demonstrate the use of blockchain technology at the registry level and employ the data structure of a Merkle tree for issuing green energy certificates. We designed our system to support prosumers in electricity generation and consumption, drawing inspiration mainly from [29]. This paper also inspired our proposal for SSI-based green energy certificate issuance and verification. Moreover, the concept of smart meters in our framework draws influence from research on REC [7].

We compared our proposed solution with the three mentioned papers that inspired us to lead to our proposed solution, and our proposed framework stands out by offering a hybrid model that combines DLT and blockchain for issuing and verifying green energy certificates. This hybrid approach allows us to integrate the strengths of both DLT and blockchain into a cohesive system. Consequently, our solution operates without transaction fees at the registry level, powered by DLT, while necessitating only a one-time transaction fee for anchoring the developed Merkle tree in Concordium's public blockchain.

Table 1 compares ReCert's solution with relevant papers, showing that all the papers share the common feature of the Merkle tree. However, the hybrid approach of utilizing blockchain and DLT is specific to the ReCert only. Each related paper also shares one additional feature, chosen from the following: *Prosumer-driven*, *Smart Meter*, and *SSI*-based certificates, as listed in **Table 1**.

8. Conclusion and future work

This study presents an evolutionary ReCert framework designed to operate the granular ReCert certificates originating and aggregated by the prosumers. The significance of our proposed ReCert framework is its ability to evolve and serve as a foundation for a next-generation, fully operational, decentralized BCTE framework. The ReCert framework enhances the overall security and reliability of the system without incurring substantial operational costs. This enhancement is realized by integrating SSI principles for bolstering security, incorporating DAG-based IOTA Tangle for feeless transactions, and utilizing the public Concordium blockchain as a single source of truth for the anchored ReCert certificates.

As a future work, we are implementing a testbed to perform the quantitative analysis of the proposed ReCert solution. The existing versions of the ReCert solution

[1, 4] have performed the qualitative analysis of the ReCert and have discussed the technical and architectural choices made on a theoretical level. Through comprehensive experimental investigations, the pivotal quantitative analysis phase helps refine and enhance the ReCert solution, thereby priming it for pragmatic deployment within real-world scenarios. This progression signifies a stride toward establishing an encompassing blockchain-based energy transaction ecosystem, resonating with the objectives articulated in the IEEE's position paper on BCTE [3]. Hence, our proposed framework signifies a seminal step toward the groundwork for the evolution of a fully functional BCTE solution [3].

The quantitative analysis will help improve layers 1 and 2 of the ReCert framework presented in **Figure 2**. For the improvements in layer 3, we suggest the addition of new modules that can transform ReCert into a decentralized BCTE framework. For example, adding a marketplace module in the third layer of the ReCert framework and transforming SSI-based ReCert certificates into an interoperability standard can enable the global trading of green energy certificates that are currently tradable only within geographical boundaries [4].

Acknowledgements

This work was funded by the Innovation Fund Denmark project GreenCOM with project number J. nr. 2079-00040B.

Author details

Saqib Rasool* and Rune Hylsberg Jacobsen
Department of Electrical and Computer Engineering, Aarhus University, Aarhus, Denmark

*Address all correspondence to: saqibrasool@gmail.com

References

[1] Rasool S, Saleem A, ul Haq MI, Jacobsen RH. Towards zero trust security for prosumer-driven verifiable green energy certificates. In: 7th International Conference on Energy Conservation and Efficiency (ICECE). IEEE; 2024. pp. 1-6

[2] Afzal M, Li J, Amin W, Huang Q, Umer K, Ahmad SA, et al. Role of blockchain technology in transactive energy market: A review. Sustainable Energy Technologies and Assessments. 2022;**53**:102646

[3] Rahimi F et al. IEEE Blockchain Transactive energy (BCTE) a bridge to a democratized energy marketplace. IEEE; 2021. Available from: https://blockchain.ieee.org/verticals/transactive-energy

[4] Rasool S, Jacobsen RH. REC to ReCert: Introducing Re-certification to empower prosumer-driven certificate aggregators. In: 15th International Conference on Smart Grid Communications, Control, and Computing Technologies (SmartGridComm). IEEE; 2024

[5] Rasool S, Saleem A, Iqbal M, Dagiuklas T, Bashir AK, Mumtaz S, et al. Blockchain-enabled reliable osmotic computing for cloud of things: Applications and challenges. IEEE Internet of Things Magazine. 2020;**3**(2):63-67

[6] Rehtla KL, Piron M, Andersen MH. Energy track and trace: Architectural concepts and insights. Energy Track and Trace. 2022

[7] Zuo Y. Tokenizing renewable energy certificates (RECs)—A Blockchain approach for REC issuance and trading. IEEE Access. 2022;**10**:134477-134490

[8] Yao S, Liu Y, Shi X. Suppliers' corporate social responsibility efforts with greenwashing concerns: Can Blockchain help? IFAC-PapersOnLine. 2022;**55**(10):1986-1991

[9] Jokumsen M, Pedersen TP, Daugaard MS, Tschudi D, Madsen MW, Wisbech T. Verifiable proofs for the energy supply chain: Small proofs brings you a long way. Energy Informatics. 2023;**6**(Suppl 1):28

[10] Rasool S, Iqbal M, Li S, Dagiuklas T, Ghosh S. Security, privacy, and Trust of Distributed Ledgers Technology. In: Blockchains: Empowering Technologies and Industrial Applications. Wiley Online Library; 2023. pp. 91-116

[11] Rehtla KL, Piron M, Andersen MH. Energy track and trace: System benefits of granular certification. Energy Track and Trace. 2022

[12] Nazir L, Sharifi A. An analysis of barriers to the implementation of smart grid technology in Pakistan. Renewable Energy. 2024;**220**:119661

[13] Mühle A, Grüner A, Gayvoronskaya T, Meinel C. A survey on essential components of a self-sovereign identity. Computer Science Review. 2018;**30**:80-86

[14] Qi Y, Zhang J, Zhang H. Research on presentation generation method of credential selective disclosure in self-sovereign identity. In: International Conference on Computing, Control and Industrial Engineering. Springer; 2023. pp. 705-718

[15] Preukschat A, Reed D. Self-sovereign identity. Manning Publications; 2021

[16] De Salve A, Maesa DDF, Mori P, Ricci L, Puccia A. A multi-layer trust

framework for self sovereign identity on blockchain. Online Social Networks and Media. 2023;**37**:100265

[17] Guggenberger T, Kühne D, Schlatt V, Urbach N. Designing a cross-organizational identity management system: Utilizing SSI for the certification of retailer attributes. Electronic Markets. 2023;**33**(1):3

[18] Kyriakidou CDN, Papathanasiou AM, Polyzos GC. Decentralized identity with applications to security and privacy for the internet of things. Computer Networks and Communications. 2023;**1**(2):244-271

[19] Dieye M, Valiorgue P, Gelas JP, Diallo EH, Ghodous P, Biennier F, et al. A self-sovereign identity based on zero-knowledge proof and blockchain. IEEE Access. 2023;**11**:49445-49455

[20] Bolgouras V, Angelogianni A, Politis I, Xenakis C. Trusted and secure self-sovereign identity framework. In: Proceedings of the 17th International Conference on Availability, Reliability and Security. ACM; 2022. pp. 1-6

[21] Rasool S, Iqbal M, Dagiuklas T, ul Qayyum Z, Mian AN. Towards reliable computation offloading in mobile ad-hoc clouds using blockchain. In: Broadband Communications, Networks, and Systems: 9th International EAI Conference, Broadnets 2018, Faro, Portugal, September 19-20, 2018, Proceedings 9. Springer; 2019. pp. 180-188

[22] Rasool S, Saleem A, Iqbal M, Dagiuklas T, Mumtaz S, ul Qayyum Z. Docschain: Blockchain-based IoT solution for verification of degree documents. IEEE Transactions on Computational Social Systems. 2020;**7**(3):827-837

[23] Rasool S, Iqbal M, Dagiuklas T, Ul-Qayyum Z, Li S. Reliable data analysis through blockchain based crowdsourcing in mobile ad-hoc cloud. Mobile Networks and Applications. 2020;**25**:153-163

[24] Bajra UQ, Rogova E, Avdiaj S. Cryptocurrency Blockchain and its Carbon Footprint: Anticipating Future Challenges. Technology in Society. Elsevier; 2024. p. 102571

[25] Daugaard TV, Jensen JB, Kauffman RJ, Kim K. Blockchain solutions with consensus algorithms and immediate finality: Toward Panopticon-style monitoring to enhance anti-money laundering. Electronic Commerce Research and Applications. 2024;**65**:101386

[26] Develco Products. Prosumer Meter - Develco Products; 2023. Available from: https://www.develcoproducts.com/products/meter-interfaces/prosumer-meter/ [Accessed: 30 December 2023]

[27] Zeydan E, Mangues J, Arslan S, Turk Y. Blockchain-based self-sovereign identity solution for vehicular networks. In: 2023 19th International Conference on the Design of Reliable Communication Networks (DRCN). IEEE; 2023. pp. 1-7

[28] Guardian. Revealed: More than 90% of Rainforest Carbon Offsets by Biggest Certifier Are Worthless; 2023. Available from: https://www.theguardian.com/environment/2023/jan/18/revealedforest-carbon-offsets-biggest-providerworthless-verra-aoe [Accessed: 30 December 2023]

[29] Ferdous MS, Cali U, Halden U, Prinz W. Leveraging self-sovereign identity & distributed ledger technology in renewable energy certificate ecosystems. Journal of Cleaner Production. 2023;**422**:138355

Chapter 8

Next-Generation Behavioral Economics: Blockchain as the Web3 Infrastructure for Experimental Studies

Luyao Zhang

Abstract

This chapter presents a research perspective that explores the transformative impact of blockchain technology on Behavioral and Experimental Economics. It addresses critical digital challenges such as subject identity verification and privacy, trust in researchers, and the design of experimental incentives. By advocating for a blockchain-integrated framework, the chapter aims to enhance data authenticity, privacy, and incentivization through decentralized mechanisms and smart contracts, thereby ensuring research that is transparent, tamper-proof, and practical. Additionally, the chapter proposes a paradigm shift toward a "play to learn" model, which bridges decentralized science with the realm of gaming finance to advance research and development. This integration signals a new era of interdisciplinary research, offering profound insights into human behavior within the digital economy and illuminating new research pathways that connect Web2 to Web3 environments.

Keywords: blockchain, behavioral experiments, Web3 infrastructure, GameFi, DeSci

1. Introduction

This chapter explores the transformative potential of blockchain technology in refining behavioral experiments, which serve as foundational methodologies in economics research and policymaking. Behavioral experiments have been instrumental in elucidating complex economic theories, as underscored by the seminal contributions of Nobel laureates such as Kahneman and Smith [1], and Thaler [2]. In an age where the World Wide Web has greatly expanded the scope of online interactions, innovative platforms like oTree [3], built on Python's versatile programming capabilities, have become critical in facilitating behavioral experiments across various contexts. oTree's advancement from its predecessor zTree [4] is notable for its internet-based deployment capabilities, eliminating the need for a shared local network and utilizing Python, a widely-used open-source programming language. This shift has democratized the accessibility of experiments, allowing them to be run on a variety of devices with internet browsers, thus broadening the potential reach and diversity of experimental subjects.

Yet, oTree and similar online experiment platforms confront challenges unique to the digital era, for instance, verifying participant identities robustly, assuring data privacy [5, 6], and mitigating the rising threat of automated bots [7, 8], especially prevalent in online recruitment. Blockchain technology offers a compelling solution to these issues, providing a framework for secure and authentic data collection [9].

This chapter, from a research perspective, proposes a blockchain-integrated approach aimed at enhancing the field of behavioral experiments by introducing enhanced privacy, reliability, and efficiency. At the heart of this framework lie decentralized identity mechanisms, which provide a way to verify individuals' identities and ensure the privacy of data without the need for third-party services [10]. Smart contract technology, defined as self-executing contracts with the terms directly written into code, ensures that experimental protocols are conducted transparently and are safeguarded against tampering [11]. Furthermore, the tokenization of digital assets [12]—the process of converting rights to an asset into a digital token on a blockchain—revolutionizes the way participants are compensated, providing unmatched security and setting a new standard for efficiency in experimental economics.

Building on these technical advancements, the chapter advocates for a paradigm shift, drawing inspiration from the "play to earn" [13] phenomenon in blockchain gaming, where participants gain real-world rewards for their virtual achievements. It proposes a "play to learn, research, and innovate" ethos, leveraging blockchain's capabilities to enhance behavioral experiments with gamification. This approach aims to foster significant progress in research and development by encouraging players to engage in strategic decision-making within game theory environments, transcending beyond the allure of short-term online game rewards. This strategy serves as a nexus between the DeSci (Decentralized Science) [14] and GameFi (Gaming Finance) domains, where DeSci champions open, decentralized scientific collaboration and GameFi integrates gaming with blockchain's financial mechanisms. By intertwining gamification with DeSci and deepening the complexity and sustainability of GameFi, this initiative seeks to cultivate a mutually beneficial ecosystem for both spheres. Such interdisciplinary collaboration is poised to have a substantial, bidirectional influence, driving societal progress through the embracement of cutting-edge, enduring technologies.

In essence, the incorporation of blockchain into experimental economics signifies the dawn of a new interdisciplinary era, catalyzing innovative studies that transcend conventional economic paradigms. By adopting this integrated approach, researchers are poised to unveil novel insights into human behavior, AI integration, and the burgeoning digital economy, leading to economic systems that are more adaptable, transparent, and attuned to human values. Section 2 delves into the challenges encountered in experimental economics with current methodologies and the prospective solutions offered by leveraging blockchain technology as foundational infrastructure. Section 3 expands on how next-generation behavioral economics, built upon the Web3 infrastructure, can lead to broader impacts across interdisciplinary fields.

2. The challenge and the solution

The development of experimental economics has been profoundly influenced by the tools and methodologies available to researchers. In this context, Charness, Jabarian, and List [15] highlight the transformative role of Large Language Models

(LLMs) in revolutionizing experimental economics. They explain how LLMs can significantly enhance experimental design, streamline implementation processes, and refine data analysis techniques. These advancements facilitate the development of more precise and efficient research methodologies.

Despite the valuable insights provided by traditional methods into human economic behavior, they pose certain methodological challenges. This section focuses on three pivotal areas: Subject Identity and Privacy, Trust in Researchers, and Experimental Incentives. It aims to delve into the complexities and challenges that pervade the contemporary experimental landscape. Moreover, it provides a deeper understanding of the obstacles researchers face and discusses the potential solutions offered by Blockchain as the Web3 infrastructure for experimental studies, as illustrated in **Figure 1**.

2.1 Subject identity and privacy

2.1.1 The challenges

In experimental economics, the challenge of striking a balance between the accurate verification of subjects' identities for research purposes and the protection of their privacy and personal data is paramount. Traditional experimental frameworks, whether conducted in lab settings or through online platforms, often necessitate the collection of personal information from participants. This reliance on centralized data management systems not only poses significant risks to subjects' privacy but also potentially influences their behavior due to concerns about anonymity and data security [16]. Such practices can compromise the authenticity of their decision-making processes [17] and raise substantial ethical concerns regarding the confidentiality and consent of the participants [18, 19].

As shown in **Figure 2**, the main issues related to subject identity and privacy in human behavior economy include:

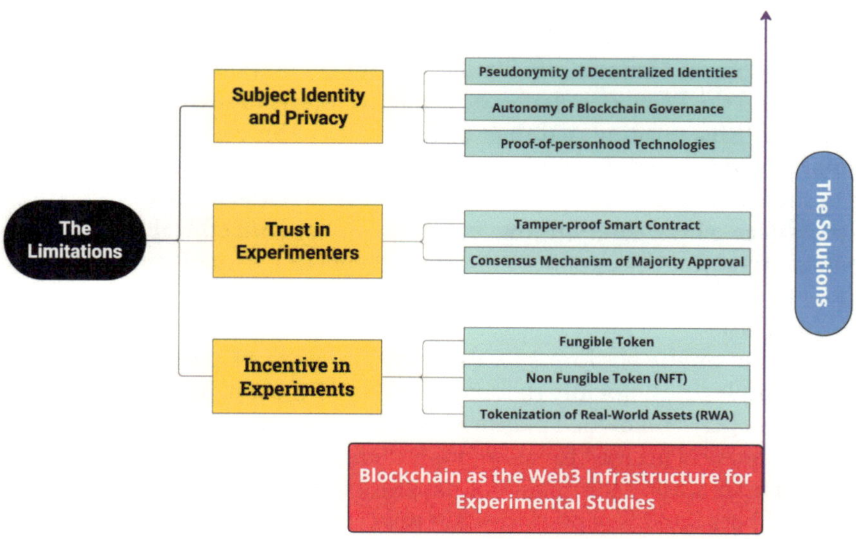

Figure 1.
The Limitations and the Solutions: Blockchain as the Web3 Infrastructure for Experimental Studies.

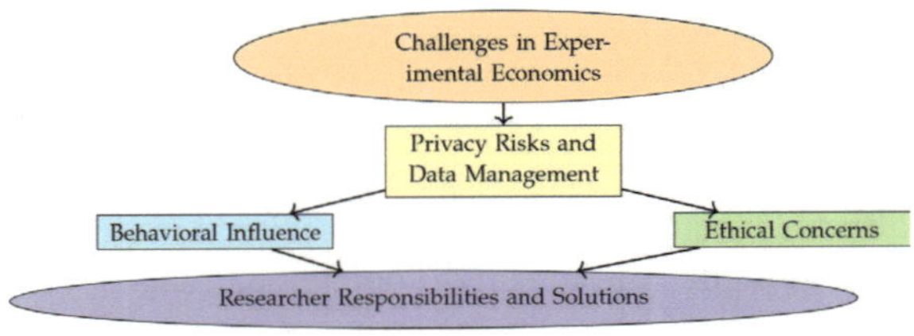

Figure 2.
Diagram of Challenges and Solutions in Experimental Economics.

- *Privacy Risks and Data Management*: The collection of personal information poses significant risks to subjects' privacy. Reliance on centralized data management systems increases the potential for data breaches and unauthorized access. Decentralized systems and advanced encryption methods are necessary to mitigate these risks.

- *Behavioral Influence*: Concerns about anonymity and data security can potentially influence participants' behavior. Participants who fear their data might be compromised may alter their responses, leading to less authentic data collection.

- *Ethical Concerns*: Practices can compromise the authenticity of decision-making and raise ethical concerns regarding confidentiality and consent. Ensuring participants' data is handled ethically is critical to maintaining trust and integrity in research.

Researchers face the responsibility of upholding ethical standards, which involves comprehensive training in Institutional Review Board (IRB) protocols, the filing of detailed applications, and the careful handling of sensitive information. "Regulating Creativity: Research and Survival in the IRB Iron Cage" [20] critiques the IRB system's broadening scope to include social sciences and humanities, resulting in an unwieldy bureaucracy that can hinder or even halt research, thereby impacting academic freedom and innovation. Similarly, Heimer and Petty's "Bureaucratic Ethics: IRBs and the Legal Regulation of Human Subjects Research" [21] evaluates the efficacy of IRBs, positing that their evolution into a bureaucratic entity often supplants refined professional ethics with inflexible, context-unaware regulations, failing to sufficiently address the nuances of ethical research practices. Tackling these issues necessitates solutions that not only comply with ethical standards and ensure data privacy but also reduce red tape and encourage innovation through the decentralization of decision-making within the IRB framework and the automation of procedural tasks.

The advent of online platforms for experimental research has introduced additional complexities, notably the susceptibility of these platforms to attacks by automated bots [22]. Renowned platforms such as Amazon Mechanical Turk and Craigslist, frequently utilized for anonymous online experiments, have experienced challenges in maintaining the quality of data for human subject research [23]. The infiltration of bots into these platforms not only jeopardizes the validity of the experimental data but also exacerbates the concerns regarding privacy and data security.

DOI: http://dx.doi.org/10.5772/intechopen.1006740

2.1.2 The solutions

Blockchain technology offers a transformative approach to addressing the challenges of subject identity verification and privacy within experimental economics. The core principles of blockchain, including its cryptographic foundation, play a pivotal role in enabling pseudonymity—an inherent feature that allows participants to engage in economic experiments without revealing their true identities [24, 25]. This pseudonymity is achieved through the use of cryptographic techniques such as hash functions and public-private key encryption, which secure transactions and data on the blockchain while masking the real-world identities of the participants.

To streamline the IRB process using blockchain technology, we propose a structured blockchain governance approach that consists of proposing, voting, and enacting changes in an automated, decentralized, and transparent manner [26, 27]. Initially, a proposal for an IRB protocol change or decision is submitted on the blockchain network. This could involve new ethical guidelines, consent forms, or research protocols. The decentralized nature of blockchain allows for a wider and more diverse set of stakeholders, including researchers, ethicists, and potentially even participants, to review and vote on these proposals. Votes are cast using blockchain's secure and transparent ledger system, ensuring that every vote is recorded and immutable. Once a proposal receives the necessary approval based on predefined criteria, it is automatically enacted through smart contracts. These smart contracts are self-executing contracts with the terms of the agreement directly written into lines of code [28]. The key features of this blockchain governance process—automation, decentralization, and transparency—ensure that IRB decisions are made efficiently, free from the undue influence of centralized authorities, and are visible to all stakeholders involved. This not only enhances the agility and responsiveness of the IRB system but also reinforces trust and accountability in ethical research practices.

To mitigate bot infiltrations in online experimental platforms, we can integrate blockchain with advanced technologies like biometric verification, CAPTCHAs, and digital identity systems to enhance the Know Your Customer (KYC) process for creating decentralized identities on blockchain networks tailored for research, coined as proof-of-personhood [29, 30]. Such integrations introduce a robust security layer, ensuring the engagement of authentic human participants in experiments. For instance, in a blockchain-based experimental setup, individuals might undergo a biometric verification step or resolve a CAPTCHA as part of their decentralized identity creation, effectively filtering out bots and maintaining the integrity of experimental data. Furthermore, blockchain ensures the authenticity and integrity of the collected data by maintaining a secure and immutable ledger of all transactions and interactions within the system. This immutable nature of blockchain means that once data is recorded, it cannot be altered without consensus from the network, thus safeguarding against fraudulent manipulation and ensuring the credibility of the experimental data. Additionally, blockchain's transparent audit trail allows for the verification of data provenance and integrity, which is crucial for upholding the ethical standards of experimental research.

In **Figure 3**, we classify the existing solutions based on the challenges identified in Section 2.1.1:

In summary, by harnessing the cryptographic underpinnings and automated processes of blockchain technology, researchers in experimental economics can conduct studies with enhanced privacy, authenticity, and integrity of data. This not only boosts participant engagement and data quality but also allows researchers to focus

Privacy Risks and Data Management

- Utilizing cryptographic techniques such as hash functions and public-private key encryption to secure participant identities.
- Enabling pseudonymity through blockchain to protect participant identities while ensuring data security.
- Ensuring the immutability and transparency of data through blockchain's secure ledger, preventing fraudulent manipulation and verifying data provenance.

Behavioral Influence

- Implementing blockchain governance for automated, decentralized, and transparent proposal, voting, and enactment of IRB decisions.
- Enhancing privacy and data security to alleviate concerns that might influence participant behavior, ensuring more authentic data collection.

Ethical Concerns

- Integrating biometric verification, CAPTCHAs, and digital identity systems within blockchain to ensure authentic human participation and uphold ethical standards.
- Ensuring the ethical handling of participants' data by maintaining a secure, immutable ledger and transparent audit trails, reinforcing trust and accountability in research.

Figure 3.
Classification of existing solutions based on the challenges identified in Section 2.1.1.

more on scientific exploration rather than being bogged down by data management and security concerns. Through the strategic integration of blockchain with other advanced technologies, the field can effectively mitigate the risks posed by automated bots, further ensuring the reliability and ethical integrity of online experimental platforms. However, future research should also be aware of the current limitations and governance and ethical issues of the blockchain infrastructure [31, 32].

2.2 Trust in experimenters

2.2.1 The challenges

Trust in the experimental framework and the researchers conducting the study is a fundamental aspect of experimental economics. Trust problems in experimental economics primarily revolve around the assurance that experiments are conducted fairly, participant data is managed ethically, and results are reported accurately. These aspects are essential for the validity of experimental findings.

As illustrated in **Figure 4**, in current systems and platforms used in experimental economics, several trust issues are prevalent:

1. *Integrity of Experimenters*: Participants may doubt the integrity of the experimenters or the fairness of the implementation process. For instance, the litera-

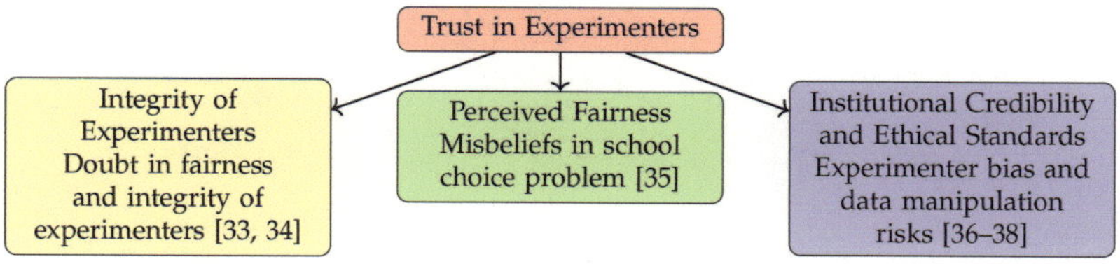

Figure 4.
Trust issues in experimental economics, highlighting the challenges related to the integrity of experimenters, perceived fairness, and institutional credibility and ethical standards.

ture indicates that participants may not behave truthfully—even when it is in their best interest according to the experimental rules—if they doubt the integrity of the experimenters [33, 34].

2. *Perceived Fairness*: A common scenario illustrating this issue is the school choice problem, where applicants are informed that requesting financial support will not influence their admission chances, which are based solely on academic merit. Despite this, many applicants believe that foregoing financial support will enhance their chances by financially benefiting the schools, thereby giving them an edge in the admission process [35].

3. *Institutional Credibility and Ethical Standards*: In traditional research settings, trust is usually built through institutional credibility, transparent communication, and adherence to ethical standards. However, experimenter bias—often referred to as the "demand effect" [36]—along with risks of inadvertent protocol deviations or data manipulation, continually threatens this trust. These issues can distort experimental results, as documented in both laboratory [37] and field studies [38].

2.2.2 The solutions

Blockchain technology, celebrated for its transparency and immutability, provides a robust foundation to foster trust in experimental economics [39]. This section provides comprehensive details on each solution, focusing on technical aspects, contributions, and limitations.

1. *Smart Contracts*: As in **Figure 5**, at the core of blockchain technology are smart contracts—programmable protocols that execute automatically once predetermined conditions are fulfilled [40]. By integrating the rules and protocols of an experiment within these smart contracts, blockchain significantly diminishes the risk of human error or bias during the implementation phase.

- *Technical Contributions*: The use of smart contracts ensures that experimental protocols are strictly adhered to without manual intervention, reducing the risk of protocol deviations. They also automate the execution of experimental rules, enhancing the consistency and reliability of experiments.

- *Limitations*: The complexity of designing and implementing smart contracts can be high, requiring specialized knowledge in blockchain programming [41]. Additionally, smart contracts are only as good as the conditions and rules they encode; any oversight in their design can lead to unintended consequences [42–45].

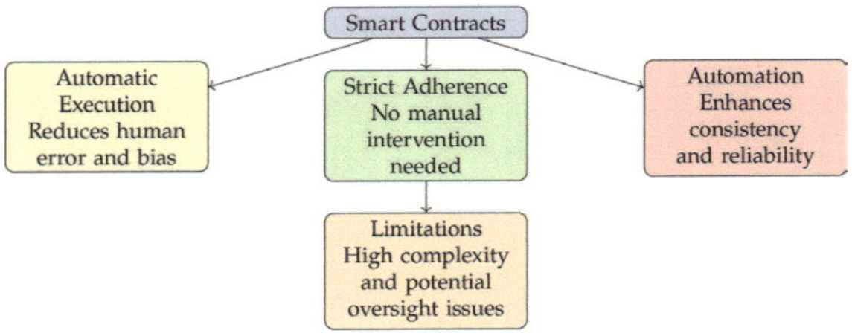

Figure 5.
Illustration of the benefits and limitations of smart contracts, highlighting automatic execution, strict adherence, automation, and potential limitations.

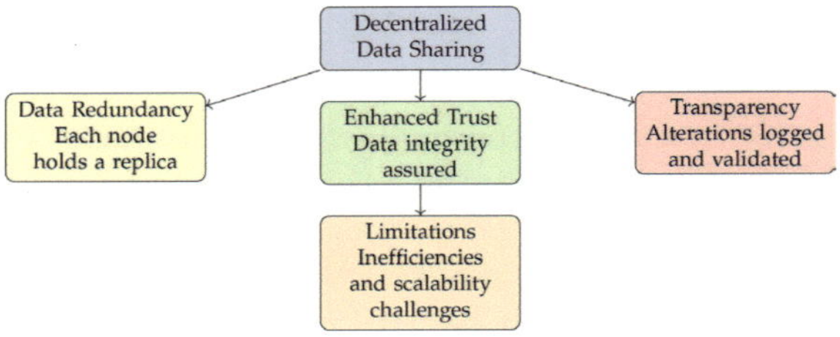

Figure 6.
Illustration of decentralized data sharing, showing the benefits of data redundancy, enhanced trust, and transparency, as well as potential limitations.

2. *Decentralized Data Sharing*: As in **Figure 6**, blockchain's architecture facilitates a transparent data-sharing environment in a decentralized system. Each node in this network holds a replica of all de-identified on-chain data, ensuring data redundancy and reliability.

- *Technical Contributions*: The decentralized nature of blockchain ensures that data is not controlled by a single entity, enhancing trust in data integrity. Any alteration to the data records is transparently logged and necessitates validation through a consensus mechanism, typically involving majority approval from the network's participants [46]. This rigorous level of transparency enables subjects to independently assess the fairness and integrity of the experimental process.

- *Limitations*: The decentralized model can lead to inefficiencies, such as slower transaction processing times [47, 48] and higher computational costs, potentially resulting in scalability challenges [49] and negative impacts on sustainability [50, 51]. Moreover, emerging literature on the measurement of blockchain decentralization raises concerns about centralization in the actual usage and applications of blockchain infrastructure [52–57].

3. *Enhanced Participant Confidence*: As in **Figure 7**, blockchain's transparency and immutability foster greater confidence among participants in the validity of research outcomes.

- *Technical Contributions*: Blockchain provides an immutable record of all transactions and interactions within the experimental system. This audit trail allows for the verification of data provenance and integrity, which is crucial for upholding the ethical standards of experimental research.

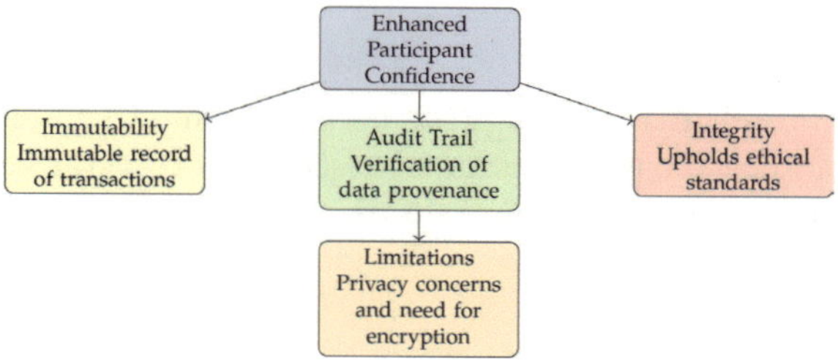

Figure 7.
Illustration of enhanced participant confidence, showing the benefits of immutability, audit trails, and integrity, as well as potential limitations.

- *Limitations*: While blockchain enhances transparency, it may also introduce privacy concerns [58]. Ensuring that participant data remains de-identified and secure is paramount, but it requires robust encryption and privacy-preserving mechanisms [59].

In summary, by harnessing the cryptographic underpinnings and automated processes of blockchain technology, researchers in experimental economics can conduct studies with enhanced privacy, authenticity, and integrity of data. This not only boosts participant engagement and data quality but also allows researchers to focus more on scientific exploration rather than being bogged down by data management and security concerns. Through the strategic integration of blockchain with other advanced technologies, the field can effectively mitigate the risks posed by automated bots, further ensuring the reliability and ethical integrity of online experimental platforms.

2.3 Incentives in experiments

2.3.1 The challenges

The design and implementation of incentive mechanisms play a pivotal role in experimental economics, significantly shaping participants' engagement and decision-making processes [60–63]. These mechanisms, whether monetary or non-monetary, are essential for eliciting behaviors that reflect genuine economic decisions in controlled settings. Traditional incentive structures face numerous challenges related to distribution logistics, customization to individual participant needs, and their relevance to real-world economic contexts [64]. These limitations can hinder the effectiveness of incentives, reducing participants' motivation and potentially impacting the ecological validity of the experimental findings [65]. To address these issues, recent studies have suggested innovative approaches to improve the alignment between experimental incentives and real-world economic behaviors. For example, Rosenboim and Shavit [65] propose a 'prepaid incentive mechanism' that mimics real-world financial transactions more closely, potentially enhancing participant engagement by making the stakes more relatable and immediate. Additionally, Voslinsky and Azar [66] discuss the effectiveness of varying incentive types and their timing (e.g., paying for all rounds or only one round in multi-round experiments), which can significantly influence decision-making processes and outcomes. These advancements underscore the need for continuous refinement of incentive mechanisms to ensure their effectiveness in eliciting genuine economic behaviors in experimental settings.

2.3.2 The solutions

The advent of blockchain technology has heralded a significant innovation in experimental economics: the tokenization of assets. This transformative process facilitates the creation of complex and customizable incentive schemes, categorized into three primary types of digital tokens: Fungible Tokens, Non-Fungible Tokens (NFTs), and Tokenization of Real-World Assets (RWA) as in **Figure 8**.

Fungible Tokens: Representing digital assets that are interchangeable, fungible tokens often possess an established exchange rate with fiat currencies [67]. These tokens can be exchanged for fiat at various cryptocurrency exchanges or used to acquire real-world assets in markets that accept cryptocurrency. This token type enables the alignment of monetary rewards in experimental settings with real-world economic transactions, offering a detailed and flexible reward structure.

Non-Fungible Tokens (NFTs): NFTs are unique digital assets that denote ownership of specific items or rights within an experimental context [68]. Available for auction on NFT marketplaces, these tokens allow participants to realize the monetary value of their rewards. Moreover, NFTs can function as Proof-of-Attendance, serving as digital certificates, intellectual property rights, or tokens of honor [69], which prove invaluable in research focused on social recognition, creative industries, and Research and Development (R&D).

Tokenization of Real-World Assets (RWA): This category encompasses tokens that digitally represent tangible real-world assets, enabling experimental economists to integrate actual asset values into their research [70]. RWA includes diverse types such as Decentralized Physical Infrastructure Networks (DePin) [71], which tokenize physical infrastructure assets, alongside other platforms that tokenize real estate, commodities, art, and intellectual property. These tokens significantly enhance the correlation between experimental behaviors and real-world economic activities, embedding physical asset-based rewards within the experimental framework.

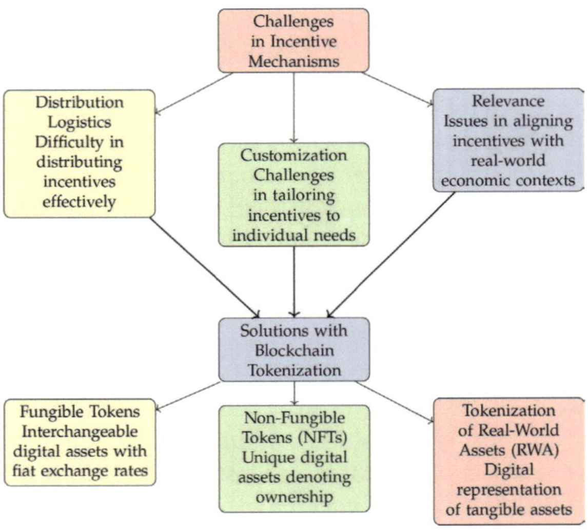

Figure 8.
Challenges in incentive mechanisms and the corresponding solutions through blockchain tokenization, illustrating the issues in distribution logistics, customization, and relevance, and how fungible tokens, NFTs, and tokenization of real-world assets can address these challenges.

Cryptoassets have empowered new financial investment opportunities on the blockchain infrastructure with trillions of market cap [72–78]. By utilizing these digital tokens, experimental economists are equipped to devise intricate incentive models that closely mirror the complexities of human economic behavior, thus enhancing the ecological validity and relevance of research findings. Such progressive approaches to incentive design are pivotal in deepening our understanding of economic decision-making processes and translating experimental results into actionable economic policies and strategies. The precision and adaptability provided by these tokenization methods not only facilitate more realistic and engaging experimental environments but also empower researchers to examine the nuanced impacts of real asset values and market dynamics within controlled experimental settings.

3. The broader impacts: an interdisciplinary approach

The integration of blockchain technology into experimental economics not only refines existing methodologies but also significantly expands research horizons, fostering an interdisciplinary approach that intersects with various domains. This section examines the role of blockchain as a foundational element of the Web3 infrastructure, catalyzing transformative changes across diverse fields. Notably, it impacts areas such as gaming finance (GameFi) [79] and decentralized science (DeSci) [14, 80, 81], enhancing human-AI interactions and facilitating a seamless transition from Web2 to Web3 paradigms. This exploration underscores blockchain's potential to revolutionize the landscape of research and development across multiple scientific and economic sectors as illustrated in **Figure 9**.

3.1 Turn GameFi into DeSci

GameFi, a synergy of "gaming" and "finance," leverages blockchain technology to merge gaming with decentralized financial mechanisms, thereby enabling players to earn real-world economic rewards in the form of crypto tokens through

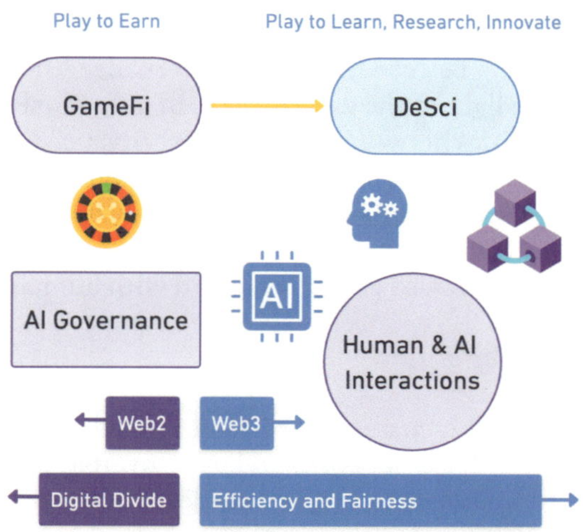

Figure 9.
The Broader Impacts: An Interdisciplinary Approach.

gameplay [79]. While this integration offers substantial benefits by compensating users for their engagement and actions within games, it also presents challenges such as the risk of addiction and potential manipulation and exploitation of users [82].

In response to these challenges, we advocate for the integration of GameFi with decentralized science (DeSci) [14, 80, 81]. This proposal aims to transform GameFi platforms into experimental laboratories where economic behaviors can be meticulously studied within gamified environments. This innovative approach not only facilitates the collection of extensive datasets on human economic behavior but also democratizes the participation in scientific research, allowing gamers and non-academics alike to contribute to scientific advancements through their gameplay. Moreover, transitioning from a "play to earn" to a "play to learn, research, and innovate" model under the DeSci framework provides participants with not only immediate financial incentives but also long-term intellectual and professional development.

Furthermore, the inherent transparency and immutability of blockchain technology provide accurate and verifiable record-keeping, which significantly enhances the reliability and reproducibility of the data collected from these virtual labs. This dual strategy promotes a more ethical and sustainable model within GameFi and positions it as a credible and valuable tool for scientific research and innovation, particularly in the fields of behavioral game theory [83] and mechanism design [84]. This integration heralds a new paradigm in research that bridges the gap between theoretical economic studies and applied gaming finance.

3.2 Human-AI interaction as piot study

The domain of human-AI interaction provides a rich arena for blockchain-enabled experimental studies, particularly as AI technologies increasingly permeate economic decision-making processes. Blockchain technology offers a secure and transparent platform for conducting pilot studies that examine the interactions between humans and AI agents across various economic scenarios. These scenarios range from automated market trading [85–87] to collaborative problem-solving in resource allocation [88–90].

These experiments are invaluable as they illuminate the dynamics of trust, collaboration, and competition between human participants and AI. They provide critical insights into how AI systems can be tailored to align with human values and economic goals, addressing key concerns in AI governance [91–94]. This research is crucial, particularly in light of the existing gaps in individual and strategic decision-making capabilities between even the most advanced generative AI and humans [95–99]. Moreover, the immutable record of interactions and decisions that blockchain facilitates provides a robust dataset for analyzing economic behaviors in human-AI interactions, contributing significantly to the development of AI systems that are not only effective but also ethically aligned with human interests.

3.3 Connect Web2 to Web3

The transition from Web2, characterized by centralized internet services, to Web3, marked by decentralized networks and user sovereignty [100], presents a complex landscape of challenges and opportunities for experimental economics. Blockchain technology is pivotal in this transition, providing a critical bridge that facilitates the integration of traditional web platforms [101] with the decentralized ecosystem of Web3 [31].

By leveraging blockchain, researchers can conduct comprehensive experiments across both Web2 and Web3 environments, examining the comparative impacts of centralized versus decentralized economic mechanisms on participant behavior [102]. This integration not only enriches the experimental landscape with diverse data sources and testing environments but also deepens our understanding of decentralization's implications for economic theory and practice. These studies are instrumental in informing the design of future digital economies, ensuring that they are founded on principles that promote fairness, transparency, and inclusivity, and are equipped to bridge rather than widen the digital divide [103].

In conclusion, the integration of blockchain technology into experimental economics marks a new frontier for interdisciplinary research, enabling innovative studies that transcend traditional economic paradigms. By embracing this interdisciplinary approach, researchers can uncover new insights into human behavior, AI integration, and the evolving digital economy, paving the way for economic systems that are more efficient, fair, and aligned with human values.

Acknowledgements

Luyao Zhang is supported by the National Science Foundation China on the project entitled "Trust Mechanism Design on Blockchain: An Interdisciplinary Approach of Game Theory, Reinforcement Learning, and Human-AI Interactions (Grant No. 12201266)". The author acknowledges the use of ChatGpt for language polishing of the manuscript.

Notes/thanks/other declarations

I would like to acknowledge the pioneering scholars in behavioral and experimental economics, including Profs. Gary Charness, Chun-Lei Yang, and John List for their invaluable inspiration.

Author details

Luyao Zhang
Duke Kunshan University, Suzhou, China

*Address all correspondence to: lz183@duke.edu

References

[1] Altman M. The Nobel prize in behavioral and experimental economics: A contextual and critical appraisal of the contributions of Daniel Kahneman and Cernon Smith. Review of Political Economy. 2004;**16**(1):3-41

[2] Earl PE, Richard H. Thaler: A nobel prize for behavioural economics. Review of Political Economy. 2018;**30**(2):107-125

[3] Chen DL, Schonger M, Wickens C. oTree—An open-source platform for laboratory, online, and field experiments. Journal of Behavioral and Experimental Finance. 2016;**9**:88-97

[4] Fischbacher U. Z-tree: Zurich toolbox for ready-made economic experiments. Experimental Economics. 2007;**10**(2):171-178

[5] Acquisti A, Brandimarte L, Loewenstein G. Privacy and human behavior in the age of information. Science. 2015;**347**(6221):509-514

[6] Harborth D, Pape S. Investigating privacy concerns related to mobile augmented reality apps–a vignette based online experiment. Computers in Human Behavior. 2021;**122**:106833

[7] Ahler DJ, Roush CE, Sood G. The micro-task market for lemons: Data quality on Amazon's mechanical Turk. Political Science Research and Methods. 2019:1-20

[8] Mason W, Suri S. Conducting behavioral research on Amazon's mechanical Turk. Behavior Research Methods. 2012;**44**(1):1-23

[9] Yu Y, Li Y, Tian J, Liu J. Blockchain-based solutions to security and privacy issues in the internet of things. IEEE Wireless Communications. 2018;**25**(6):12-18

[10] Ferdous MS, Chowdhury F, Alassafi MO. In search of self-sovereign identity leveraging blockchain technology. IEEE Access. 2019;**7**:103059-103079

[11] Chen YH, Chen SH, Lin IC. Blockchain based smart contract for bidding system. In: 2018 IEEE International Conference on Applied System Invention (ICASI). IEEE; 2018. pp. 208-211. Available from: https://ieeexplore.ieee.org/document/8394569

[12] Wang G, Nixon M. SoK: Tokenization on blockchain. In: Proceedings of the 14th IEEE/ACM International Conference on Utility and Cloud Computing Companion. 2021. pp. 1-9. Available from: https://dl.acm.org/doi/10.1145/3492323.3495577

[13] Vidal-Tomás D. The new crypto niche: NFTs, play-to-earn, and metaverse tokens. Finance Research Letters. 2022;**47**:102742

[14] Ding W, Hou J, Li J, Guo C, Qin J, Kozma R, et al. DeSci based on Web3 and DAO: A comprehensive overview and reference model. IEEE Transactions on Computational Social Systems. 2022;**9**(5):1563-1573

[15] Charness G, Jabarian B, List JA. Generation Next: Experimentation with Ai. National Bureau of Economic Research; 2023

[16] Scarpi D, Pizzi G, Matta S. Digital technologies and privacy: State of the art and research directions. Psychology & Marketing. 2022;**39**(9):1687-1697

[17] Liu B, Wei L. Unintended effects of open data policy in online behavioral research: An experimental investigation of participants' privacy concerns and research validity. Computers in Human Behavior. 2023;**139**:107537

[18] Phillips T. Ethics of field experiments. Annual Review of Political Science. 2021;**24**(1):277-300

[19] McDermott R, Hatemi PK. Ethics in field experimentation: A call to establish new standards to protect the public from unwanted manipulation and real harms. National Academy of Sciences of the United States of America. 2020;**117**(48):30014-30021

[20] Bledsoe CH, Sherin B, Galinsky AG, Headley NM. Regulating creativity: Research and survival in the IRB iron cage. Northwestern University Law Review. 2007;**101**:593

[21] Heimer CA, Petty J. Bureaucratic ethics: IRBs and the legal regulation of human subjects research. Annual Review of Law and Social Science. 2010;**6**:601-626

[22] Lu L, Neale N, Line ND, Bonn M. Improving data quality using Amazon mechanical Turk through platform setup. Cornell Hospitality Quarterly. 2022;**63**(2):231-246

[23] Chen AT, Komi M, Bessler S, Mikles SP, Zhang Y. Integrating statistical and visual analytic methods for bot identification of health-related survey data. Journal of Biomedical Informatics. 2023;**144**:104439

[24] Kosba A, Miller A, Shi E, Wen Z, Papamanthou C. Hawk: The blockchain model of cryptography and privacy-preserving smart contracts. In: 2016 IEEE Symposium on Security and Privacy (SP). IEEE; 2016. pp. 839-858

[25] Raikwar M, Gligoroski D, Kralevska K. SoK of used cryptography in blockchain. IEEE Access. 2019;**7**:148550-148575

[26] Lumineau F, Wang W, Schilke O. Blockchain governance—A new way of organizing collaborations? Organization Science. 2021;**32**(2):500-521

[27] Kiayias A, Lazos P. SoK: Blockchain governance. In: Proceedings of the 4th ACM Conference on Advances in Financial Technologies. 2022. pp. 61-73

[28] Almasoud AS, Hussain FK, Hussain OK. Smart contracts for blockchain-based reputation systems: A systematic literature review. Journal of Network and Computer Applications. 2020;**170**:102814

[29] Borge M, Kokoris-Kogias E, Jovanovic P, Gasser L, Gailly N, Ford B. Proof-of-personhood: Redemocratizing permissionless cryptocurrencies. In: 2017 IEEE European Symposium on Security and Privacy Workshops (EuroS&PW). IEEE; 2017. pp. 23-26

[30] Ford B. Identity and personhood in digital democracy: Evaluating inclusion, equality, security, and privacy in pseudonym parties and other proofs of personhood. arXiv preprint arXiv:201102412. 2020

[31] Quan Y, Wu X, Deng W, Zhang L. Decoding social sentiment in dao: A comparative analysis of blockchain governance communities. arXiv preprint arXiv:231114676. 2023

[32] Liu Y, Zhang L. The economics of Blockchain governance: Evaluate liquid democracy on the internet computer. arXiv preprint arXiv:240413768. 2024

[33] Rosenfeld A, Hassidim A. Too smart for their own good: Trading truthfulness

for efficiency in the Israeli medical internship market. Judgment and Decision Making. 2020;**15**(5):727-740

[34] Zhang L. Bounded Rationality and Mechanism Design. 2018. Available from: http://rave.ohiolink.edu/etdc/view?acc_num=osu1532692312980569

[35] Hassidim A, Romm A, Shorrer RI. The limits of incentives in economic matching procedures. Management Science. 2021;**67**(2):951-963

[36] De Quidt J, Haushofer J, Roth C. Measuring and bounding experimenter demand. American Economic Review. 2018;**108**(11):3266-3302

[37] Krawczyk M. "Trust me, I am an economist." a note on suspiciousness in laboratory experiments. Journal of Behavioral and Experimental Economics. 2015;**55**:103-107

[38] Riach PA, Rich J. Deceptive field experiments of discrimination: Are they ethical? Kyklos. 2004;**57**(3):457-470

[39] Lo SK, Xu X, Chiam YK, Lu Q. Evaluating suitability of applying blockchain. In: 2017 22nd International Conference on Engineering of Complex Computer Systems (ICECCS). IEEE; 2017. pp. 158-161

[40] Mohanta BK, Panda SS, Jena D. An overview of smart contract and use cases in blockchain technology. In: 2018 9th International Conference on Computing, Communication and Networking Technologies (ICCCNT). IEEE; 2018. pp. 1-4

[41] Zhang LS. The design principle of blockchain: An initiative for the sok of soks. arXiv preprint arXiv:230100479. 2023

[42] He D, Deng Z, Zhang Y, Chan S, Cheng Y, Guizani N. Smart contract vulnerability analysis and security audit. IEEE Network. 2020;**34**(5):276-282

[43] Fu Y, Zhuang Z, Zhang L. Ai ethics on blockchain: Topic analysis on twitter data for blockchain security. In: Science and Information Conference. Springer; 2023. pp. 82-100

[44] Zhang L. Machine learning for blockchain: Literature review and open research questions. In: NeurIPS 2023 AI for Science Workshop. 2023

[45] Huang J, Huang K, Jackson K, Zhang L, Toren J. Web3 and AI security. In: Web3 Applications Security and New Security Landscape: Theories and Practices. Springer; 2024. pp. 153-179

[46] Lashkari B, Musilek P. A comprehensive review of blockchain consensus mechanisms. IEEE Access. 2021;**9**:43620-43652

[47] Liu Y, Lu Y, Nayak K, Zhang F, Zhang L, Zhao Y. Empirical analysis of eip-1559: Transaction fees, waiting times, and consensus security. In: Proceedings of the 2022 ACM SIGSAC Conference on Computer and Communications Security. 2022. pp. 2099-2113

[48] Zhang L, Zhang F. Understand waiting time in transaction fee mechanism: An interdisciplinary perspective. arXiv preprint arXiv:230502552. 2023

[49] Sanka AI, Cheung RC. A systematic review of blockchain scalability: Issues, solutions, analysis and future research. Journal of Network and Computer Applications. 2021;**195**:103232

[50] Schinckus C. The good, the bad and the ugly: An overview of the sustainability of blockchain technology. Energy Research & Social Science. 2020;**69**:101614

[51] Fu Y, Jing M, Zhou J, Wu P, Wang Y, Zhang L, et al. Quantifying the Blockchain trilemma: A comparative analysis of Algorand, Ethereum 2.0, and beyond. arXiv preprint arXiv:240714335. 2024

[52] Zhang L, Ma X, Liu Y. Sok: Blockchain decentralization. arXiv preprint arXiv:220504256. 2022

[53] Ao Z, Horvath G, Zhang L. Is decentralized finance actually decentralized? A social network analysis of the Aave protocol on the Ethereum blockchain. arXiv preprint arXiv:220608401. 2022

[54] Zhang Y, Chen Z, Sun Y, Liu Y, Zhang L. Blockchain network analysis: A comparative study of decentralized banks. In: Science and Information Conference. Springer; 2023. pp. 1022-1042

[55] Chemaya N, Cong LW, Jorgensen E, Liu D, Zhang L. Uniswap daily transaction indices by network. arXiv preprint arXiv:231202660. 2023

[56] Xiao Y, Deng B, Chen S, Zhou KZ, Lc R, Zhang L, et al. "Centralized or decentralized?": Concerns and value judgments of stakeholders in the non-fungible tokens (NFTs) market. Proceedings of the ACM on Human-Computer Interaction. 2024;**8**(CSCW1):1-34

[57] Yan T, Li S, Kraner B, Zhang L, Tessone CJ. Analyzing reward dynamics and decentralization in Ethereum 2.0: An advanced data engineering workflow and comprehensive datasets for proof-of-stake incentives. arXiv preprint arXiv:240211170. 2024

[58] Peng L, Feng W, Yan Z, Li Y, Zhou X, Shimizu S. Privacy preservation in permissionless blockchain: A survey. Digital Communications and Networks. 2021;7(3):295-307

[59] Augusto A, Belchior R, Correia M, Vasconcelos A, Zhang L, Hardjono T. SoK: Security and privacy of Blockchain interoperability. In: 2024 IEEE Symposium on Security and Privacy (SP). IEEE Computer Society; 2024. pp. 234-234

[60] Smith VL. Experimental economics: Induced value theory. The American Economic Review. 1976;**66**(2):274-279

[61] Azrieli Y, Chambers CP, Healy PJ. Incentives in experiments: A theoretical analysis. Journal of Political Economy. 2018;**126**(4):1472-1503

[62] Grove WA, Wasserman T. Incentives and student learning: A natural experiment with economics problem sets. American Economic Review. 2006;**96**(2):447-452

[63] Kamenica E. Behavioral economics and psychology of incentives. Annual Review of Economics. 2012;**4**(1):427-452

[64] Ochoa-Mora AG. Human behavior in response to incentives and opportunity costs : Experimental method. Tamansiswa Management Journal International. 2021

[65] Rosenboim M, Shavit T. Whose money is it anyway? Using prepaid incentives in experimental economics to create a natural environment. Experimental Economics. 2012;**15**:145-157

[66] Voslinsky A, Azar OH. Incentives in experimental economics. Journal of Behavioral and Experimental Finance. 2021;**30**:100483

[67] Cong LW, Xiao Y. Categories and functions of crypto-tokens. The Palgrave

Handbook of FinTech and Blockchain. 2021:267-284

[68] Kugler L. Non-fungible tokens and the future of art. Communications of the ACM. 2021;**64**(9):19-20

[69] Bamakan SMH, Nezhadsistani N, Bodaghi O, Qu Q. Patents and intellectual property assets as non-fungible tokens; key technologies and challenges. Scientific Reports. 2022;**12**(1):2178

[70] Tokenized Real-World Assets (RWA) in DeFi. CoinTelegraph. 2021. Available from: https://cointelegraph.com/learn/tokenized-real-world-assets-rwa-in-defi

[71] Ballandies MC, Wang H, Law ACC, Yang JC, Gösken C, Andrew M. A taxonomy for Blockchain-based decentralized physical infrastructure networks (DePIN). arXiv preprint arXiv:230916707. 2023

[72] Liu Y, Zhang L. Cryptocurrency valuation: An explainable ai approach. In: Science and Information Conference. Springer; 2023. pp. 785-807

[73] Zhang L, Wu T, Lahrichi S, Salas-Flores CG, Li J. A data science pipeline for algorithmic trading: A comparative study of applications for finance and cryptoeconomics. In: 2022 IEEE International Conference on Blockchain (Blockchain). IEEE; 2022. pp. 298-303

[74] Liu Y, Zhang L, Zhao Y. Deciphering bitcoin blockchain data by cohort analysis. Scientific Data. 2022;**9**(1):136

[75] Zhang L, Sun Y, Quan Y, Cao J, Tong X. On the mechanics of nft valuation: Ai ethics and social media. arXiv preprint arXiv:230710201. 2023

[76] Yu H, Sun Y, Liu Y, Zhang L. Bitcoin Gold, Litecoin silver: An introduction to cryptocurrency valuation and trading strategy. In: Future of Information and Communication Conference. Springer; 2024. p. 573-586

[77] Zhu J, Zhang L. Educational game on cryptocurrency investment: Using microeconomic decision-making to understand macroeconomics principles. Eastern Economic Journal. 2023;**49**(2):262-272

[78] Fu Y, Zhou M, Zhang L. DAM: A universal dual attention mechanism for multimodal Timeseries cryptocurrency trend forecasting. arXiv preprint arXiv:240500522. 2024

[79] Proelss J, Sévigny S, Schweizer D. GameFi: The perfect symbiosis of blockchain, tokens, DeFi, and NFTs? International Review of Financial Analysis. 2023;**90**:102916

[80] Wang FY, Ding W, Wang X, Garibaldi J, Teng S, Imre R, et al. The DAO to DeSci: AI for free, fair, and responsibility sensitive sciences. IEEE Intelligent Systems. 2022;**37**(2):16-22

[81] Miao Q, Zheng W, Lv Y, Huang M, Ding W, Wang FY. DAO to HANOI via DeSci: AI paradigm shifts from AlphaGo to ChatGPT. IEEE/CAA Journal of Automatica Sinica. 2023;**10**(4):877-897

[82] Young K. Understanding online gaming addiction and treatment issues for adolescents. The American Journal of Family Therapy. 2009;**37**(5):355-372

[83] Camerer CF. Progress in behavioral game theory. Journal of Economic Perspectives. 1997;**11**(4):167-188

[84] Kucuksenel S. Behavioral mechanism design. Journal of Public Economic Theory. 2012;**14**(5):767-789

[85] Mohan V. Automated market makers and decentralized exchanges: A DeFi primer. Financial Innovation. 2022;**8**(1):20

[86] Xu J, Paruch K, Cousaert S, Feng Y. Sok: Decentralized exchanges (dex) with automated market maker (amm) protocols. ACM Computing Surveys. 2023;**55**(11):1-50

[87] Wu X, Deng W, Quan Y, Zhang L. Trust dynamics and market behavior in cryptocurrency: A comparative study of centralized and decentralized exchanges. arXiv preprint arXiv:240417227. 2024

[88] Dafoe A, Bachrach Y, Hadfield G, Horvitz E, Larson K, Graepel T. Cooperative AI: Machines Must Learn to Find Common Ground. Nature Publishing Group; 2021

[89] Dafoe A, Hughes E, Bachrach Y, Collins T, KR MK, Leibo JZ, et al. Open problems in cooperative ai. arXiv preprint arXiv:201208630. 2020

[90] Zhang L, Tian X. On blockchain we cooperate: An evolutionary game perspective. arXiv preprint arXiv:221205357. 2022

[91] Dafoe A. AI governance: A research agenda. Governance of AI Program, Future of Humanity Institute, University of Oxford: Oxford, UK. 2018;**1442**:1443

[92] Schiff D, Biddle J, Borenstein J, Laas K. What's next for ai ethics, policy, and governance? A global overview. In: Proceedings of the AAAI/ACM Conference on AI, Ethics, and Society. 2020. pp. 153-158

[93] Wirtz BW, Weyerer JC, Sturm BJ. The dark sides of artificial intelligence: An integrated AI governance framework for public administration. International Journal of Public Administration. 2020;**43**(9):818-829

[94] Kuziemski M, Misuraca G. AI governance in the public sector: Three tales from the frontiers of automated decision-making in democratic settings. Telecommunications policy. 2020;**44**(6):101976

[95] Mei Q, Xie Y, Yuan W, Jackson MO. A Turing test of whether AI chatbots are behaviorally similar to humans. National Academy of Sciences of the United States of America. 2024;**121**(9):e2313925121

[96] Chen Y, Liu TX, Shan Y, Zhong S. The emergence of economic rationality of GPT. National Academy of Sciences of the United States of America. 2023;**120**(51):e2316205120

[97] Zhang Y, Gosline R. Human favoritism, not AI aversion: People's perceptions (and bias) toward generative AI, human experts, and human–GAI collaboration in persuasive content generation. Judgment and Decision Making. 2023;**18**:e41

[98] Horton JJ. Large Language Models as Simulated Economic Agents: What Can we Learn from Homo Silicus? National Bureau of Economic Research; 2023

[99] Brynjolfsson E, Li D, Raymond LR. Generative AI at Work. National Bureau of Economic Research; 2023

[100] Weyl EG, Ohlhaver P, Buterin V. Decentralized society: Finding web3's soul. Available at SSRN 4105763. 2022

[101] Tong X, Li Y, Li J, Bei R, Zhang L. What are people talking about in# blacklivesmatter and# stopasianhate? Exploring and categorizing twitter topics emerged in online social movements through the latent Dirichlet allocation model. In: Proceedings of the 2022 AAAI/

ACM Conference on AI, Ethics, and Society. 2022. pp. 723-738

[102] Zhang L. The future of finance: Synthesizing CeFi and DeFi for the benefit of all. In: Miciuła DII, editor. Financial Literacy in Today's Global Market. Rijeka: IntechOpen; 2023. Available from:. DOI: 10.5772/intechopen.1003042

[103] Van Dijk J, Hacker K. The digital divide as a complex and dynamic phenomenon. The Information Society. 2003;**19**(4):315-326

Chapter 9

Perspective Chapter: The Web 3.0 – Brief Literature Considerations, Use Cases, Sustainability and Risks

Claudio Juan Tessone and Carlos Alberto Durigan Junior

Abstract

This chapter explores some general definitions about Web 3 and blockchain technology, along with some applications. Moreover, it mentions definitions of related terms like DAOs. Additionally, this chapter presents some use cases, risks, and sustainability of Web 3. Final considerations and future perspectives are presented at the end.

Keywords: Web 3.0, decentralized governance, blockchain, trust, technology

1. Introduction

Before we go directly into the field of Web 3, it is important to mention some definitions that are related to and from the fundament Web3 applications. It is important to bring definitions of blockchain, decentralized autonomous organizations (DAOs), and decentralized applications (DApps).

2. Blockchain

Since 2008, Bitcoin brought along with it the concept of blockchain, the technology that supports cryptocurrency but is not limited to it. Blockchain enables a decentralized economy and applications. It can be understood as a distributed system that deals with information. This system has many features. Blockchain is a type of Distributed Ledger Technology (DLT). This is a system that records a ledger of transactions or a history of changes to the system state [1]. Examples of blockchain are Bitcoin, Ethereum, Hyperledger Fabric, and IOTA. According to CoinDesk [2], the annual revenue of blockchain-based enterprise applications (globally) will reach almost $20 billion by the year 2025 [2].

According to Tabatabaei et al. [1], there are five findings (or definitions) that altogether support the meaning of the term blockchain. **Table 1** below brings these findings.

Findings	Details
Finding 1	Blockchain is a system utilizing the data structure of bitcoin but extends the functionality.
Finding 2	Blockchain is a system that maintains a chain of blocks. This definition allows for generalization of Definition 1: it allows data structures other than those used in bitcoin. For example, Ethereum and Hyperledger match these points.
Finding 3	Blockchain is a system that maintains a ledger of all transactions. The blockchain does not need to be stored as a chain of blocks; however, IOTA is an example of a system that follows this definition.
Finding 4	Blockchain is a system with distributed non-trusting parties collaborating without a trusted intermediary.
Finding 5	Blockchain is a system that provides support for smart contracts. Ethereum is the first one to support them along with Ethereum Virtual Machines (EVMs).

Source: Adapted from Ref. Tabatabaei et al. [1].

Table 1.
Blockchain definitions.

3. Decentralized applications (DApps)

Decentralized applications (DApps) can be defined as software applications that are able to run on decentralized computer networks. These applications are based on the blockchain. Hence, data are stored and executed across many distributed networks of nodes, which also helps them more resistant to Fraud. Some examples of DApps are decentralized finance (DeFi), decentralized exchanges (DEXs), blockchain-based games, and social media platforms. Decentralized applications (DApps) have some main features: they are decentralization (there is no need for central authority or intermediaries); transparency (recorded on Public Blockchains); security (decentralization helps to be less susceptible to attacks); autonomy (using smart contracts and consensus mechanisms); and open source (Developers can contribute toward improvements). **Table 2** below brings some opportunities and challenges for decentralized applications.

4. Decentralized autonomous organizations (DAOs)

According to Wang et al. [4], there is no single definition of DAO. The authors point out that, to them, DAO stands for a blockchain-based organization that can run independently without any central authority or hierarchy. In a DAO, all the

Opportunities of decentralized applications	Challenges of decentralized applications
• Greater financial inclusion	• Regulatory uncertainty
• Lower transaction costs	• Lack of user adoption
• Greater transparency and accountability	• Technical limitations
• Enhanced privacy and security	• Energy consumption
• Increased innovation and competition	• Cybersecurity risks

Source: Based on Ref. [3].

Table 2.
Opportunities & challenges of decentralized applications.

DAO characteristics	Details
Distributed and decentralized	There is no central authority and hierarchical architecture in DAO; there is coordination and cooperation among distributed network nodes. Interactions among nodes follow the principles of equality, voluntariness, reciprocity, and mutual benefit.
Autonomous and automated	In a DAO, the code is supposed to be law, the organization is distributed, power is decentralized, and management is based on community autonomy. As DAOs are expected to have agreement among stakeholders, consensus and trust within a DAO are also expected to be less costly.
Organized and ordered	As DAOs use smart contracts, their operational rules, participants' responsibility and authority, and the rewards and penalties terms are open and transparent. Through efficient governance rules, the rights and interests of participants are differentiated and dimensioned, that is, individuals who pay, contribute, and assume responsibility are aligned with corresponding powers and benefits to promote the division of labor and the unification of power. This works as a mean of coordination and transparency.

Source: Adapted from Ref. Wang et al. [4].

Table 3.
DAOs' characteristics.

management and operational rules are recorded on the blockchain in the form of smart contracts, and the distributed consensus protocols and token economy incentives are consumed into the organization itself [4]. According to Wang et al. [4], there are three main features of a DAO. They are listed on **Table 3**.

5. Metaverse

The metaverse considers advanced human-computer interface (HCI) technologies, allowing users to stablish interactions. The Web 3 is the internet of the Metaverse [5]. According to Zhang et al. [6], it is possible to integrate Web 3 with Artificial Intelligence (AI), along with blockchain and the metaverse. Moreover, this complex architecture can provide a ubiquitous immersive experience to users during real-time interaction with digital avatars in the metaverse. The architecture involves two parallel worlds (physical and virtual ones) [6].

6. The Web 3

Web 3 stands for a decentralized architecture based on blockchain technology offering democracy and ownership to its users. Although Web 3 has many potential applications, it is still necessary to explore more about scalability, compliance, sustainability, among other topics. Web 3 is user-centered and offers the possibility of multiple connections. The Web 3 can integrate developers, entrepreneurs, and individual users to work together to shape the future of the Internet. Web 3 can bring about innovation in many sectors, from finance and governance to data privacy and digital identity management. Web 3 expects to be equitable, secure, and interconnected. The metaverse will also be associated with Web 3 for some solutions [3].

Since the year 2020, Web 3 (or Web 3.0) has made connection with crypto markets once this new version of Web is based on cryptocurrency networks (Weyl et al. [7] and Consensys [8]). According to the concept proposed by Wood [9], the Web 3 may provide distributed internet services without trusted third parties (TTP), in this scenario, users have control over their data. Users are not controlled by centralized agents. Web 3 can be seen as a broader term used to describe the next generation of internet services including many components and infrastructure. Web 3 applications are deployed on decentralized networks, such as blockchain platforms or related distributed systems hosted by many peer-to-peer (P2P) servers [10].

Web 3 transforms the static, consumer-oriented Web 1.0 and the dynamic producer and platform-oriented Web 2.0 into a decentralized web ecosystem. Web 3 can be implemented in terms of decentralized autonomous organizations (DAOs) and other Distributed Ledger Technologies (DLT) that enable the exchange of digital assets. Once Web 3 is a decentralized ecosystem, it is supposed to reduce or solve problems like over-centralization, improve security and information usage and trade, along with remuneration to the users [11].

According to Wang et al. [10], Web 3 brings some benefits that can be listed (i) open, as data are stored in an open network developed by public communities; (ii) trustless: a user can make connections and exchange assets with an unknown user without the reliance of a trusted third party; (iii) permissionless: not pending on central authorities neither on identity validation; (iv) anonymous: users can have some anonymity and pseudonyms or off-chain storage; (v) high availability: Web 3 provides a high availability architecture; and (vi) compatibility: deployed services and applications are not limited to a specific blockchain network. Users only need to connect the wallet to their targeted sites [10].

Regarding governance, users from the Web 3 space can expose much personal data which users can freely browse the internet as well as perceive their data without compromising its privacy. According to Ethereum [12], the Ethereum foundation makes much more progress by drafting an RFP for defining a formal specification. By controlling data and assets, an individual can make profits through incentive mechanisms. This helps in reaching a sustainable ecosystem [10].

According to Gilbert [13], the majority of the existing Web 3 projects fit into one of the following three categories: (1) decentralized Finance (DeFi) – peer-to-peer, blockchain-based financial services including savings, borrowing, payments, and credit scoring. (2) Digital services – decentralized internet service provision, cloud storage, web infrastructure, data analytics, and identity management. (3) Collectibles – digital artwork, sports memorabilia, and virtual goods [13]. The author also points out some examples of Web 3 unicorns (companies valued at more than one billion USD). They are:

- Ripple (international payments provider).
- Aave (protocol for borrowing and lending crypto assets that runs on Ethereum).
- Chainalysis (data analytics platform for compliance, risk management, and cybercrime investigations).
- Forte (gaming infrastructure platform).
- OpenSea (digital collectibles marketplace).
- Sorare (Ethereum-based fantasy football game in which virtual player cards can be bought and traded).

About tokens in the Web 3, there are several different types, including utility tokens, which grant rights of access to a product or service, and governance tokens, which grant voting rights on decisions [13]. Currently, the Web 3 is an application of blockchain, which is having a profound impact on society and the global economy. The potential impact of Web 3 technologies (based on blockchain) is still not fully estimated. Web 3 applications are related to decentralized finance (DeFi), law (data privacy), research (data sharing), new forms of ownership (NFTs), and education, among many possible unlisted applications [14].

Web 3 applications may commonly be related to decentralized autonomous organizations (DAOs). DAOs can be governed by a community and through smart contracts use. In Web 3, users have more control over their data. Web 3 tools can provide interoperability that is immutable and trustless. DAOs are also understood as participatory governance structures in which rules can be mediated by software code [14].

Ray [3] listed some potential applications and context for Web 3, and these are listed on **Table 4** below.

Web 3 is about to result more user-centralization over their data and remuneration, resulting in the democratization and ownership to users. In **Table 5**, there are listed the main use cases (so far) for the Web 3:

The main topics that are related to some risks of the use and adoption of Web 3 are mentioned on **Table 6**. The related risks are not impeditive factors once effective controls are adopted to solve and or reduce them.

Web 3 application/ solution	Details
Interoperability and cross-chain solutions	Decentralization in Web 3 is encouraged by the interoperability between blockchains, allowing them to communicate. Cross-chain solutions, such as Polkadot, Cosmos, and Avalanche, are designed to connect different blockchain networks, enabling transfers among them. Interoperability allows multi-chain applications, providing users with the possibility of customized services.
Digital identity and privacy	Web 3 decentralized applications foster user identity solutions, giving them control over their personal data. Decentralized identity solutions can improve privacy once it reduce centralized data storage. Web 3 also allows for the use of secure and interoperable identity management tools. These decentralized identity solutions can allow users to monetize their data and connect in data-sharing agreements, fostering a user-centric digital ecosystem.
The role of governance In Web 3	The decentralized governance in Web 3 can make users share and allocate resources collectively. This governance can be based on DAO ecosystem and rely on smart contracts. Governance in Web 3 can address many points, such as security, scalability, interoperability, and user-centered, through collaboration, innovation, and consensus-based solutions.
The role of Web3 in the metaverse	The metaverse considers many digital environments, such as social media, gaming, and virtual reality. Web3, along with the Metaverse can enable interoperable and decentralized digital experiences, being user-centered and promoting monetization appropriately to all users.
The potential of Web3 for decentralized healthcare	Web 3 applications can also foster Decentralized Healthcare (DeH) solutions, once these are guided by the same user's principles and rights in Web 3. DeH platforms allow innovation, collaboration, and patient-centered care.

Source: Based on Ref. [3].

Table 4.
Web 3 applications and solutions.

Field of application	**Description**
Decentralized Finance (DeFi)	Smart contracts-based solutions (like Ethereum) are used to enable decentralized economic systems.
Decentralized Applications (DApps)	Used to ensure transparency and create decentralized networks & applications.
Blockchain-based identity	Avoid centralized identity management. Helps users have control over their data and transparency.
Tokenization of assets	Helps to prove ownership over assets.
Data ownership and privacy	Users can have the ability to share and monetize their assets.
Interoperability	Efforts have been made here. The topic is not fully solved.
Content monetization	Using microtransactions and cryptocurrencies.
Source: Authors.	

Table 5.
Main use cases for web 3.

Main topics related to possible risks	**General comments**
Scalability	There are many blockchain protocols that still suffer from scalability issues.
Interoperability	This is still a big issue once Web 3 transacts data among many networks.
User experience	Users still need to have better experiences when dealing with Decentralized Applications (Dapps).
Regulatory uncertainty	The regulatory guidelines for both crypto and Web 3 are still under development and consideration.
Security	Security approaches must always be considered constantly when dealing with new technologies and their new governance mechanisms.
Energy consumption	It is still a sustainability challenge once blockchains (mainly the ones that use Proof-of-Work (PoW)) consume a great amount oof energy.
Legal and ethical issues	Topics regarding smart contracts, local regulations, and compliance overall need to be addressed in every use case.
Adoption and education	As Web 3 is a technology relatively new, under adoption and use, users need to be well educated.
Privacy concerns	Like a risk management culture, privacy concerns should always be controlled and assisted.
Governance	Governance should guarantee that it is indeed decentralized and transparent to all users.
Not observing homogeneous or full levels of decentralization toward: • Economic Power. • Governance & Decision Making. • Implementation (i.e. Development)	For all these aspects (Economic Power, Governance & Decision-Making, and Implementation) it should be observed a considerable (reasonable) level of decentralization. Once the technology does exist to promote decentralized governance and user-centered features/rights. Protocols' design and adoption should avoid economic concentration, promote inclusive and democratic decision-making processes, and decentralized implementation. Hence, if we observe these features, it will not be expected to see hybrids forms of governance (when there are expressive levels of centralization in the network).
Source: Authors.	

Table 6.
Main topics and related risks about web 3.

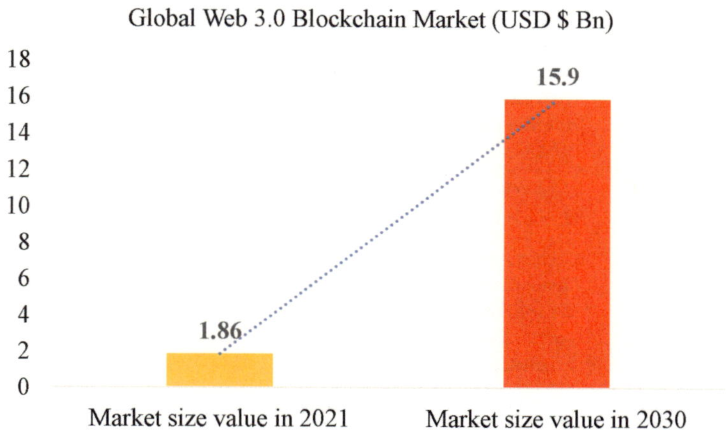

Figure 1.
Global Web 3 blockchain market in size ($ USD Bn). Source: Authors based on Ref. Skyquestt [15].

According to the website Skyquestt [15], the Web 3.0 Blockchain Market size was valued at around USD 1.86 Billion in 2021 and is expected to reach a value of USD 15.9 Billion by 2030. In nine years, the market is expected to grow more than eight times its size from 2021. The website also says that the growth can be associated to the increasing demand for data privacy through Web 3.0's decentralized identity and the growth of the technologies based on internet, along with cryptocurrencies and 5G/6G. Web 3 can support the growth of whole blockchain industry, along with crypto transactions [15]. **Figure 1** shows the global Web 3 Blockchain Market in size ($ USD Bn) for the years of 2021 and 2030 (forecast).

7. Web 3 and sustainability

The emergence of Web 3.0 has called attention to its potential implications for sustainability. However, the literature about this is still limited. Sustainability encompasses various fields that together preserve or contribute to the natural environment, human health, and ecosystem balance along with the creation of innovation. The circular economy concept may also walk together with sustainability [16].

Web3.0 is related to sustainability as these last principles can be applied to environmental, economic, technological, and social fields. By being based on decentralized technologies, Web 3 fosters sustainability. However, there are only a few industry reports and research papers in the literature that have discussed sustainability issues related to Web 3.0. Web 3.0 allows to advance sustainability objectives through various mechanisms, including transparency, energy optimization, promotion of trust, innovation, and inclusivity [16]. According to Rathor et al. [16], there are some Web 3.0 and blockchain applications that help achieve sustainability goals. They are listed on **Table 7** (these are just some samples, and there are others existent).

8. Final considerations and future research

According to what has been shown in this chapter, it is possible to claim that the adoption of Web 3 is something already in use, with an expressive market

Web 3/blockchain project - sustainability	Description
World Food Programme (WFP)	Provides food assistance, and leverages decentralized financial (DeFi) applications to enhance distribution efficiency and enable secure money transfers, empowering refugees.
Chinese blockchain-based carbon asset markets	Allow the efficient generation of carbon assets in alignment with China's Carbon Emissions Reduction goals for the Paris Agreement.
Blockchain-based peer-to-peer energy systems	Tends to reduce energy waste by eliminating the need for long-distance transmission and energy storage, while various blockchain-powered platforms such as Echchain, ElectricChain, and Suncontract aim to optimize supply chain efficiency in the energy sector.
Open earth foundation	Leverages Web 3.0 technologies to build an advanced carbon pricing mechanism.
The social plastic project	There are collection centers in developing nations to convert plastic waste into currency, services, or goods, with the goal of addressing plastic pollution and poverty and is currently developing a blockchain-powered app for exchanging plastic for cryptographic tokens.
Green world campaign	Uses cryptocurrencies and a hybrid smart contract application. This project aims to start a global campaign to restore degraded land, raise living standards increasing healthcare and living standards in rural areas, replenishing soil, and mitigating climate change.

Source: Based on Ref. [16].

Table 7.
Web 3 and blockchain projects that foster sustainability.

capitalization. Web 3 has been applied to many industries, although it is also based on crypto-economics networks, it is not only applied to the financial industry, going beyond such as healthcare solutions. In the future, it is expected that the use of Web 3 will be even more expressive and related to many processes. Moreover, the market capitalization tends to be even more significant by the year of 2030 (nearly USD 16 billion). We have also seen in this chapter that there are many projects already in use that consider Web 3 and blockchain solutions to reach sustainability (**Table 7**).

This chapter also lists the use cases and applications of Web 3 (**Tables 4** and **5**) along with some risks or challenges (**Table 6**). It is necessary to mention that these challenges (or related risks) do not mean that we should avoid using Web 3 solutions. It does mean that some controls or appropriated actions must be considered and taken toward them. For future research, we suggest that researchers and industry players consider thinking about better practices to use the Web 3 as an inclusive, sustainable, decentralized, and inclusive approach. The Web 3 is indeed promising for the upcoming years.

Author details

Claudio Juan Tessone[1*] and Carlos Alberto Durigan Junior[1,2]

1 UZH Blockchain Center, University of Zurich, Switzerland

2 The University of São Paulo, Brazil

*Address all correspondence to: claudio.tessone@uzh.ch

References

[1] Tabatabaei MH, Vitenberg R, Veeraragavan NR. Understanding blockchain: Definitions, architecture, design, and system comparison. Computer Science Review. 2023;**50**:100575

[2] Coindesk. State of blockchain-Q4 2017 enterprise blockchain summary. 2018. Available from: https://s3-us-west-2.amazonaws.com/guizishanren/pdf/Coindesk-201712-State-of-Blockchain-2018.pdf

[3] Ray PP. Web3: A comprehensive review on background, technologies, applications, zero-trust architectures, challenges and future directions. Internet of Things and Cyber-Physical Systems. 2023

[4] Wang S, Ding W, Li J, Yuan Y, Ouyang L, Wang FY. Decentralized autonomous organizations: Concept, model, and applications. IEEE Transactions on Computational Social Systems. 2019;**6**(5):870-878

[5] Gadekallu TR, Huynh-The T, Wang W, Yenduri G, Ranaweera P, Pham QV, et al. Blockchain for the metaverse: A review. arXiv. 2022. Available from: https://arxiv.org/

[6] Zhang X, Min G, Li T, Ma Z, Cao X, Wang S. AI and blockchain empowered metaverse for web 3.0: Vision, architecture, and future directions. IEEE Communications Magazine. 2023;**61**:60-66

[7] Weyl EG, Ohlhaver, P, Buterin V. Decentralized society: Finding web3's soul. 2022. Available from: https://ssrn.com/abstract=4105763

[8] Consensys. The web3 report q3 2021 (consensys). 2021. Available from: https://consensys.net/reports/web3-report-q3-2021/

[9] Wood. Wood Gavin. Why we need web 3.0. 2022. Available from: https://gavofyork.medium.com/why-weneed-web-3-0-5da4f2bf95ab

[10] Wang Q, Li R, Wang Q, Chen S, Ryan M, Hardjono T. Exploring web3 from the view of blockchain. arXiv. 2022

[11] Cao L. Decentralized ai: Edge intelligence and smart blockchain, metaverse, web3, and desci. IEEE Intelligent Systems. 2022;**37**(3):6-19

[12] Ethereum. Request for proposals (rfp): Sign-in-with-ethereum. 2022. Available from: https://notes.ethereum.org/@djrtwo/sign-in-with-ethereum-RFP

[13] Gilbert S. Crypto, web3, and the Metaverse. Cambridge, Policy Brief: Bennett Institute for Public Policy; 2022

[14] Filipčić S. Web3 & DAOs: An overview of the development and possibilities for the implementation in research and education. In: 2022 45th Jubilee International Convention on Information, Communication and Electronic Technology. Opatija, Croatia (MIPRO). IEEE; 2022. pp. 1278-1283

[15] Skyquestt. 2024. Available from: https://www.skyquestt.com/report/web-3-0-blockchain-market [Accessed: March 9, 2024]

[16] Rathor S, Zhang M, Im T. Web 3.0 and sustainability: Challenges and research opportunities. Sustainability. 2023;**15**(20):15126